Other Theatres

*The Development of Alternative
and Experimental Theatre
in Britain*

Andrew Davies

MACMILLAN
EDUCATION

© Andrew Davies 1987

First published 1987

Published by
MACMILLAN EDUCATION LTD
Houndmills, Basingstoke, Hampshire RG21 2XS
and London
Companies and representatives
throughout the world

Typeset by Wessex Typesetters
(Division of The Eastern Press Ltd)
Frome, Somerset

Printed in Hong Kong

British Library Cataloguing in Publication Data
Davies, Andrew
Other theatres: the development of
alternative and experimental theatre in
Britain.—(Communities and culture)
1. Experimental theater—Great Britain—
History
I. Title   II. Series
792   PN2582.E9
ISBN 0–333–32433–1 (hardcover)
ISBN 0–333–32435–8 (paperback)

Series Standing Order

If you would like to receive future titles in this series as they are
published, you can make use of our standing order facility. To place a
standing order please contact your bookseller or, in case of difficulty,
write to us at the address below with your name and address and the
name of the series. Please state with which title you wish to begin your
standing order. (If you live outside the United Kingdom we may not
have the rights for your area, in which case we will forward your order
to the publisher concerned.)

Customer Services Department, Macmillan Distribution Ltd
Houndmills, Basingstoke, Hampshire, RG21 2XS, England.

Communications and Culture

Communications has been defined as the conveying or exchanging of information and idea. This wide definition is taken as the starting-point for this series of books, which are not bound by conventional academic divisions. The series aims to document or analyse a broad range of cultural forms and ideas.

It encompasses works from areas as esoteric as linguistics and as exoteric as television. The language of communication may be the written work or the moving picture, the static icon or the living gesture. These means of communicating can at their best blossom into and form an essential part of the other mysterious concept, *culture.*

There is no sharp or intended split in the series between communication and culture. On one definition, culture refers to the organisation of experience shared by members of a community, a process which includes the standards and values for judging or perceiving, for predicting and acting. In this sense, creative communication can make for a better and livelier culture.

The series reaches towards the widest possible audience. Some of the works concern themselves with activities as general as play and games; others offer a narrower focus, such as the ways of understanding the visual image. It is hoped that some moves in the transformation of the artful and the scientific can be achieved, and that both can begin to be understood by a wider and more comprehending community. Some of these books are written by practitioners – broadcasters, journalists and artists; others come from critics, scholars, scientists and historians.

The series has an ancient and laudable, though perhaps untenable, aim – an aim as old as the Greeks and as new as holography: it aspires to help heal the split between cultures, between the practitioners and the thinkers, between science and art, between the academy and life.

PAUL WALTON

COMMUNICATIONS AND CULTURE

Executive Editors   STUART HALL, PAUL WALTON

Published

Forthcoming

Contents

Preface

When I mentioned to a friend that I was writing a book on the history of experimental and alternative theatre in Britain since the early nineteenth century, his reaction was 'well, that will be a short book – and of pretty limited interest too'.

I hope that *Other Theatres* proves him wrong on both counts. Again and again alternative and experimental drama has anticipated changes and innovations which only took place later within mainstream theatre, but the very existence let alone the work of groups like the suffragettes' Actresses' Franchise League, Group Theatre, Unity Theatre or the ABCA Play Unit is barely known other than to specialists. And if it is 'Big Names' which attracts readers, then a glance through the following pages reveals figures such as William Cobbett, William Morris, George Bernard Shaw, W. B. Yeats, W. H. Auden, Joan Littlewood. . . .

But just what is 'alternative', 'experimental', 'fringe' or 'other' theatre – the variety of terms used indicating both the welter of such activity and its resistance to neat categorisation? The answer to this question should become clear during the course of the book, but as a working definition one might use the phrase 'non-commercial', i.e. theatre whose primary objective is something other than the making of a financial profit. This distinguishes it from the West End theatre and also from the popular theatre of circus and music hall. It also means that the boundaries of alternative and experimental theatre are not drawn in too narrow or sectarian a manner – and if it is pointed out that the dividing line is often difficult to make out, well, that is one of the book's themes.

Little has been written about this history: the best books so far have been Catherine Itzin's *Stages in the Revolution*, exploring developments since 1968, and Norman Marshall's pioneering *The Other Theatre*, which was published in 1947 and looked at the inter-war years. Reading Marshall's book eight years ago started me researching into this whole subject and my choice of a similar title is in part a tribute to his study.

Other Theatres is the first overall history of British alternative theatre, but I would like to stress that the book does not record a simple linear tradition in which, like a relay race with the passing on of the baton, groups handed down their accumulated experiences to the next generation. Many individuals and companies did not know anything of their forerunners or even their contemporaries. Raphael Samuel has rightly written of this history as resembling more a 'series of moments'; yet these moments, however disparate and often contradictory, remain united by their opposition towards the commercial or West End theatre.

Alternative and experimental theatre is often associated with a didactic humourlessness, an emphasis on 'the message' at the expense of 'entertainment'. Certainly this has often been the case, but to tar the whole with this brush is wrong. In 1964 Joan Littlewood issued a statement which contained the following passage:

> Shakespeare's company was made up of leary misfits, anarchists, out of work soldiers and wits who worked at their ideas in pubs and performed them as throwaways to an uninhibited pre-Puritan audience. My Company works without the assistance of smart direction, fancy dress, beards and greasepaint and was prepared for the wave of opposition which we knew would come. I hope the audience will enjoy our work as much as we do.

I have tried to write *Other Theatres* in such a spirit, bringing out the humour and excitement as well as the frictions and disagreements which are inevitably involved in the process of putting together 'other theatres'. I have quoted extensively from those involved within this tradition at various times in order to convey the mood and flavour of each period or venture.

In addition I have attempted to place this history within its social context – how, for example, can one discuss alternative theatre without at least sketching out what it is that it is meant to be alternative to? – in contrast to those historians of theatre and drama, few of whom, in Eric Bentley's words, 'seem to have noticed anything in this universe except theatre and drama'.

Two final points. Academic books nowadays are often clogged up with lengthy footnotes, so exhaustive as to rival the text itself. I have referenced all quotations from whatever source together with references for contentious or little-known 'facts'. There is also an essay on further reading at the end. I think this should enable anyone who wants to explore the subject further to do so. The footnotes contain neither additional information nor asides, queries or jokes and therefore can be safely ignored by the general reader.

If any interested reader of this book would care to enter into correspondence with me, whether to praise, damn or query a statement or reference, then please write to me c/o Macmillan Publishers, Higher and Further Education Division, Houndmills, Basingstoke, Hampshire RG21 2XS

Finally, *Other Theatres* does cover a great deal of ground, oblivious to the 'no entry' signs which separate academic disciplines from each other – 'English', 'Drama', 'Politics', 'Sociology' and so on – but then, as R. H. Tawney once wrote:

When we reach years of discretion – which I take to mean when youth shows signs of getting over its education – part of our business is to join those naturally connected interests which the demands of examinations and the exigencies of time-tables have temporarily put asunder.

Introduction

Before starting to examine one particular area of this country's theatrical history I thought it might be helpful if the reader was offered a general overview. Although this introduction is entirely self-contained, the story of the nineteenth and twentieth centuries are covered more fully in the following chapters. This is the context in which 'other theatres' have existed.

English medieval drama rested upon three foundations: folk drama; the secular tradition of the wandering entertainers; and Church drama. If we know a certain amount about the last, the history of the first two comes down to us only in scattered form. The strand of folk drama acted not so much as conscious 'theatre' but rather as an expression of the local community's self-identity – demonstrated in certain activities which today would be referred to as 'dramatic'. In a static and virtually illiterate society where communication was almost non-existent and few people ever travelled outside the immediate district, the villagers' seasonal festivals and rituals confirmed their own existence by excluding outsiders.

The strolling bands of entertainers moving from village to village also sprang from an oral culture far removed from printing presses, libraries and noblemen's halls. Fragments testify to their activities, and much of it is negative in the sense that it derives from the fulminations of Church councils condemning the clerical presence at the entertainments which followed on from feasts and marriages. St Augustine in his *Confessions* owned up to a youthful love of such festivities, and the Laws of Charlemagne passed between 800 and 814 further reprimanded ecclesiastical laxity.

No doubt the acrobats, the jugglers and the mimes, poking fun at the authorities in market places, continued on their own way, more concerned with pleasing that mass of the population which paid and fed them. Edgar of England in 960 called for the reform of the monasteries, yet again berating those who should have known better than allow strolling entertainers to perform in front of them, and in the twelfth century William of Malmesbury referred to 'dramatic gestures', an indication perhaps that the mimes were acting out parts. But however slight, what little we know of these strollers points to the existence of a secular tradition that was irreverent, crude and satiric.[1]

On the other hand the tradition of Church drama emerged from a desire to extend religious belief by dramatising biblical episodes, thus livening up services conducted in the sung Latin which meant nothing to the bulk of the congregation. The *Visitatio* exchanges from the later half of the tenth century, for example, sought to bring home in more visual and telling ways the significance of Christ rising from the dead, as well as ensuring that these dramatic activities took place under the watchful eye of the ecclesiastical authorities themselves. However, before long things began to get out of hand: movement around the whole interior of the church was followed by the introduction of vernacular dialogue, an innovation that threatened clerical control.

The upshot was the ejection, whether voluntary or otherwise, of the drama from the churches and its maintenance by trade guilds responsible for separate sections of the plays. These mystery cycles continued as dramatisations of stories from the Bible but found themselves intermingled with the comic secular tradition which did not take anything too seriously. There are countless examples of this: in the York version Joseph listens disbelievingly to Mary's story that her pregnancy was purely the result of divine intervention. Mrs Noah is a gossiping old shrew in the Chester, York and Towneley plays, constantly nagging her husband and holding him up for ridicule by her neighbours. Herod is invariably portrayed as a laughably ranting idiot, and linked to this is the depiction of the Devil as a comic villain, anticipating characters seen in cheap Hollywood westerns or children's Christmas pantomimes. Even the torturers snigger and have a lot of fun in the Wakefield cycle.

The medieval plays also demonstrate a bewildering mix of forms: jugglers' tricks and a frequent use of fireworks jostle with the Last Supper and the Crucifixion. Topical criticism abounds too, as in the Second Shepherds' Play where the shepherds complain of their lords' high and mighty ways, grousing about the extortionate level of taxation. Finally, quite apart from the presentation of the plays being the collective responsibility of the whole town, the medieval audience were direct participants in the plays themselves, cast in the role of Mankind – thus in the Towneley version Christ appeals directly to them from the Cross.[2] The staging of the episodes on pageant wagons surrounded by a boisterous crowd could not but establish close contact between performers and spectators.

Academic specialists have noted the popular characteristics of these productions. Allardyce Nicoll argued that 'It can hardly be emphasized too much that the great cycles of the fourteenth and fifteenth centuries could not have become the popular things they were had it not been for the efforts of the comic actors to make sport and the machinists to make wondrous entertaining shows.'[3] Glynne Wickham has likened them to community games: 'Song, dance, wrestling, sword-play, contests between animals, disguise, spectacle, jokes, disputation and ritual all figure, separately or compounded, in the drama of the Middle Ages which was devised in celebration of leisure and for a local community.'[4]

The morality plays which superseded the earlier mysteries and miracles retained many of their characteristics, in particular their abundant exuberance; now it is the figure of Vice who banters and spars with the audience. However as the sixteenth century wore on a number of other influences increasingly began to make themselves felt. The Reformation led to the extinction of anything supposedly papal in origin, and so the mysteries and miracle plays were gradually suppressed: the Hereford plays were ended by 1548 and the last performance of the Chester cycle occurred in 1575 – but they left behind a rich dramatic legacy.

The growing professionalism of the players themselves was reflected in the spread of touring companies from the 1550s which were primarily composed of actors rather than the more versatile entertainers of the past. Allied to this trend were the draconian laws and whipping campaigns aimed at those discontented hordes tramping the roads in the sixteenth century dispossessed by the more profitable sheep; the statute of 1572, which outlawed rogues and vagabonds unless carrying a licence from two Justices of the Peace, drove a further wedge between such authorised companies as the Earl of Leicester's Men and the rest. A more permanent location was only a matter of time and finally came with the construction of the Theatre in 1576. However important this event – the first such theatre building in this country – James Burbage and his company were only reflecting the commercial expansion and self-confidence of Elizabethan times.

Christopher Hill has written that 'The financial genius of James Burbage brought playing from a small-scale private enterprise to a big business.'[5] From 1572 Burbage had been the head of the leading troupe of players, the Earl of Leicester's Men, and quickly realised the lucrative gains to be extracted from constructing a more permanent venue in preference to tramping the highway. Borrowing £100 from his brother-in-law he invested the money in tagging a theatre onto the back of an inn called The George in Shoreditch and, most importantly, initiated the box office, stationing gatherers at the entrance who ensured pre-payment – a marked contrast from the traditional stampede that occurred, and still does, when the busker sends round the hat after his or her performance.

Burbage's Theatre was soon imitated by the Curtain and then by the Rose, and their growth out of the inn-yard and bear-yard was illustrated by the wide variety of the entertainments presented. The plays themselves contained a fantastic mix of mood and styles, the coexistence of tragedy and comedy welcomed by an audience convinced that the spice of variety was all. Everyone knows of the gravediggers, the ghost and the strolling players in *Hamlet*, the drunken porter and the witches in *Macbeth*, the antics of Falstaff and his friends, Feste's songs in *Twelfth Night*, Prospero's role of magician throughout *The Tempest*, Juliet's Nurse and Henry V's soldiers before the Battle of Agincourt, the wrestling match in *As You Like It* – all of these ingredients counterpointed the rhetoric of other more lofty protagonists. The thrusts and gibes of the Fool in *King Lear* often today seem rather boring, but then they would have full of topical satire and innuendo which altered from performance to performance.

The use of contrast is evident in Shakespeare's plays – for instance, there are the very different views on honour expressed by Falstaff and Hotspur in *Henry IV* – as is his relish in dealing with contemporary political issues: in Hamlet's phrase, 'the forms and pressures of the age'. With the theatre replacing the pulpit as a dominant influence, the history plays concerned not so distant events, and the subjects dramatised – questions of civil war, power, justice – remained of especial relevance in a country with an ageing Queen and no heir, beset by religious factions and a feudal system in the throes of disintegration. It is vital to remember too that although Shakespeare today is universally revered, at the time he was regarded as no more than another member of the company. The reason for this lay in the 'sharing system', a democratic means of organisation whereby the company took collective responsibility for opportunities and rewards, making their own rules and electing their own officers, thus discouraging what later emerged as the 'star system'.[6]

By 1598 friction with the landlord prompted Burbage's company to build a new playhouse, and although this building, the Globe in Southwark, was the first to be constructed as a theatre per se, the continuities were symbolised by the fact that it was the wooden timber from the Theatre which formed the seating of the new property. The Globe was soon followed by other public playhouses such as the Fortune and the Swan, and the comparative cheapness of admission – anything from a penny upwards – encouraged their enormous popularity: of London's total population of 140 000 at this time, over 20 000 went to the playhouses each week.[7] An equivalent today would mean something like one million Londoners going to the theatre each week.

But of course the theatrical conditions of the time were forever changing, and the playhouses began to introduce a more ordered programme upon which their regular customers could depend. The role of the fool, for example, formerly occupied by Richard Tarleton with his penchant for crude jokes and Will Kempe's singing and dancing, was now, by 1600, being more fully integrated into the play itself – as is seen in *King Lear*.[8] Some of the more 'extraneous' entertainers were banished from the boards, and in Shakespeare's plays too a more pessimistic tone increasingly appears, a reflection of his loss of contact with the teeming mass that thronged the public playhouses.

Why was this? Alongside the tradition of the popular theatre there had always existed the very different tradition of private theatres and court masques. One of the former establishments, Blackfriars, had been opened in the same year as the Theatre, but its restricted clientele and expensive admission spawned a more literary and stylised form of theatre very different from the crude vigour of the public playhouses. When James I came to the throne in 1603 one of his first acts was to set up Burbage, Shakespeare and company as King's Men or part of his royal household. In effect this entailed their transference from one tradition of theatre to another.

It was a move from open air playhouses to the private theatres charging admission to their indoor, evening and artificially lighted performances. Of prime consideration now was just how close one sat to the monarch, and the spectators' responses were conditioned by how the King reacted to the play rather than by their own spontaneous feelings. The design of the theatres was influenced by continental Renaissance ideas of the picture-frame stage with the proscenium barrier emphasising the growing sense of distance between performers and spectators, something indicated also by the more self-conscious and elitist language and forms used by playwrights like Marston and Tourneur who worked primarily within this tradition. The court masques designed by Inigo Jones heightened this introspection and glorification of the monarch.[9] Not surprisingly, Shakespeare's use of contrast and much else was lost, and his reputation suffered a serious decline in court circles precisely because of the popular – or, by now, vulgar – elements in his poetry and plays.[10]

The distinction between public playhouse and private theatre is not of course an absolute one, but within it one can already discern the seeds of the literary West End theatre and the popular, lively, all-embracing variety tradition.

The expansion in size and influence of the commercial middle classes – their worship of profit satirised by Ben Jonson in his play *Volpone* of 1606 – accelerated the growth of puritan attitudes which disapproved of the theatre as an unnecessary diversion from the virtues of hard work and industry. These forces were particularly strong in London and the outbreak of the Civil War ensured the closing down of all theatres in 1642. Scholars have traced the fragile existence of dramatic activities over the course of the next eighteen years, but it was only with the Restoration of 1660 that the theatre emerged from the twilight.

Most importantly its emergence was in a manner that reinforced the literary or West End tradition, finally ending that national drama which had flourished for the greater part of Shakespeare's career. Charles II decreed that henceforward drama was to be confined to the theatres to which he granted royal patents and which turned out to be Covent Garden and Drury Lane. In such circumstances the two theatres could be little more than royal toys, dependent totally on court patronage and with an audience of courtiers and hangers-on. The 'sharing system' was abandoned as the patents were granted personally to Messrs D'Avenant and Killigrew, who now hired the actors as paid employees and had total and untrammelled control over the productions.

In many respects the theatres were little more than reservoirs in which the male members of the aristocracy could fish for suitable mistresses, especially as actresses were now permitted to appear on stage for the first time. The differences between the Restoration theatre and the Elizabethan public playhouse should not be overemphasised – for example the apron stages at both patent theatres projected deep into the audience and so retained some of the former intimacy between performers and spectators, and a notable figure like Nell Gwyn with her repartee and mischievous wink looked back to the Shakespearean fools and forward to music hall favourites like Marie Lloyd – but the seventeenth century was crucial in British theatrical history. A truly popular form of drama based upon improvisation, variety and the absence of any rigid distinction between stage and audience was replaced by a tradition of theatre which was elitist and spoke only to and for a few. The puppets, the performing animals, the jugglers and the acrobats who had occupied an honourable place on the Elizabethan stage found themselves banished to the fairgrounds and market squares, back again with the old pitfalls and the sharing of the stroller's life.

In the eighteenth century the key event was the passage of the Stage Licensing Act of 1737, a statute which introduced a systematic method of censorship. The consequences of this measure reverberated throughout the theatre, and this at a time when there was already taking place a gradual expansion of the audience as puritanical tenets waned amongst the middle classes and they developed more of a theatre-going habit. Instead of the often topical and provocative ballad opera which did not survive the 1737 legislation, it was productions which offered familiar settings and problems for this new middle-class audience that held sway, overlaid by a generous helping of sentimentalism.

The neutering of the drama represented by the Stage Licensing Act was also reflected in the greater ascendancy of the players themselves, especially in the cases of David Garrick and Sarah Siddons. With the plays of such a uniformly mediocre standard the focus of the spectators was more firmly on the actors, in turn hastening the advent of the 'star' syndrome which would have seemed so misplaced to Shakespeare. The tedium of the plays further encouraged an interest in the diversions of spectacle and extravagant presentation, and Garrick employed as his scene designer Philip de Loutherbourg, a man whose ingenuity showed itself in the fires, volcanoes and thunder storms regularly on show at Drury Lane. This emphasis on ostentation, together with the sumptuous costumes, had of course the effect of distancing the productions from the spectators and it is notable that, for instance, Garrick when delivering a soliloquy now spoke as if there was no audience more than but a few yards from him.[11]

Although the growth of the theatrical performance as an illusion accelerated during the eighteenth century, still many features of the popular theatre remained. The entertainment kept its compendious flavour, beginning at 6 o'clock in the evening and ending at midnight, and the plays would be sandwiched between dancing and comical after-pieces. The audience could still handle widely contrasting emotions and reactions; as Allardyce Nicoll has noted of this period: 'There seemed nothing extraordinary to the audience in their listening to Lear's agony at 7.30 and laughing hilariously at pantomime or farcical afterpiece at 8.'[12]

The growth of the eighteenth-century theatre-going audience was not a phenomenon exclusive to London, and provincial theatres were constructed throughout these years. Building upon the esteem and prestige built up by the more respectable troupes of strollers such as the Norwich Company of Comedians, enterprising business men began to conduct campaigns to persuade the authorities to allow them building permission. Generally they were successful: in the twenty years after 1768 patents were granted to eight provincial theatres, including those at Norwich, York, Liverpool and Manchester. In Birmingham, however, local hostility prevented the erection of a theatre until 1807.

The widespread economic and social changes at the end of the eighteenth century consequent upon the development of industrialisation resulted in migration from the countryside and the rapid growth of towns and cities. Within the theatre sheer weight of numbers reintroduced the 'popular' back into the playhouses both in London and in the provinces, infiltrating even Covent Garden, Drury Lane, and also the Haymarket which had been informally admitted to the ranks of the patents. By the 1840s melodrama and pantomime – then working-class entertainments – held sway both at these theatres as well as at the new minor (as opposed to the majors or patents) and penny theatres. The music halls and circuses were also a reversion to the undifferentiated fare characteristic of the Shakespearean era. Despite the industrialised nature of much of Victorian Britain folk drama continued in its own relatively self-enclosed fashion.

However towards the end of the nineteenth century the theatre's character changed yet again, a transformation which this time centred on the creation of 'the West End theatre' as an institution appealing predominantly to the leisured and prosperous. A rash of new playhouses was built in Charing Cross Road and Shaftesbury Avenue, whilst in the provinces too the middle classes were lured back. Not everyone was happy with this trend and certain groups and organisations condemned the West End theatre on a variety of grounds, trying instead to set up the 'other theatres' which are the subject of this book.

Where then did the working-class audience disappear to when they left the theatres at the end of the nineteenth century? To the cinema, where spectators were provided with the old melodramas which their predecessors had once enjoyed in the theatre – today of course this popular form is more readily available within television 'soap operas'. Ironically enough it is this elusive and huge audience which the other theatres have spent so much time, often unsuccessfully, in trying to attract. The West End theatre has also rested on rather insecure foundations, appealing only to a small, albeit wealthy, minority of the population and tending to reflect that group's tastes and interests. The subsidised companies which have grown up since the Second World War have been allowed a certain freedom to experiment whilst largely protected from commercial pressures – although in recent years the reduction in public subsidy in relation to rising costs and inflation has meant that commercial criteria are beginning to dominate these companies' programmes and methods.

Chapter 1

The Great Bard and All That: Some Traditions of British Theatre

What are the images most widely conjured up by the word 'theatre'? The indoor stage, the lights dimming and curtain rising as the evening performance begins, the darkened auditorium, the irritation at late-comers groping for their seats or people who insist on talking throughout the play? The ice-creams and programmes, the scramble for the bar at the interval, the splendid scenery and costumes, the impatient wait for the entrance of the star, the burst of applause at the end?

However powerful these associations may be, the various elements within them – scenery, evening performances, the curtain and so on – relate only to one particular type of theatre which, although it may predominate today, has no monopoly on the notion of what constitutes 'theatre'. Examples of very different theatrical events in the past, such as the penny gaffs or cheap neighbourhood theatres of the nineteenth century and the Shakespearean public playhouse, help to emphasise that what is called 'theatre' at any one time is always the product of historical and cultural forces and therefore continually changing.

The penny gaffs sprang up in the working-class districts of the overcrowded cities from the 1820s onwards, catering for those adults and children working inordinately long hours. Converted shops, stables and warehouses were all turned into gaffs, and the ramshackle nature of the entertainment was demonstrated by the bare stage which might be no more than a few planks raised on some barrels. The length of the show fluctuated according to the number of customers waiting outside for the next performance, but a spectator would be lucky if he or she saw more than half an hour's worth. Cut-down versions of Shakespeare were popular (that is, *Othello* or *Hamlet* in 20 minutes!) and all the pieces, in true melodramatic fashion, veered between blackest tragedy and broadest farce.

An impermanent and temporary form of entertainment, we are fortunate in possessing some eyewitness accounts of these gaffs. The journalist James Grant visited several in the 1830s, describing them in his book *Sketches in London*, published in 1838:

> The dramatis personae of the Penny Theatres keep up, in most cases, a very close intimacy with the audience. In many instances they carry on a sort of conversation with them during the representations of the different pieces. It is no uncommon thing to see an actor stop in the middle of some very interesting scene, to answer some question asked by one of his audience, or to parry any attempted witticism at his expense. This done, the actor resumes his part of the performance as if nothing had happened; but possibly before he has delivered half a dozen sentences more, some other question is asked, or some other sarcastic observation made by one of the auditory, in which case the performer again stops to answer or retort, as if by way of parenthesis. A cross fire is thus sometimes kept up between the audience and the actors for several minutes at a time, and, to my taste, such 'keen encounters of the wits' of the parties are much more amusing than the histrionic performances themselves.

James Greenwood in his *Wilds of London* (1874) tells of an incident at a gaff when the singer, on being barracked by his audience, proceeded to fight it out with one of the spectators in the pit before getting back on stage to finish his song.

Going further back in time to the public playhouse of Shakespeare's time, one is again struck by the very different conventions of behaviour in theatres than from those of today. The bustling and boisterous crowds were a frequent cause for condemnation by critics, and the diversity of the dramatic fare was demonstrated by the dancing bears, acrobats, sword swallowers and magicians that disported themselves before the spectators and whose entertainments were interlaced between the plays. The stage itself was usually crowded: not only would 'gallants' sit up there, but if a pickpocket was caught in a theatre he was tied to a post on the platform.[1]

The flavour of the entertainment and its contempt for dramatic 'rules' is brought out by hostile witnesses, in this case the Lord Mayor and aldermen of the City of London who had conducted a running battle with the players, in a letter dated 1597 to the Privy Council:

> They [the plays] are a special case of corrupting their youth, containing nothing but unchaste matters, lascivious devices, shifts of cozenage, and other lewd and ungodly practices, being so as that they impress the very quality and corruption of manners which they represent, contrary to the rules of art prescribed for the making of comedies even among the heathen, who used them seldom and at certain set times, and not all the year long as our manner is.[2]

A pamphleteer of the time underlines the vigour and demonstrativeness of the audience, referring to plays 'which commonly ends in six acts, the spectators frequently mounting the stage, and making a more bloody Catastrophe amongst themselves, than the Players did'. In 1602 an advertised play at the Swan was suddenly withdrawn and the frustrated audience 'revenged themselves upon the hangings, curtains, chairs, stools, walls and whatsoever came in their way, very outrageously, and made great sport'.[3]

But although there have existed, and still do, different traditions or types of theatre in this country, it is clear that not all of them are accorded equal status. To go back to the penny gaffs, it is difficult to hazard even rough estimates of the size of their audiences, but James Grant thought that something in the region of 24 000 people visited London's gaffs each evening. A recent historian has suggested that the figure would be nearer 50 000 at Christmas.[4] By contrast, Covent Garden and Drury Lane at this time, even if full, attracted less than 5 000 people an evening. Yet our knowledge of the gaffs in comparison with the latter two theatres remains minimal, and most historians neglect even a mention of their very existence – there is nothing about them, for instance, in Allardyce Nicoll's encyclopaedic histories of the nineteenth-century drama, nor in George Rowell's standard work *The Victorian Theatre*.

Why should this be the case? Is there some pattern or model which helps to explain these curious imbalances and omissions? There is indeed if one distinguishes four different traditions of theatre which have recurred in Britain over the last few centuries: 'West End' theatre, popular theatre, alternative and experimental theatre, and folk theatre. While emphasising that this is intended as a broad description rather than a rigid categorisation, and that some companies or even performances straddle two or more traditions, what are the characteristics of each?

The West End tradition is not so much a geographical definition, although it is most obviously found in London, but indicates the 'serious' form of drama that is today laden with prestige. Its most famous practitioners, such as Henry Irving, Laurence Olivier, John Gielgud and Edith Evans, are awarded titles and honorary degrees, and its literary qualities are affirmed by the generally inflexible scripts that are learnt off by heart – thus leaving little room for improvisation or spontaneity – and then published as definitive texts. Architectural considerations – in particular the ubiquitous proscenium arch – tend to reinforce the barrier between performers and audience, the latter sitting in darkness and discouraged from any participation other than that of applause at conventional moments, in case they break the 'illusion'. Theatre censorship ensured that for many years productions shied away from controversial subjects, granting privilege to the 'well made' play whose boundaries and horizons remain firmly inside the theatre itself. Allied to this West End tradition is a whole network of social indicators and symbols, with both these factors and the high price of seats accounting for the generally, but not exclusively, middle-class background of the West End audience.

The popular theatre is marked by its informality and diversity. Locations are often temporary and unpretentious, encouraging a crude and straightforward presentation rather than expensive production values, and the lack of a proscenium barrier encourages a close and intimate relationship with the audience who are very much a part of the performance. All the most popular entertainers in this tradition, such as Joe Grimaldi the clown, Marie Lloyd the music hall singer and today's stand-up comics, thrive upon the contact, ad-libbing and enjoying the banter with the spectators. Improvisation, spontaneity and topicality are uppermost, and the bill of fare usually swings from farce to tragedy within the same piece, ignoring literary dictates as to unity of style. The fluidity of popular theatre is illustrated by the scantiness of written texts. Sir Barry Jackson has written of seeing performances in the early years of this century where 'the actors were told the outlines of the plot and were then thrown onto the stage to fill out the dialogue to the best of their ability'.[5]

Alternative, experimental or fringe theatre – the variety of terms employed to describe it reflecting its elusive and changeable nature – is distinguished by a more self-conscious antagonism towards the West End or commercial theatre, which is usually seen as bankrupt on political and artistic grounds. Arguing that the commercialism of the West End stifles artistic innovation and excludes controversial subject matter in its search for bland entertainment, alternative theatres invariably issue manifestoes and statements of aims and strive to create new forms of theatre for 'new' audiences (that is, those people who do not go to the West End), often using a bewildering array of experimental techniques and devices. Experimental companies are often organised and run on collective lines in an effort to get away from the 'star syndrome' and specialised functions seen as part of the West End tradition's malaise. Usually such ventures are not self-supporting – financial backing may come from a wealthy individual, a political organisation or in recent years from state subsidy – and are generally short-lived.

Finally, there is folk theatre, a form of communal ritual which often appears meaningless to outsiders and is typically the expression of a close-knit parish or village. One commentator has decided it as an 'annual restatement of a small community's self-definition'.[6] The essential features of the performance are not written down but instead pass orally and in the vernacular from generation to generation, with participants undergoing a slow graduation from menial tasks to more important contributions. Folk theatre is not easily transplanted to industrial centres where a sense of community is conspicuously absent, in contrast to the more urban context of popular theatre.

In setting up this model of the four traditions of British theatre, it should be stressed that these are descriptive and not evaluative terms – unlike in Peter Brook's *The Empty Space* where he distinguishes a 'Deadly', a 'Holy', a 'Rough' and an 'Immediate' theatre. But however approximate this division into four traditions, it does clarify why, for example, subsidised theatre in Britain today is so often caught between different stools: trying to be commercial, experimental and also popular. Responding to a cut in the Arts Council's grant to the Royal Shakespeare Company, its joint artistic director Terry Hands expressed the dilemma: 'There really is no such thing as subsidized theatre in England. What we have is commercial theatre in which there is public investment. We have always been concerned with box office. That building-in of commercial potential has now become mandatory.'[7] The intermingling of commercial backing for the company's musical *Les Miserables* provided a graphic demonstration of this trend.

The model of the four traditions of British theatre also explains the relative prominence of, say, Drury Lane and the penny gaffs. The former belongs securely in the West End tradition, its status guaranteeing that all the theatre's productions were extensively reviewed, its plays published and its financial and administrative details recorded. The gaffs on the other hand come from the popular tradition, until recently ignored by critics and historians.

The dominance of the West End tradition arose from the changes which transformed the theatrical world in the late nineteenth century, sketched out more fully in Chapter Three, and the introduction at that time of dramatic criticism into newspapers and magazines conveys the judgements and assumptions which effectively dismissed the existence of other forms of theatre. Emphasis was placed on the 'literary-critical', that is the words on the page, and away from the popular theatre where performance is paramount. Arising from this came a dramatic hierarchy whose pecking order still remains intact today. The best way to bring out these attitudes is to quote from two influential reviewers and 'men of letters' of the Victorian period.

For example, Henry Morley wrote in 1866: 'in our provinces and colonies the form of entertainment will be, as it now is, mainly determined by the example of the eight or nine theatres in or near the West-end of London of which I hold the performances to be worth serious attention.' Thirty years later William Archer considered that 'at the Princess's and the Opera Comique the entertainments presented have occasionally been so distinctly of the East End or provincial order that I felt they did not come within my critical province.'[8]

Such attitudes, if not always expressed with quite that tone of patronising complacency, can be multiplied endlessly, and the equation West End = theatre lives on today. One recent book, for instance, states that 'Between 1865 and 1914 (and afterwards, to a lessened degree) West End theatre *was* British theatre',[9] a view which exterminates many of the groups and organisations dealt with in the first half of this book as well as the penny gaffs and strollers of the late Victorian period.

The magnitude of this sort of bias has meant that few research students or historians tackle 'non-West End' subjects such as the popular theatre. Shakespeare was once a strolling player and thus one of the 'rogues and vagabonds' scourged by Elizabethan statutes; but there is virtually nothing available on the history of strollers since Shakespeare's time. Innumerable biographies have been published of the great actors and actresses who graced the stage in the eighteenth and nineteenth centuries; not one of John Richardson, the man whose travelling theatre with its booth capable of holding a thousand spectators was 'theatre' for many more people than Covent Garden or Drury Lane. Bearing out Morley's and Archer's implicit view that to be popular is somehow to be by definition superficial or insubstantial, Joe Grimaldi's biographer Richard Findlater has observed:

Scores of 'straight' players who were not much better than serviceable artists were more fully commemorated at the time than was a great buffoon like Grimaldi, because they were employed in a *respectable* branch of the theatre, while pantomime was despised as vulgar or childish nonsense by the majority of educated playgoers.[10]

That both playgoers and critics looked down on the pantomime underlines the fact that it is not a conspiracy that we know relatively little about popular theatre: bedevilled by a lack of records, being primarily an oral form, by its very nature the popular theatre is impermanent and temporary. But the dramatic hierarchy ensures that little effort is made on behalf of popular theatre, and we can see the process at work around us.

It is the popular drama of radio and television which is now largely ignored. Writing about radio drama, one critic has suggested:

None of the people one might expect to be sufficiently enthusiastic about the subject to research it and write about it – dramatic critics, literary scholars, cultural historians, sociologists of the mass media – have shown much interest in it, especially in Britain, even though BBC Radio has serious claims to provide the best radio service in the world and is the envy of many countries.[11]

Similarly with television drama; although the huge size of the audience it attracts is recognised, 'sections of the intellectual Establishment are still averting their eyes from it. The modest role that television drama plays in university syllabuses is clear evidence of this. How many English Departments consider making a TV play a prescribed text?'[12]

The feebleness of much television reviewing in the press indicates this prejudice. Why does this bias exist? Because literary critics and academics are dismissive of anything that smacks too obviously of 'entertainment': to be educational or artistic requires seriousness and, as Christopher Bigsby has noted, to be not too freely or widely available.[13]

If popular theatre has suffered, then so too has folk drama of which little is known, even though the work which has been carried out hints at the wealth of material waiting to be discovered. As for experimental and alternative theatre in

Britain, the last few years have seen greater interest and some excellent work has been published on, for example, suffragette theatre and Joan Littlewood's Theatre Workshop. But here the political leanings of most researchers have meant that most attention has been devoted to the overtly political groups such as the Workers' Theatre Movement of the 1920s and early 1930s, thus tending to ignore or reject, in Colin Chambers' words, 'the work of those not openly committed to a revolutionary politics'.[14] Often missing too is the placing of experimental and alternative theatre within the rest of British drama and its context: what is alternative theatre alternative to?

It might be thought that such a survey of research done and the sketching out of critics' prejudices is of little interest or significance to anyone other than drama critics themselves. But in fact the more powerful of these values do affect us all, mainly through the educational system. Shakespeare is the best case in point: the only authentic representation – the 'Chandos' portrait hanging in the National Portrait Gallery – shows him as a swarthy stroller wearing a golden earring; but subsequent images invariably depict him as 'Our National Bard', dignified, respectable and very dull. As we saw earlier in the chapter, the conditions in which Shakespeare's plays were performed were akin to a music hall or circus, catering to a popular audience with its taste for excitement and action: an audience well able to encompass rapid switches from tragedy to comedy and back again in the same play or even within the same act. Thus the treatment of his plays down the years has often been irreverent and selective. The nineteenth century witnessed performances of *Macbeth* with fifty 'Singing Witches', a *Hamlet* with a happy ending when King Hamlet marries Queen Ophelia, and dog and equestrian versions of Shakespeare's plays. In the 1840s the wandering showman D. P. Miller could be found staging *Richard III* twenty times in seven hours.[15]

The love of Shakespeare nevertheless penetrated deep into the working classes: quite apart from the popularity of Shakespeare adaptations at the Victorian gaffs and circuses, one comes across cases of the girl factory employees in the late 1840s who used to read his plays together at 5 o'clock in the morning for an hour before going off to work.[16] As a final case, a clergyman in the 1870s came across a little boy in the street reciting *Richard III* to his companions:

> After a time, he asked the lad how much he knew. 'All but the last Act, sir,' was the reply; 'and that I'll learn as soon as I get sixpence!' 'Why sixpence?' 'To go to Sadler's Wells with. I learnt it all there, and I know one or two more.' 'And can't you read?' 'No, sir, nobody never taught me.'[17]

But alongside this popular regard for Shakespeare was another attitude which frowned upon the playwright for what was seen as his 'low' side. Already in the court circles of Charles I's day Shakespeare's reputation had declined, and in the middle-class London theatres of the eighteenth century his plays were cut and excised: unsavoury parts such as those of the Fool in *King Lear*, the porter in *Macbeth* and the gravediggers in *Hamlet* were omitted. In 1818 Dr Thomas Bowdler published his 'family' edition of Shakespeare, leaving out those phrases thought unsuitable to be heard or seen by women and children.

After the Education Act of 1870 which established a system of primary education in Britain, Shakespeare's plays began to be studied and read in schools but in a context which emphasised above all the 'texts' themselves and disregarded the conditions under which the plays were performed and written. It was impossible to guess that Shakespeare produced only acting scripts or that he possessed a thorough knowledge of 'bawdy'. The Newbolt Report of 1921 on *The Teaching of English in England*, which has been carefully dissected by Derek Longhurst, exemplifies this highly distorted approach to 'The National Bard'. There we are told that his plays are true 'not of an age, but for all time', thereby ignoring the social context of drama. Some of Shakespeare's plays should be treated with caution: 'Boys and girls should never be allowed to see the wood-magic of *A Midsummer Night's Dream* destroyed by the protracted clowning of Bottom, or to find the flower-sweet loveliness of *Twelfth Night* sullied by extravagant orgies of would-be comic drunkenness.'[18] Such an approach was given further intellectual validation by the criticism of the Cambridge don F. R. Leavis who focused on the words on a page before a reader and dismissed the notion of drama in performance.

In other words, the process attempted to transfer Shakespeare from the popular tradition towards a more West End tradition, playing down those elements within his plays which made him stand out in his own time. It is this attitude which has held ever since, demanding that great chunks of his plays set by examination boards are learnt off by heart and then regurgitated on to thousands of exam papers.

In the light of this example, it is worth asking whether the different traditions of British theatre do not need revaluation, particularly in respect of their varying weight and authority. Although the mainstream or commercial theatre is always likely to occupy the most prominent position, the other traditions deserve much greater attention from critics, historians, publishers and theatre-goers. *Other Theatres* is a small step in this direction.

Chapter 2

Castles, Ghosts and Chartists: Stage Melodrama in the Nineteenth Century

Melodrama, which simply means music with action, plays an important part within popular entertainment. Turn to any 'soap opera' on television and its principal features soon become apparent: the stereotyped characters, the background music which keys in the audience's intended response, the mix of violence and farce, tragedy and comedy, the happy ending, the emphasis placed on sensation and physical events, the sentimental appeal to the emotions rather than the mind.

The origins of melodrama in this country can be traced back many centuries, back for instance to the Robin Hood ballads of the Middle Ages which were recited aloud before an illiterate audience. Chapbooks, broadsides and almanacs of the seventeenth and eighteenth centuries — the whole phenomenon of the 'street literature' described as 'non-books' of the poor[1] – continued in the same mould, supplemented in the later eighteenth century by the 'Gothic novel' such as Horace Walpole's *The Castle of Otranto* (1764) and Ann Radcliffe's *The Mysteries of Udolpho* (1794).

As for stage melodrama, its beginnings are sometimes dated from Schiller's play *The Robbers* of 1782, but it first came of age with the birth of the Parisian boulevard theatres of the 1790s which catered for a largely working-class and uneducated audience, stirred up by the momentous political events taking place around them. Pixerecourt, the most prolific of the boulevard playwrights, once remarked that 'I am writing for those who cannot read', and the plays themselves were rather like today's strip cartoons.[2] By the 1800s melodrama was starting to dominate the British stage too, primarily because the far-reaching political, social and economic changes transforming everyday life – most notably the impact of industrialisation and of major migration from the countryside to the towns and cities – rendered this form of entertainment especially attractive.

Britain's population rose from 9 million in 1750 to 10 million in 1800, an increase of just over 10 per cent; but then it doubled in the next 50 years to 20 million and almost doubled again by 1900 to 37 million. Simultaneously there took place a huge expansion of many towns and cities: Manchester's population, for instance, jumped from 17 000 in 1760 to 180 000 in 1830, and Bradford's from 13 000 in 1801 to 104 000 in 1851. The growth of London was the most spectacular: from just under a million inhabitants in 1800, the capital numbered 4½ million by 1900. The extent of Britain's urbanisation was such that by the time of the 1851 census more people lived in towns and cities than in rural areas – decades before a similar landmark was reached elsewhere in Europe.

Within these rapidly developing towns the introduction of new forms of production within factories created very different conditions of work, this division of labour ensuring the decline of small-scale handicraft industry. The workforce now lived near to the factories, unlike their masters, and the rows of unhealthy tenements and cellars reinforced the separation between employer and employee. For the first time 'the language of class', in Asa Briggs' phrase, began to be heard.[3]

In view of these massive changes it was inevitable that traditional forms of recreation and leisure would be largely reshaped. Most important within the context of this book were the new or transformed entertainments which appealed to this irreverent and urban working-class public searching for welcome relief from the rigours of factory discipline. Older venues and habits were turned upside down: the Drury Lane and Covent Garden theatres, for example, hosted the clown Joe Grimaldi as he refashioned the pantomime by shifting its subject-matter to the town settings which his audience recognised and enjoyed, and Sadler's Wells fell in with the vogue for 'aqua-drama' by installing a huge tank – just as the new Drury Lane of 1794 incorporated a lake.[4]

Many novel types of entertainment grew up: Philip Astley pioneered the circus with his Amphitheatre from 1769, penny theatres or 'gaffs' abounded, and saloon theatres like the Bower created a form known as 'burletta', an attempt to evade the prohibition that only the patent or established theatres should stage 'legitimate' plays. These saloon theatres later developed into music halls. Finally, enormous new East End or 'minor' theatres were built: there was the Pavilion from 1828, the Standard from 1835, and the Britannia in Hoxton from 1843, all of them capable of holding several thousand people.

The demand was not for nuanced and subtle plays but for lashings of emotion and physical sensation, supported by an orchestra thundering and scraping in accompaniment and the players roaring out their words: in a word, melodrama. Anything and everything was grist to this mill, from 'bird' drama to *Hamlet* done by dogs. It was a popular theatre which characteristically resisted categorisation or neat definitions, exemplified by the well-known play *Black-Eyed Susan* with its combination of dialogue, song, dance and music. Performers like Edmund Kean, who had started out as a 'barnstormer', were ideally suited to such conditions, the frenzy of his and other actors' playing whipped up by the shouts and encouragement of the spectators.

It was an audience both eager and determined to make its feelings known. What the socialist Robert Blatchford, who began his career working for the saloon theatres, recalled of the spectators at the Bower in the mid-nineteenth century remained true for much of the century: 'the audience at the Bower were uncritical and had a robust taste. They demanded ghosts and pirates, smugglers and slave-drivers, Jack Tars and brigands: combats, abductions, love, treachery, battle, murder and blue fire – and they got them.'[5]

The influx of these new theatre-goers reversed the trend which had held since the theatres were reopened after the restoration of Charles II: drama became once more, as it had been during Shakespearean times, frequented by the majority of the nation. But unaccustomed to or unconcerned by previous modes of behaviour within the playhouse, these new working-class audiences proved highly demonstrative. For instance when a play called *The Tailors* was performed at the Haymarket in 1805, a group of tailors objected with such force to what they considered to be a slur on their trade that seventy of them were arrested.[6] In 1812 pitched battles were fought at the Theatre Royal, Nottingham, over the refusal of some spectators to stand up when the National Anthem was played.[7] At the Royal Coburg (later the Old Vic) in 1827 a particular play caused the audience to throw so much rubbish at the stage that the actors and musicians had to perform with their hats on.[8] Most famously of all, the Old Price Riots of 1809 at Covent Garden, sparked off by the decision of the proprietor Kemble to raise the prices and increase the number of private boxes, lasted for sixty-seven consecutive nights: spectators turned the theatre into a fairground, dancing, blowing trumpets and horns, and even letting birds and pigs loose in the auditorium.

Again and again description and comment on the early and mid-nineteenth century theatre bring out the disgust felt by some at the new theatre-goers. Take for example John Hollingshead's remarks on the audience at the Victoria Theatre in 1861 at a performance of *Oliver Twist*:

> Half the evil, low-browed, lowering faces in London are wedged in, twelve-hundred deep, perspiring, watchful, silent. Every man is in his yellow shirt sleeves, every woman has her battered bonnet in her lap. The yell when Bill Sykes murders Nancy is like the roar of a thousand wild beasts, and they show their disapprobation of the act, and their approbation of the actor, by cursing him in no measured terms.[9]

It was not a process confined to London. A typically moralistic judgement was passed on the Manchester theatre in 1844: 'The theatre does nothing to purify and elevate the taste, and furnishes little but what is necessary to attract the crowd habituated to gross pursuits . . . The more moral portion of the community, therefore, shun it, and wisely so, as fraught with immoral tendencies.'[10] The middle classes were indeed leaving the playhouse for the rather more staid and genteel pleasures of the opera. As F. G. Tomlins summarised in 1851: 'The conclusion, then, we must come to is, that the cultivated and propertied classes have mostly forsaken the English theatres; the portion that like theatrical performances transferring their patronage to the opera and musical entertainments.'[11]

Clearly then stage melodrama at this time was a working-class form so far as the composition of the audience was concerned – although it appears that the hack playwrights themselves rarely were. At least one half of the English melodramas staged in the first half of the nineteenth century were plagiarisms from the French stage, which thus required writers to be able to travel to that country and understand the language well enough in order to write the plays down word for word and then translate them. But is it possible to go on from the working-class character of stage melodrama and treat it as a radical form, possibly containing a critique of an emerging capitalist society?

Certainly an undercurrent of generalised discontent runs through some of the plays, especially the 'factory plays'. For example John Walker's *The Factory Lad*, which was put on at the Surrey Theatre in London for a few nights in 1832 and is often advanced as confirmation of the radical tendencies of melodrama, includes the familiar figure of a stony-hearted squire who is 'rationalising' his factory by introducing new steam looms. As well as having his factory burnt to the ground, this squire Westwood receives his final come-uppance when he is shot dead by the local poacher Rushton. Throughout the play various asides and remarks question the justice of the legal system; the magistrate is called Justice Bias and he asserts at one stage:

> The law is made alike for rich and poor.
> RUSHTON: Is it? Why, then, does it so often lock the poor man
> in a jail, while the rich one goes free?[12]

Other factory plays of the period tackled the same kind of subjects – poaching, unemployment, bad housing, upper-class designs on working-class maidens, the hypocrisy of the church – and had broadly similar titles; amongst them were Douglas Jerrold's *Factory Girl* and *Factory Lad* of 1832, Atkyne's *The Life of a Labourer*, Stirling's *Mary of Manchester; or, the Spirit of the Loom*,

Richard Peake's *The Climbing Boy; or, the Little Sweep*, and J. T. Haines' *The Factory Boy*. Dramatisations of Charles Dickens' novels, particularly *Oliver Twist*, often linked crime together with the horrific social conditions.

But by and large the oppression shown in these plays is of a personalised nature and does not portray let alone condemn the structures of this new society. In other words individuals are blamed and not the social order itself, just as the ballads of previous centuries had suggested that if only the King's 'evil counsellors' were removed then all would be well. Usually too the plays have a happy ending, similar to those in the 'industrial novels' of the 1840s and 1850s written by authors like Disraeli and Charles Kingsley.

Significant within the genre of melodrama were the highwaymen plays in which such outlaws as Dick Turpin and Jack Sheppard played the starring roles. This phenomenon had been stimulated by the novels of Harrison Ainsworth with his *Rookwood* published in 1834 about Turpin, and *Jack Sheppard* in 1840. Both novels were dramatised all over the country, setting off a vogue for Turpin canes, masks and other 'memorabilia'. The plays invariably concluded with a repentant or dead criminal – but only after the audience had spent the major part of the play delighting in his exploits. However in the 1860s this type of play was banned from the stage by the Lord Chamberlain,[13] a ruling which leads on to the question: what part did censorship play in toning down the political content of stage melodrama?

From 1737 the theatres had been governed by the Stage Licensing Act, a statute which granted the Lord Chamberlain complete and arbitrary powers. Scripts had to be submitted to his office at least two weeks before performance and he could cut out what he wished without the theatre manager or writer having any right of appeal. Because of this legislation, writers like Henry Fielding who had produced many political satires before 1737 turned their backs on the stage and devoted their energies to the fledgling art of the novel. With words such as 'thigh' excised and lines like 'For your country fight and be free' censored for being too controversial, what issue of any substance could be raised on the stage?[14]

But although the 'legitimate' theatres of Covent Garden and

Drury Lane were thus hamstrung by the Lord Chamberlain's catch-all tests of 'Nature, Taste and Good Sense', the popular theatre of fairground, strolling players, minors and penny gaffs were often able to evade the provisions of the 1737 Act. One method was by accompanying the action with musical passages and then arguing that the piece was thus a 'Burletta' and not a play. Another form of entertainment which eluded the Examiner of Plays – to whom the Lord Chamberlain in practice delegated his powers – was the pantomime, primarily because of its non-verbal qualities. In the hands of a performer like Joe Grimaldi the pantomime burlesqued Regency fashions and foibles, ridiculed figures of authority like squires, magistrates, the clergy and lawyers, and poked fun at the vanity of army officers parading around in their opulent uniforms. Grimaldi's Clown relied on ad-libbing and improvisation, and although technically illegal it proved difficult for the Examiner of Plays to pin down the offence, especially as the audience delighted in just such spontaneity. Parliamentary reform, the Peterloo massacre, and the issue of the Corn Law were all broached by the pantomime but ignored by the established theatres.[15]

In 1843 the Theatres Act was passed in order to clarify a legal situation which had been confused by the activities of the minors. As well as breaking the hold of Covent Garden, Drury Lane and the Haymarket theatres on the legitimate drama, the statute redefined the scope of censorship. Plays were to be shown to the Lord Chamberlain in script form at least seven days before the proposed performance, and he was empowered to prohibit the whole or part of a play whenever 'he shall be of opinion that it is fitting for the preservation of good manners, decorum or of the public peace so to do'. This piece of legislation remained in being until 1968 and casts its shadow over the rest of this book.

The 1843 Act was comprehensive in that it also applied to minor theatres, and its wide powers meant that much would depend on the character and attitudes of the Examiner of Plays himself. From 1849 until 1874 that post was occupied by William Bodham Donne whose forbidden territory comprised the unholy trinity of sex, religion and politics. Factory plays like adaptions of Disraeli's *Coningsby* and Elizabeth Gaskell's *Mary*

Barton were either severely cut or banned entirely; and even a version of Victor Hugo's *Ruy Blas* was vetoed because a valet has the temerity to have a queen fall in love with him. Such a draconian policy inevitably led to self-censorship: 'Authors and managers could ill afford to place before the Examiner a play that in the last few days before production would require extensive overhauling.'[16]

But even when we bear in mind the work of the censor and also the fact that only a fraction of the 25 000 to 30 000 plays performed in the nineteenth century was ever published and has therefore come down to us today, the claims made for the radical tendencies of Victorian melodramas appear misplaced. It is revealing in this respect that historians of the penny dreadfuls and other such 'street literature' of the time have come to similar conclusions. One commentator has described them as revealing a mood that failed to find 'a direct expression';[17] and Victor Neuberg has gone further: 'There is little evidence in the sheets of anything more than a vaguely sketched class-consciousness – class and economic antagonisms are, indeed, played down.'[18]

Intrinsic to stage melodrama as a highly popular entertainment was the welter of noise and excitement, the providential endings, the two-dimensional plots and characters – elements which by themselves precluded rational analyses of situations, quite apart from the conditions within the playhouses where they were staged, let alone proposals for political change. But worse than this, however, for those few individuals in the nineteenth century who wished to use the drama as a part of the reform movement: the very ubiquity and pervasiveness of melodrama meant that it was difficult to produce or even conceive of alternatives to it as a pattern of theatre. The one section of early nineteenth-century society which had an interest in so doing was the nascent labour movement engendered by industrialisation and the growth of towns and cities.

Yet again this whole subject is often frustrated by the paucity of surviving evidence, with tantalising references or allusions leading nowhere. To take one example: an article in the *Anglo-Soviet Journal* of Autumn 1958 mentions 'the theatrical shows organised by the Corresponding Societies' in the 1790s, but further details as to quite what these early radical clubs actually put on have not been unearthed.[19] But even if one is aware of the tenuous routes by which material is passed down to future generations, it does seem that the majority of effort and energy expended by members of the labour movement in the cultural field was poured into the publication of radical newspapers and pamphlets, amongst them William Cobbett's *Political Register*, Wooler's *Black Dwarf* and the Chartist journals of the 1830s and 1840s such as the *Northern Star*.

We do know that theatre riots often took on an overtly political character. During the Old Price (OP) Riots of 1809, one of the placards paraded in the theatre read 'John Bull Will Have His Rights' and historians have referred to the outbursts mounted by sections of the audience at this time, one commentator observing that theatre riots generally were tantamount to 'a species of class-war'.[20] There is no sign however that the riots and disturbances were anything other than of a negative and short-lived character (other than the OP Riots), or that political orators and activists attempted to make use of these rowdy theatre-goers.

Perhaps the first documented instance of a play intended for a 'non-commercial' theatre was William Cobbett's three-act comedy entitled *Surplus Population* and published in his periodical *Two-penny Trash* in June 1831, and it does appear that this was indeed staged before audiences. R. K. Webb, in his *The British Working-class Reader 1790–1848*, asserts, without a supporting reference, that 'it was played with great success in rural areas in southern England'; fortunately George Spater in his biography of Cobbett is more forthcoming: the play was republished in 1835 and acted in the neighbourhood of Normandy farm. Cobbett himself said that it was to be taken on a tour of Hampshire, Sussex and Kent villages, and certainly the performance at Tonbridge, which was to have been attended by Cobbett, was vetoed by the local authorities. Whether the intended tour took place we do not know.[21]

Surplus Population testifies to the pervasive hold of melodrama as a form in the nineteenth century. Betsy Birch, a buxom eighteen-year-old lass, is engaged to marry Dick Hoyle but menaced by the lecherous advances of Sir Gripe Grindum. The other main protagonist is Squire Thimble who trots out the arguments of the Reverend Thomas Malthus in favour of limits on population growth in general, and on Betsy in particular. But to no avail:

> SQUIRE THIMBLE: she laughs at the idea of moral restraint.
> SIR GRIPE GRINDUM: I dare say she does. [Aside] And so shall I, too, if I can get her into my clutches.

As expected, everything turns out happily. Cobbett's hostility towards Malthusian ideas is made known by means of a discussion between a farmer and a shoemaker; and Grindum's evil plans being discovered, he is run out of the village leaving the young men and women to 'live and love in peace'. Cobbett planned to write another play on *Bastards in High Life* but it appears that he failed to do so.[22]

The Owenites – the followers of the factory owner and philanthropist Robert Owen – set up a thriving alternative culture of their own in the 1830s and 1840s, 'a social world in which members could move during their leisure hours'.[23] Activities included choirs and bands, festivals, hymn singing and dancing, libraries and 'Halls of Science' – but nothing substantial has yet come to light about any dramatic events, other than vague references to 'occasional theatrical performances'. The chances are against them organising such initiatives on any sustained basis, for two reasons. First, the puritanical strain within the movement frowned on the frivolous and make-believe nature of theatre; and secondly, Owenite literature tended to be, in the words of J. F. C. Harrison, 'expository and didactic, with occasional pieces of romantic or millennial rhetoric' – a stance that would not encourage the development of a dramatic programme.[24]

The Chartists in the same period established a lively range of cultural projects in marked contrast to mainstream culture, publishing their own books, newspapers, and poetry. But one area which they shied away from was the theatre, despite the fact that one of their leaders, Feargus O'Connor, as a young man wrote a number of plays. Another, Ernest Jones, did once attack the theatre in an article of 1847 for its political bias; it is worth quoting at some length because it is the first instance of such criticism and the forerunner of many others:

Can no new fire be infused into what is called the 'expiring drama'? – expiring, because it has been dedicated to an expiring cause – because it has been the pander to wealth and fashion, instead of the vindicator of manhood and industry. Whenever, indeed, it has ridiculed or chastised an aristocratic vice, it has done so playfully and kindly, shewing it in a sportive light, and, at any rate depicting how it made an equal suffer, not how it crushed a 'subordinate'. We have had the misfortunes of younger sons, the mishaps of injured daughters of noble houses, but when has the Bastille victim, when the lost child of labour, when has the hapless operative (the martyrs of the nineteenth century), when have these been brought before the public eye in the drama, or when will they?[25]

Jones ended his article with a warning and a hope: 'Let our dramatic talent be on the lookout. Chartism is marching into the fields of literature with rapid strides; the precincts of the drama it has not yet passed.' From the evidence which we have, it seems that it never did.

The Chartist Thomas Cooper did form a Shakespearean Society in Leicester, putting on *Hamlet*, with himself in the title part (he knew the whole play off by heart), in order to pay some legal expenses and support his wife when he was in prison. In his autobiography Cooper claims that the performance of January 1843 was a big success with crowds of 3000 attending each production, but that income barely covered expenses – which is odd as they could not have amounted to much. The local press of the time suggests that Cooper's memory had let him down.[26]

As for original material written at that period of the 1830s and 1840s, the handful of plays still in existence are characterised by their inflated rhetoric which was clearly modelled on the worst of Shakespeare. For instance John Watkins' *Oliver Cromwell, the Protector*, published in 1848, demanded a cast of 38, impractical for small groups of Chartists, even if several parts were doubled. It also cost 2s 6d to purchase a printed copy, putting it well out of the price range of those scraping together a penny for a newspaper like the *Poor Man's Guardian*.

John Watkins wrote another historical play called *Runnymede, or the Magna Carta*, costing 1s 6d to buy, and a more topical play about John Frost, the man who had led the Newport rising in 1839 in an attempt to provoke a national insurrection. Published in 1841 in the *Northern Star*, Watkins from the start seemed unsure as to quite what his play was meant to convey: 'This drama is not so much intended to illustrate the characters of the dramatis personae in it, nor the insurrection at Newport, on which the plot turns, as it is an attempt to illustrate Chartism itself.'

A Soviet commentator has claimed that the play was produced at the time by 'workers' collectives', but this seems unlikely in view of its cumbersome style.[27] Here John Frost is in his cell waiting to be transported:

> Transported! – 'tis to drag on death alive.
> Such mercy is the worst of cruelty.
> The fiends alone can call it mercy.
> Oh, 'tis sardonic! transport! aye, indeed!
> Transport in penal flames! – transported, ha!
> They'll next call hell, – heaven – devils too.
> They'll christen angels – so, indeed, they are,
> Compar'd with those who make their hell of England.

In view of the unsuitability of these Chartist plays for performance, some groups fell back on earlier work, notably Robert Southey's dramatic poem *Wat Tyler*. Written by Southey in 1817 as 'one impatient of all the oppressions that are done under the sun', the poem reads – and no doubt could be recited – with great fire and gusto. That Chartists had to rely on such material written some years before their own movement indicates the weakness and virtual non-existence of their own plays. Lacking any guidelines at all as to what a radical literature and drama might actually look like, Chartist writers fell back on laboured imitations of sonnets, epics and Shakespeare.

Apart from this scanty Chartist theatrical activity, we are left with scattered references that promise more than they begin to deliver. For example, a benefit performance was given at the Coburg in May 1832 for Spanish refugees in England who had

fled from the Carlist disturbances. The bill included a five-act
tragedy and some other Spanish pieces. Was this production
attended only by Spanish refugees, or did Londoners also
provide moral and financial support?[28] We do not know. When
the stonemasons went on strike in 1841, they hired the Victoria
Theatre in order to present a dramatised version of their own
case.[29] The headquarters of the National Union of the Working
Classes in the early 1830s, the Rotunda in Blackfriars Road,
London was also a theatre: some overlap there? Finally, the
Select Committee of 1832 looking into Dramatic Literature was
anxious about the political drama which they suspected was
being staged at minor theatres – but it is important to note that
the manager of the Coburg denied this assertion, stating that if
he had done so he would have run the risk of opposing groups
tearing his theatre apart, a consideration which must have
weighed heavily with many other managers.

It does not add up to much, at least so far. Why should this
be the case? Here one returns to the whole question of
melodrama itself: in the early and mid-nineteenth century its
very popularity inhibited the development of other forms of
'non-commercial' drama. There was simply no other model of
theatre available on which playwrights could draw in an
attempt to get away from the crude characterisations and
stereotypes of melodrama. This is not to argue that melodrama
can never function as a political force in the theatre or
elsewhere, but merely that during this period it did not do so. A
second problem lay in the difficulty of producing theatrical
events – drama is the most social of forms and therefore
requires a great deal of organisation. The labour movement at
this time clearly did not think, or even actively consider, that
such effort was worthwhile.

However in the last few decades of the nineteenth century
British theatre was transformed yet again, and one major
consequence was the severe weakening of the hold of
melodrama on the stage: did this development offer an
opportunity for the creation of forms of alternative and
experimental theatre?

Chapter 3

The Rise of the West End – and Some Independent Theatres

The Theatres Act 1843 broke the control of the 'legitimate' drama exercised by Covent Garden, Drury Lane and the Haymarket, thus permitting other playhouses to present spoken drama. But it was some years before this opportunity was fully taken up – no new theatres were built in London between 1845 and 1866[1] – mainly because the working-class audiences attending the melodramas did not represent a financially attractive proposition for theatrical entrepreneurs. Gradually, however, from the late 1860s this began to change, and over twenty-five new theatres were built in London's West End before the turn of the century, together with many others in the London suburbs and the provincial centres.

That such an expansion took place at this time indicated the enormous changes affecting the British theatre in the later nineteenth century, a process which centred on the wooing back of the middle-class audience which had earlier in the century transferred its patronage to the opera. The key to this change lay in the creation of a respectable and prestigious West End theatre very different from the noisy melodramas of the old playhouses.

The landmarks in this episode come in a rush. Madame Vestris, the manageress of the Olympic theatre, began to put on specific, well-organised programmes rather than the sprawling six-hour entertainments favoured by, say, Sadler's Wells. At the Adelphi in 1858 the apron stage was discarded in

25

favour of a picture-frame stage – the apron jutting out into the auditorium encouraged performers to 'play to' the spectators. Henry Irving at the Lyceum in the 1870s began the practice of rehearsals, introduced the lit stage and darkened auditorium, and ended the custom of the recall of actors and actresses at the end of bravura passages but in the middle of the play. Programmes, reservations, an 8 o'clock start, evening dress, much higher admission prices of up to a guinea and a half in the stalls, carpets, and fixed, upholstered and numbered seats were other innovations introduced throughout London's more 'up market' theatres in the last decades of the Victorian period.

New patterns of theatre management were fostered by the actor–managers, men who controlled individual playhouses and ran them in an autocratic fashion ensuring that no breath of impropriety or scandal should ever touch their establishments, unlike the excesses associated earlier in the century with Edmund Kean. The very concept of West End theatre was assisted by the redevelopment taking place within the centre of the city, involving the migration of the poor away from central districts into the East End – the terms 'West End' and 'East End' were familiar and accepted by the 1880s[2] – and the construction of new thoroughfares such as Shaftesbury Avenue and Charing Cross Road in place of the slums that had once existed in the middle of the capital. Transport improvements too played their part, with the Underground permitting those who lived in the suburbs to visit the West End with ease. All these changes had the effect of excluding the 'rough' working-class spectators who had patronised the old melodrama.

The changes within the theatres diminished the closeness which had formerly existed between performers and audience. For instance the 'Fourth Wall' convention, encouraged by the proscenium arch which was a standard feature in West End theatres led to actors and actresses ignoring the spectators as if they were just another 'wall'. Not surprisingly the audience gradually became much more staid in their behaviour and conduct, as a series of eyewitnesses testified. A German observer, Prince Puckler-Muskau, commented on the boisterousness of theatre-goers in 1826:

English freedom degenerates into the rudest license, and it is not uncommon in the midst of the most affecting part of a tragedy, or the most charming cadenza of a singer, to hear some coarse expression shouted from the galleries in stentor voice. This is followed, according to the taste of the bystanders, either by loud laughter and approbation, or by the castigation and the expulsion of the offender.[3]

But by 1877 the writer Henry James could write of the London audience: 'It is well dressed, tranquil, motionless; it suggests domestic virtue and comfortable homes; it looks as if it had come to the play in its own carriage, after a dinner of beef and pudding.'[4] Similarly Karl Marx's wife Jenny, an avid theatre-goer, complained of the audience's restraint in an article published in the mid-1870s: 'It sat in deadly silence, with only an occasional timid clapping: no such applause as might encourage the young actor. Everyone sat passive and immovable.'[5]

Such a transformation was not confined to London. Writing about the Theatre Royal in Hull for example, Donald Roy notes the hierarchical divisions enshrined in the architecture of the new building and concludes of the changes between 1850 and 1880: 'the theatre can now afford to project a markedly different image of itself; the likely corollary is that it has already begun to retrieve the custom of the prosperous middle classes and their social superiors.'[6] The same process was occurring in virtually all the provincial cities.

Within other forms of entertainment such as the music hall, parallel developments were taking place. The earlier halls had grown out of pubs and saloon bars, but by the second half of the century proprietors were realising the financial benefits which accrued both from economies of scale and a family audience. As with the theatre, new halls like the London Pavilion in 1886 penetrated the West End, putting on a highly respectable face: bars were cut off from the auditorium; the chairmen and tables were phased out; chorus singing and encores discouraged; uniformed commissionaires and individual, tip-up seats introduced. The new Certificates of Suitability required safety curtains and fire exits, and the prohibitive cost of installing them closed down many of the more sleazy music halls and penny gaffs. By the time Edward Moss and Oswald Stoll combined forces in 1899 with a joint capital of £1½ million, the lively and alcoholic music hall had been turned into the more refined and genteel Theatre of Variety.[7]

Several of the changes within the theatre did meet with some opposition – there were riots when the pit at the Haymarket was abolished in 1880. When Emma Cons took over the Old Vic and transformed it into a coffee house with elevating lectures, some spectators carried on as before: 'play-goers accustomed to exchanging back-chat with red-nosed comedians saw no reason why they should not also exchange back-chat with professors.'[8] But the tide was flowing all in one direction.

Although it is difficult to prove this point, many commentators remarked at the time on what they saw as more sophisticated audience expectations, perhaps because of the expanding educational system: after the Education Act of 1870 average school attendance jumped from 1¼ million in 1870 to 4½ million in 1890, and in 1902 a further Education Act dealt with secondary and technical education.

Other rival entertainments offered an attractive alternative to the theatres and penny gaffs. The railways prompted the growth of seaside excursions and resorts. Football was reorganised on a mass basis with larger stadiums. The *Daily Mail* was launched in 1896 as a cheap tabloid based upon a massive circulation and heavy advertising. Bioscope shows were introduced into this country by February 1896, and photography became a popular hobby in the 1890s after the advent of the simple Box Brownie camera. With the first faltering steps of the radio and gramophone, the age of mass entertainment was looming large.

In such a changed context, stage melodrama could not survive. First melodrama at the minor theatres began to be laughed at and then disappeared, followed by the theatres themselves. On the West End stage it was replaced by the more respectable 'teacup and saucer' drama epitomised by Tom Robertson's plays of the 1860s where decent aristocrats and other well-bred people could be relied upon to observe the proprieties. That they sometimes did not formed the plot for many plays. For example, take Robertson's *Caste* of 1867: it concerns a member of the nobility who falls in love with, of all people, a ballet dancer and tries hard to get his mother, the Marquise de St Maur, to come to terms with their marriage.

One significant indication of the way in which the theatre had changed was the fate of the orchestra, indispensable to melodrama: the new West End theatres phased out the orchestra pit, unnecessary because the productions were played in near silence. The settings of the plays shifted too, away from the public locations of melodrama and into private drawing-rooms. Intimate staged dialogue replaced the action and heroics enjoyed by working-class audiences. Censorship remained in force.

The trend away from melodrama towards the West End style of theatre was confirmed and reinforced by the advent of independent drama criticism in newspapers. The critics were only too glad to participate in this new status of their profession and several like J. F. Nisbet of *The Times* and Clement Scott of the *Daily Telegraph* saw themselves as 'men of letters', publishing their reviews in book form. Their dramatic theory centred on upholding the Aristotelian unities which exalted restraint and moderation at the expense of variety and spontaneity.

There was also a reversal in the character of writers attracted by the stage. The usually anonymous hack turning out melodrama after melodrama was superseded by learned and sophisticated authors who once more looked on the drama as a suitable receptacle for their talents, especially when the Copyright Act of 1883 and regulations against American piracy of their work in 1891 gave them various legal powers to protect their plays from plagiarism or mutilation. The financial rewards were also much larger: a well-known playwright like H. A. Jones could expect to make thousands of pounds from each of his works, whereas the melodramatists were paid barely in tens let alone hundreds.

But although old-style melodrama largely died out on the commercial stage it remained a potent genre, simply being transplanted to that form of entertainment to which the popular audience had also switched its patronage: the new 'moving pictures'. In any case these early films were simply a return to mime with music, and the *Pearl White* serials and others were no more than stage melodrama in a different medium. Comics like *Ally Sloper's Half Holiday*, *Chips* and *Comic Cuts* displayed many features of the genre, and crime fiction was another area in which melodrama's attitudes and style survived: impossibly brave heroes such as Bulldog Drummond, cardboard villains like Carl Peterson – the action, the stereotypes, the xenophobia. One historian of the crime story has remarked that 'early crime fiction was simply melodrama in print'.[9]

Much of Hollywood's output, particularly the early Westerns, was pure melodrama. Today of course, quite apart from the romances of the Mills and Boon and Barbara Cartland school, it is the melodrama of the 'soap opera' or the imported American 'high life' serials which are so popular. We will return to the question of melodrama again in the last chapter when we look at the relationship between the theatre and television since the 1950s.

Yet ironically enough, even though melodrama's decline in the latter part of the nineteenth century removed, seemingly, the major obstacle in the way of the development of an experimental theatre which would be an alternative to the commercial stage, the situation proved hardly promising. In other countries the opportunities were much greater, primarily because there existed an effective counter-balancing force to the established theatre: a culturally orgnaised labour movement.

In Germany for instance, which in any case possessed a tradition of educational drama going back to Goethe and Schiller, over eight hundred workers' educational associations existed by 1860, providing the foundations for both the Social-Democratic Workers' Party which had half a million members by the end of the 1870s, and the workers' theatre, the Freie Volksbuehne, set up in 1890.[10] Similarly in Finland the establishment of various trade unions led to the creation of workers' acting groups and in 1887 to the People's Theatre. Norway had a National Theatre of which Ibsen had been the director, and in France Maurice Pottecher built an open-air people's theatre in the Vosges in 1895.

In Britain, on the other hand, following the decline of the Chartist movement in the late 1840s, such trade unions and organisations as existed showed little interest in anything other than 'bread and butter' issues. During the mid-Victorian period there was a falling away of that separate identity sometimes called 'the world of labour', undermined by the relatively high wage-levels paid at the time. Trade unions catered mainly for skilled craftsmen, and their leaders' concern to display moderation and reasonableness led to policies which drew upon traditional bodies like the Liberal Party and away from their own distinctive political let alone cultural organisations.

Without the cultural foundations secured in other European countries, those few efforts made at producing an alternative theatre were bound to be conducted in a half-hearted and uncertain fashion. An example of this is revealed by the case of William Morris. Private means enabled Morris to experiment in many areas of the arts such as textiles, wallpapers, weaving and printing, but one field he avoided was the 'drama', largely because of his hostility to the West End stage. As George Bernard Shaw put it: 'Morris would have written for the stage if there had been any stage that a poet and artist could write for.' His daughter May wrote that 'As all his intimate friends well knew, my Father's antagonism to the Victorian stage was inveterate.'[11]

Morris did write one short play, an interlude. *The Tables Turned; or Nupkins Awakened*, which was performed at the offices of the Socialist League, the political group to which Morris was then committed, in Farringdon Road, London, in October 1887. The plan contains a satirical picture of British justice, showing the trials of three people: a middle-class swindler, a woman accused of stealing some loaves of bread, and a socialist arrested for obstruction caused during an open-air meeting. The court is presided over by the biased Justice Nupkins; as he sums up to the jury after the prosecution has put the case against Mary Pinch and despite the police evidence having conflicted wildly:

> show this mistaken woman the true majesty of English Law by acquitting her – if you are not satisfied with the abundant, clear, and obviously unbiassed evidence, put before you with that terseness and simplicity of diction which distinguishes

our noble civil force. The case is so free from intricacy, gentlemen, that I need not call your attention to any of the details of that evidence. You must either accept it as a whole and bring in a verdict of guilty, or your verdict must be one which would be tantamount to accusing the sergeant and constables of wilful and corrupt perjury; and I may add, wanton perjury; as there could be no possible reason for these officers departing from the strict line of truth. Gentlemen, I leave you to your deliberations.

But Nupkins and his court are overtaken by the 'Social Revolution' when people march into the court singing the Marseillaise. The second act takes place in the new society (a forerunner of Morris' utopian *News from Nowhere*, first published in 1890). Everyone is happy and fulfilled, apart from Citizen Nupkins who is on the run, wrongly convinced that if people find out about his past career he will be strung up from the nearest tree. The play ends with people dancing and Nupkins in tears: 'A world without lawyers! – oh, dear! oh dear! To think that I should have to dig potatoes and see everybody happy!'

Apart from the character of Nupkins, the humour in the play is provided by the appearance in court of expert witnesses such as Tennyson and the Archbishop of Canterbury. Morris himself played the Archbishop, but with typical enthusiasm he got carried away and forgot his words. Shaw was in the audience and by his account Morris brought the house down, entering with a dignity which 'several minutes of the wildest screaming laughter at him . . . could not disturb'.[12]

One biographer of Morris has claimed that although *The Tables Turned* was a 'slight jest', 'it broke new ground in the creation of agitprop. Morris was doubtless stimulated in pioneering with this form by the thought of medieval popular plays: hence his name for it of interlude.'[13] The play has been performed a few times since the 1880s and reads quite well, but it was more of an amateur theatrical 'one-off' than part of any sustained dramatic movement.

Morris was by no means the only person to dislike the commercial stage of the late Victorian period. Others seized upon the works of the Norwegian playwright Henrik Ibsen in an effort to conceive of and develop a different form and pattern of theatre. Today it is difficult to see what it was in Ibsen's plays that caused such a furore when his works reached England in the last two decades of the nineteenth century. After *Ghosts* was produced in March 1891, a leader in the *Daily Telegraph* judged it hard 'to expose in decorous words the gross and almost putrid indecorum of the play', and the *Evening Standard* called the audience 'lovers of prurience and dabblers in impropriety who are eager to gratify their illict tastes under the pretence of art'.[14] But at the time, Ibsen's plays, with their discussion of personal and emotional topics totally ignored by the 'teacup and saucer' drama were highly provocative.

The plays were taken up by some individuals in the labour movement largely because Ibsen's 'New Drama', quite apart from its focus on the specific problems of women in middle-class society, portrayed sympathetically the dilemmas of people rebelling against their own background – obviously a matter of concern to middle-class socialists such as the Fabians. The actress Elizabeth Robins later recalled the effect of one of the first of Ibsen's plays to be staged in England, *A Doll's House* produced in 1889: 'The unstagey effect of the whole play . . . made it, to eyes that first saw it in '89, less like a play than like a personal meeting – with people and issues that seized us and held us, and wouldn't let us go.'[15]

This performance was a private production, for legal reasons. The man who had succeeded W. B. Donne as Examiner of Plays and held the post between 1874 and 1895, Edward Pigott, thought that all the characters in Ibsen's plays were 'morally deranged', thus refusing to licence any of his works. The commercial actor-managers also detested Ibsen, and with few translations of his plays available in the 1880s it looked as if performances of them would be non-existent. But in 1886 the Shelley Society hit upon the idea of presenting Shelley's notorious play about incest, *The Cenci*, by means of club membership, whereby members paid an entrance fee and constituted themselves a private club, thus evading the censorship regulations which applied only to public shows. *A Doll's House* was put on privately at the Gaiety Theatre, London, in 1889 followed by performances of *Ghosts*, *Hedda Gabler* and *Rosmersholm* in 1891.

Two people heavily influenced by Ibsen were Edward Aveling and Eleanor Marx, Karl's youngest daughter. Aveling had once run a troupe of strolling players which was shipwrecked when returning from a tour in Ireland. Aveling then became a lecturer, offering to talk on such subjects as Shakespeare, Ibsen, and 'The Theatre and the Working Classes', as well as working as a dramatic critic for a number of periodicals. His articles berated the London stage for its irrelevance, asserting that: 'the really great modern play, when it comes, will deal not with the struggle in two human beings only, but with that class-struggle which is the epic of the nineteenth century also.'[16]

Such strongly expressed views make it all the more peculiar that Aveling's own plays, written under the name Alec Nelson, are so disappointing. Plays like *The Love Philtre* were nothing more than sentimental comedies or else adaptations of French plays, something the established West End theatre did handle with verve and confidence. Aveling's plays never met with any success.

The divorce between Aveling's writings and his practical efforts reflects yet again the absence of a strong cultural platform able to sustain forms of experimental drama. The one organisation which might have developed a suitable framework was the working men's clubs of the later nineteenth century, of which there were well over nine hundred by 1880. By 1900 they claimed a total membership of a quarter of a million men (and a few women).

The clubs functioned as places where members could come and relax after a day's work, but they also sponsored debates and lectures. Amongst these activities were the Elocution Classes popular in the 1880s and from which emerged amateur dramatic groups. A glance at the titles of the plays produced by some of them reveals, for instance, a sketch called *Eviction*, put on at the Borough of Hackney Club in December 1885 and written by members Gaston and Willis. Other clubs hosted 'Democratic Readings' from the works of writers such as Shelley and Dickens, and there were occasional stagings of Shakespeare's plays.

By the 1890s few clubs did not possess stages or scenery, and audiences for plays sometimes numbered well over six hundred. In 1894 a Clubs Dramatic Association was formed which claimed eleven members by the next year. But in the main the usual dramatic fare at the clubs confined itself to farces and comedies, as exemplified by the piece, *Retiring*, of which a club journal gave this synopsis:

> One Samuel Snaffles retires from business, and he and his wife, worthy people in Tottenham Court Road, feel out of place among elegant surroundings. A charge of receiving some stolen property is made against Mr. Snaffles, but the real culprit makes a confession, and all ends happily by the marriage of Miss Snaffles to the son of a proud stockbroker.[17]

Not much scope there for a prospective alternative theatre.

In the course of the 1890s the character of club entertainment began to change, away from the amateur provision of earlier days towards professional performers operating on a circuit with all the trappings of agents and stardom. The educational and political side of the clubs also wilted away, as Tim Ashplant has noted: 'although the 1880s had witnessed political plays, and political themes emerging in the Judge-and-jury mock trials and in the Democratic Readings, these disappeared completely in the 1890s, and were never revived.'[18]

It is not the case that no one in the labour movement at the end of the nineteenth century was interested in the arts. Certainly some Fabians like Beatrice Webb distrusted the theatre, but others such as Stewart Headlam called for the provision of 'public theatres'. Headlam had already founded the Church and Stage Guild in 1879 in an attempt to overcome the church's antipathy towards all forms of public entertainment – an undertaking which resulted in Headlam's being unable to obtain an ecclesiastical post. Other Fabians like Graham Wallas, Sidney Oliver and George Bernard Shaw called for municipal corporations to support theatres; and some Fabian branches also put on plays by Strindberg and Galsworthy amongst others: the Liverpool Fabian Society for instance produced Ibsen's *An Enemy of the People*. Lectures on aspects of drama were held at Fabian summer schools.[19]

Despite these endeavours however, the audience for such

plays and lectures remained small. One observer, Holbrook Jackson, pointed out in his book on the 1890s:

> The new drama was in the main an occasional affair, highly experimental, and appealing only to a small and seriously minded group of intellectuals in London. They belonged very largely to the literary fringe of the Fabian Society and other reform and revolutionary organisations, and these were practically the sole supporters of the efforts of the Independent Theatre, the Stage Society and the New Century Theatre.

The most important of the bodies mentioned above by Jackson was the Independent Theatre, set up by the Dutchman J. T. Grein in 1891; Grein had made large sums of money by producing the plays of English playwrights like H. A. Jones and Pinero in Amsterdam, and his decision to form a theatre reflected a European-wide movement against the commercial theatre, a mood which also brought forth the French Théâtre Libre of 1887 and the Moscow Arts Theatre started in 1897. As the prospectus of the Independent Theatre stated, their aim was 'to give special performances of plays which have a literary and artistic rather than a commercial value'.

Set up as a club in order to escape censorship, the Independent Theatre's membership never rose to more than 175 people. The major difficulty they faced was quite what plays to produce; in 1921 Shaw wrote to Grein and recalled: 'When you declared that you would bring to light treasures of unacted English drama grossly suppressed by the managers of that day, you found that there was not any unacted English drama except two acts of an unfinished play (begun and laid aside eight years before) by me.'[21] It was a problem that was never solved: in the six years of its existence 28 plays were staged, but the only memorable works were those by Shaw himself. The Stage Society, the Independent Theatre's successor from 1899, was undermined by a similar dilemma.

The enterprise was plagued from the start by ambiguity – even the name begged the question 'independent of what or whom? If it was the West End stage then that never happened; Grein later summed up the whole Independent Theatre and

Stage Society venture as having been 'a splendid auxiliary channel to increase the repertoire of the Commercial Theatre'.[22] This capacity of the commercial theatre to benefit from innovations pioneered outside of itself – a recurrent theme throughout this book – had already been demonstrated when the actor-manager Beerbohm Tree staged Ibsen's *An Enemy of the People* in 1893, knowing that the air of notoriety which clung to his plays would guarantee a full house.

Other participants in the Independent Theatre project like Shaw had claimed that 'it was the business of the theatre to come to the people', but although Ibsen's *A Doll's House* and *An Enemy of the People* and Shaw's *Candida* were amongst the plays toured, it remained an overwhelmingly London-based and London-orientated organisation. The high subscriptions ensured that only an exclusively middle-class membership would be able to afford the fees: the Stage Society for instance charged £1 membership and a further £1 for each performance.

But whatever the drawbacks and failings of the Independent Theatre, it did at the very least provide a forum for the energetic and provocative figure of George Bernard Shaw. Heavily influenced by the works of Ibsen, in 1890 Shaw gave a series of lectures to the Fabian Society which were published the next year under the title *The Quintessence of Ibsenism*. The book contained the first thorough critique of the West End commercial stage.[23]

The bulk of *The Quintessence* consists of an outline of Ibsen's plays – more imperative then than today because few of them had been translated let alone performed by 1890 – and a reprinting of the more violent denunciations of the playwright and his English admirers. The two features of the West End stage at which Shaw aimed his fire in particular as being responsible for the low standards prevalent were the system of censorship and the critics. Regarding the first, Shaw pointed out that: 'The licenser has the London theatres at his mercy through his power to revoke their licences; and he is empowered to exact a fee for reading each play submitted to him, so that his income depends on his allowing no play to be produced without going through that ordeal.' As for the critics, Shaw's withering scorn of them occupied a dozen pages: 'It is not too much to say that very few of the critics have yet got so far as to be able to narrate accurately the stories of the plays they have witnessed.'

But *The Quintessence*'s force derived from its negative attacks, and Shaw had little constructive to propose relating to the creation of alternatives to the West End. He expressed support for Grein's Independent Theatre venture, but said nothing for example about how the range of theatre-goers might be extended – an especially telling omission in view of the opinion sometimes expressed by Shaw that there was a need to take 'the theatre to the people'.[24]

Throughout the 1890s Shaw's distaste for the commercial stage continued to be voiced in vehement terms. In his obituary notice of Morris written in 1896 he asked: 'Why, then, did he seldom go to the theatre? Well, come, gentle reader, why doesn't anybody go to the theatre? Do you suppose that even I would go to the theatre twice a year except on business? . . . We have no theatre for men like Morris: indeed, we have no theatre for quite ordinary cultivated people.'

In the 1913 edition of *The Quintessence of Ibsenism*, Shaw added additional chapters and here he was more forthcoming in his proposals. Praising Ibsen for his introduction of 'the discussion' into drama, Shaw emphasised the Norwegian's opposition to the melodrama which had dominated the theatre for much of the nineteenth century; instead of the clearcut heroes and villains and the stereotyped plots, Ibsen's characters were praised for being more ambiguous and complex. Shaw also applauded the commonplace settings and stories of Ibsen's plays which were in marked contrast to the spectacular extravaganzas of the later melodramas: 'Ibsen saw that, on the contrary, the more familiar the situation, the more interesting the play. . . . The things that happen to his stage figures are things that happen to us.'[25]

There is a supreme irony here: Shaw is enthusing over Ibsen's 'naturalism' or depiction of probable behaviour within believable and everyday settings. At first a welcome relief from the posturings of the worst kinds of melodrama, this form was soon to dominate the West End, other than musicals, but in the guise of the 'well-made play'. Naturalism, yes, yet only within a middle-class framework. Not until the 1950s were serious attempts made to break this stranglehold on the West End theatre.

But if the new edition of *The Quintessence* was more detailed as to the kind of topics and the manner in which writers antipathetic to the commercial stage should treat them, once again Shaw barely hinted at concrete, practical proposals. There was no analysis either of the star system or of the 'long runs' fostered by the West End; nothing on the Actresses' Franchise League or the repertory theatres which were in well-publicised existence by 1913. None of this ties up with the critic who had confidently asserted that 'If the speculators will not give us decent theatres . . . why, we shall sooner or later provide them for ourselves.'[26]

Both editions of *The Quintessence of Ibsenism* (a third in 1926 offered a new preface but nothing more substantial), have more of an 'armchair' feel about them than the sense of day-to-day involvement, which is especially disappointing in Shaw's case because of the fact that the plays which he himself wrote before the First World War were in marked contrast to the society dramas dominating the commercial stage.

His first play, *Widowers' Houses*, was a study of slum and absentee landlords obsessed with financial profit rather than the conditions in which their tenants were forced to live. In the 1893 Preface to the play, Shaw stated that the purpose behind the work had been to prompt people to vote for the Progressives in the forthcoming London County Council elections. Predictably enough, it was banned by the Examiner of Plays. The action centres around the realisation of the young doctor Harry Trench that his private income is derived from slum property, just as his future father-in-law is engaged in the same racket. His weak attempts at protest are soon overcome by Blanche, and the play ends with Trench arm in arm with his father-in-law Sartorius and his agent Lickcheese, all thought of social reform forgotten. With its frank depiction of human greed and sexual passion, *Widowers' Houses* was a far cry from the material presented each night on the West End stages.

Shaw's next play, *Mrs Warren's Profession*, was written in 1893 but because of the censor's ban did not appear on the professional stage until 1924. It brings out what Shaw saw as the links between prostitution and a grasping capitalist society. Slowly it begins to dawn on Mrs Warren's daughter Vivie that the origins of her mother's wealth lie in the selling of sex for money. Although Vivie is at first shocked and appalled, Mrs Warren forcefully argues that her anger is misplaced in such a greedy and money-obsessed country, especially when women lack opportunities to support themselves: 'The only way for a woman to provide for herself decently is for her to be good to some man that can afford to be good to her.'

Other Shaw plays poked fun at the platitudes and conventionalities paraded on the West End boards. *Arms and the Man*, for instance, ridiculed the romantic haze which surrounded war – and this some twenty years before the outbreak of the First World War – by showing the hero leading a cavalry charge, but only because his horse has bolted. *John Bull's Other Island* was written in 1904 for the Abbey Theatre, Dublin, at the request of W. B. Yeats, and was a satire on imperialism, exposing amongst other evils the land syndicates which cynically dispossessed the Irish peasant proprietors. *Major Barbara* of 1905 was a study of the moral and economic consequences of the flourishing armaments industry, depicting the brutally realistic manufacturer Andrew Undershaft: 'Poverty and slavery have stood up for centuries to your sermons and leading articles: they will not stand up to my machine guns.'

Several contemporary observers heaped praise upon Shaw's plays. The anarchist and avid theatre-goer Emma Goldman for instance thought that '*Major Barbara* is one of the most revolutionary plays. In any other but dramatic form the sentiments uttered therein would have condemned the author to long imprisonment for inciting to sedition and violence.'[27]

Certainly Shaw's plays were very different from the rest of the conventional drama, but the plays themselves – as Goldman for one seemed to overlook – reached only small audiences at select private performances. Furthermore, as John Elsom and others have pointed out, Shaw's plays occur within very restricted settings, in the now ubiquitous drawing-room where his characters could be shown in the conversations and debates in which he specialised.

It should be noted too that the discussions in his works were often highly ironic and complex, making them difficult to understand and in many ways reflecting Shaw's isolation from non-middle-class audiences. As Holbrook Jackson expressed it, 'Bernard Shaw had to write *The Quintessence of Ibsenism* to show what Ibsen's plays meant, and long prefaces and appendices to show what his own plays meant.'[28]

But whatever the drawbacks of his plays and other writings, Shaw's influence on the development of forms of non-West End theatre was significant, both in the short term and in the long. Most immediately, his plays encouraged other writers to follow in his footsteps, the most significant case being John Galsworthy, who produced three important works during the Edwardian period. *The Silver Box* of 1909 compared the very different punishment meted out to a rich and a poor offender against the law. *Strife* of the same year focused on an industrial dispute at a Welsh tin plate works. *Justice*, performed in 1910, was about a clerk who had forged cheques and it attacked the conditions within English prisons and their treatment of offenders – with such effect that the then Home Secretary, Winston Churchill, consequently tightened up prison regulations and restricted the maximum period of solitary confinement to a month.

These three plays by Galsworthy contained a level of debate and conflict not usually seen on the stage; for instance, David Roberts in *Strife* criticises the whole basis of society and its present organisation: 'That's Capital! A thing that will say – "I'm very sorry for you, poor fellows – you have a cruel time of it, I know," but will not give one sixpence of its dividends to help you have a better time.' As George Rowell has written, John Galsworthy's plays left the society drawing-room for the factory, and it was a process paralleling the 'industrial novel' of the 1840s and 1850s written by Dickens, Disraeli and Mrs Gaskell among others. The reason for the 'drama' lagging seventy years behind the novel lies in the work of the Examiner of Plays.

Shaw also influenced Harley Granville Barker, the man most responsible for actually presenting Shaw's plays to a wider public. Building upon the spadework already carried out by the Independent Theatre and the Stage Society, in 1904 Granville Barker and J. E. Vedrenne took over the Court Theatre in

Sloane Square. Their innovation was to run it, not as elsewhere like a 'long run' theatre in which the same play if successful was staged night after night until audiences finally dwindled and it was replaced, but on repertory lines. It is important to say something here about repertory, as it has been an ideal which has much influenced alternative theatre since the early twentieth century.

The notion of repertory had originated in the economic and social changes shaping the theatre in the late nineteenth century: most significantly, the spread of the railways had boosted the touring dramatic companies, usually led by a star like Sir Henry Irving, at the expense of the more local stock companies. It was a transition which strengthened the influence of the West End commercial stage because it was this theatre's plays and methods of production which were now on display throughout the country. The repertory ideal, in contrast, was based on the local company which would build up a repertoire and rotate the plays every few nights. The critic William Archer put it thus:

> when we speak of repertory we mean a number of plays ready for performance which can be acted in such alteration that three, four and five different plays may be given in the course of a week. New plays are from time to time added to the repertory and those of them which may succeed may be performed fifty, seventy, a hundred times in the course of a season, but no play is ever performed more than two or three times in uninterrupted succession.[29]

As we shall see in Chapter Four, the introduction of a repertory system in Britain was to be dogged by personal, administrative and financial difficulties, but the first attempt to approximate to it were the Barker–Vedrenne seasons at the Court Theatre – although strictly speaking it operated on a 'short run' basis. Another experiment which Barker pioneered during these seasons was to have productions centre on group or ensemble acting, rather than the star syndrome practised throughout the West End in which the minor parts in plays were simply hurried through as quickly as possible in order to reach the roles played by the leading performers.

The Court Theatre put on 988 performances in all between October 1904 and June 1907, and the fact that 701 of them were of plays by George Bernard Shaw demonstrates Barker's pivotal part in bringing Shaw's works out of coteries and studies and before a larger public. Their success pointed to the existence of a substantial audience not wholly enamoured by the typical West End drama. Some of the Court's other productions also challenged theatrical conventions; for instance Elizabeth Robins' *Votes for Women* included a scene of a suffragette rally held in Trafalgar Square, and Granville Barker's own play *The Voysey Inheritance* launched a blistering attack on human greed as exemplified by haggling over wills and legacies.

In 1907 Barker wrote a new play, *Waste*, which was intended for production as the Court, a work examining the in-fighting of government politics and its personal consequences. An important part of the play concerned a married woman's abortion, and true to form the Examiner of Plays demanded that all references to this episode should be removed. Barker's refusal to do so meant that a licence was not granted – there was no public performance of *Waste* until 1936.

Such an episode underlines the limits within which the Court was working, a situation made worse by financial worries. The theatre itself could only hold 670 spectators and in 1907 Barker and Vedrenne decided to make the plunge into the heart of the West End by hiring the Savoy Theatre. It was a case of expand or die, but unfortunately the venture managed to do both, the crippling rents destroying the whole project. As Shaw expressed it: 'Vedrenne got out with nothing but a reputation; Barker had to pawn his clothes; and I disgorged most of my royalties; but the creditors were paid in full.'[30]

The Court Theatre seasons had an enormous influence on the repertory theatres which were established in the next few years at Manchester, Liverpool, Birmingham and Glasgow. But it is worth asking whether the Court Theatre did not function, in J. T. Grein's words, as 'a splendid auxiliary channel' for the commercial theatre rather than a genuine alternative to that system. Within a few years, for example, actor-managers like Beerbohm Tree were making large sums of money from productions of Shaw's plays. And, shades perhaps of another Court Theatre 'revolution' in the 1950s, one result of the Barker–Vedrenne seasons was, as its historian concluded, that 'it has expanded enormously the conception of what kind of story is suitable for the stage . . .'.[31]

For Granville Barker in particular, the failure of the Court Theatre and his unwillingness to compromise with either the commercial stage or the Examiner of Plays led to an isolation from the practicalities of stage production. He campaigned both for the ending of theatre censorship and the establishment of a National Theatre, neither of which came about in his lifetime. Without suitable plays or organisations to hand, Barker instead turned his attentions to Shakespeare, putting on at the Savoy in 1913–14 a season which, sponsored by a wealthy benefactor, stressed the virtues of simplicity and movement. Out of the productions came his five-volume *Prefaces to Shakespeare*. It is indicative that much of the best experimental work before the First World War went into reinterpreting Shakespeare–William Poel had founded his Elizabethan Stage Society in 1894 whose productions took place without scenery and often in halls or out of doors in courtyards.

In 1922 Barker published *The Exemplary Theatre*, a book which, in its emphasis on the values of group collaboration, of the building up of a company and of the need for continuous training and study, anticipates many later developments within alternative theatre, especially in the case of Joan Littlewood's Theatre Workshop.[32] Apart from that virtually nothing: that Barker's opportunities within the theatrical world were so meagre illustrates the huge problems facing those hostile to the West End tradition of drama.

Aside from his short-term impact on the Court and on Barker, Shaw's influence over the next few decades was vast. Whatever the complexities of his plays and Prefaces, their challenge to conventional attitudes and to ways of writing and producing plays inspired many of the groups beginning to fashion a tradition of alternative and experimental theatre, whether it was the suffragettes, or the People's Theatre in Newcastle or abroad in the United States where the Federal Theatre in the 1930s put on over 10 000 performances of his works.[33] The number of times that Shaw's name appears in the following pages testifies to his lasting position within the non-commercial tradition – even if he himself had little inclination for it or idea as to how it should be developed.

Chapter 4

Regional, Nationalist and Yiddish Theatre

The establishment of the West End stage as the fulcrum of British theatre from the late nineteenth century provided further evidence of the growing centralisation taking hold of the country. For a large portion of the Victorian period, London had played a relatively less significant role; in the early nineteenth century Manchester had seized the initiative, and in the middle of the century it had been Birmingham's turn. Manchester's dynamism was founded upon the expanding textile industry, and the ferment which this provoked led to the creation of powerful political organisations – the Anti-Corn Law League was begun here, and the Chartists built up a formidable presence – and important cultural institutions like the Free Library (1852), the 1857 Art Exhibition, the Hallé Orchestra and the *Manchester Guardian*.

Birmingham's prominence resulted from the impact of its Liberal Association formed in 1865, which introduced the paraphernalia of modern politics such as organised voting and membership, but more especially because of the influence of Joseph Chamberlain as Lord Mayor between 1873 and 1876. Chamberlain launched a series of sweeping reforms including the municipalisation of the gas and water supplies, the introduction of libraries and the architectural reshaping of the city centre – schemes that seemed to demonstrate the viability of enterprise other than the private. But by the last two decades of the nineteenth century London was once more reasserting its position in political, economic and cultural affairs.[1]

There were several reasons for this. First of all, London's

population had continued to grow at a rapid pace, increasing from 3 million in 1860 to 4½ million in 1900, and both the underground and the cheap workmen's fares on the trains had led to the spread of the suburbs. The standard of its local government had been considerably improved by the founding of the London County Council in 1888; the national railway system centred on London; political parties and trade unions all had their headquarters in the capital; London was the centre of an Empire, as the Jubilees of 1887 and 1897 visibly demonstrated; and finally, the coming of mass circulation magazines like *Tit Bits* from 1881 and more importantly newspapers such as the *Daily Mail* from 1896 and the *Daily Express* from 1900, buttressed by the new advertising industry – all these factors enhanced London's dominance. As Malcolm Bradbury has written: 'London had now become the outright point of concentration for English culture, overtaking and preempting the role of the provincial large cities.'[2]

The West End theatre was founded upon two components: the star (usually the actor-manager himself) and the long run system. Appealing to a largely middle-class and metropolitan clientele, the plays tended to reflect their background and share its assumptions. But London's theatrical hold, although powerful, was never complete, and several nationalist and regional movements did manage to develop their own distinctive work, in part as a protest against the West End ideas and values which appeared to be of minimal relevance: the drawing-room comedy or genteel well-made play meant little in Dublin or Glasgow. One of the best and most important examples of this determination to resist the centrifugal pull exerted by London was the Abbey Theatre of Dublin.

The Dublin theatres of the early nineteenth century had been subject to the same pressures as elsewhere in Britain: the public demand for melodrama. Irish audiences had always been noted for their volatility – in 1754 when the manager of the Dublin Theatre refused to encore politically significant passages from a play the spectators stormed the stage and cut the scenery to ribbons with their swords – and in 1814 there were riots when the dog playing the main role in a dog drama ran away. None of the plays written for the Irish stage at this time are still produced or even read, but in 1860 a playwright who had been born in Dublin, Dion Boucicault, put on his Irish play *The Colleen Bawn*, spawning whether intentionally or not the quickly familiar figure of the stage Irishman: lively, irrational and over-talkative.[3] Other Irish writers like Oscar Wilde and even George Bernard Shaw were absorbed by the London theatre.

But in the 1890s, following on from Parnell's Home Rule campaign, a cultural upsurge spread through the country, leading to the creation of organisations like the National Literary Society founded in 1892 and the Gaelic League in 1893 which both recognised the need for a specifically Irish identity. In 1897 the Irish National Players were formed, a body which, although held back by its lack of a permanent location and the necessity of drafting English actors into the company, began to encourage thoughts of an 'Irish Theatre'. W. G. Fay, the leader of the Irish Players, had been influenced by the example of Ibsen and the French Théâtre Libre, and he sought, like J. T. Grein of the London Independent Theatre a few years before, unacted masterpieces; again like Grein, Fay found none forthcoming. But fortunately for the whole venture a certain W. B. Yeats came forward. Although Yeats lived in London and had had his play *Land of Heart's Desire* produced by the Independent Theatre in 1894, he had concluded that the 'naturalism' of Ibsen's New Drama was a dead end:

> Put the man who has no knowledge of literature before a play of this kind and he will say as he has said in some form or other in every age at the first shock of naturalism: 'Why should I leave my home to hear but the words I have used there when talking of the rates?'[4]

In 1898 Yeats and his friend Lady Gregory issued a prospectus which, apart from appealing for the sum of £300 in order to establish a permanent and regular venue in Dublin, stated their hopes and objectives:

> We propose to have performed in Dublin, in the spring of every year certain Celtic and Irish plays, which whatever be their degree of excellence will be written with a high ambition, and so to build up a Celtic and Irish school of dramatic literature. We hope to find in Ireland an

uncorrupted and imaginative audience trained to listen by
its passion for oratory, and believe that our desire to bring
upon the stage the deeper thoughts and emotions of Ireland
will ensure for us a tolerant welcome, and that freedom to
experiment which is not found in theatres of England, and
without which no new movement in art or literature can
succeed.[5]

The result of this appeal was the setting up of the Irish
Literary Theatre, formed in January 1899, and in the May of
that year Yeats' *The Countess Cathleen* was staged. It was a play
which aroused a great furore because of its depiction of an Irish
girl selling her soul to the devils so as to save those of the poor;
Lady Gregory recalled that: 'There was hooting and booing in
the gallery. In the end the gallery was lined with police, for an
attack on the actors was feared.'[6]

The next few years saw several productions and some
successes. One of the new plays staged was Douglas Hyde's
Casadh an TSugain ('The Twisting of the Rope'), the first Gaelic
play ever to be staged. In 1902 a policy was implemented of
performing the plays only with Irish actors and actresses. It did
however remain an amateur company, and in 1903 when a
weekend series of performances was arranged in London
members had to ask their employers for the Saturday off.

This London visit turned out to be a momentous
engagement. In the audience was a Miss Annie Horniman, a
woman of private means derived from the family tea-business,
who had travelled extensively throughout Europe in the last
few years of the nineteenth century. Her experiences had
revealed the very different attitudes prevailing as to the
provision of theatre: on the continent, state support of the
drama was accepted and welcomed. In Britain on the other
hand, although the older doctrine of laissez-faire was being
steadily discredited in the fields of health and education, it still
reigned supreme in the arts.

Horniman had helped out W. B. Yeats financially for a
number of years, but her attendance at the London
performances of the Irish Players convinced her that here was a
venture very different from the West End theatre and which
deserved help. In 1904 therefore she paid for the conversion of

the old Mechanics' Theatre and of the adjacent morgue into the Abbey Theatre, Dublin, at a cost of £13 000. She also subsidised the running of the Abbey until 1910 at a rate of £600 per year.[7]

From its opening in December 1904 the Abbey carried out its promise of staging Irish plays. As befitted what was largely a group enterprise, there was a great deal of collaboration in the writing of the plays. Lady Gregory specialised in comedies – particularly in the one-act form, a medium now vanished from the contemporary West End stage – which drew upon Irish country dialect. W. B. Yeats wrote peasant verse-plays such as *On Baile's Strand* which included Kings, a Blind Man and a Fool amongst the characters, and makes use of masks, chorus, legend, myth and romance – a type of drama inimical both to the society drama of the London commercial theatre and the New Drama of the Ibsenites.

The plays had not lost their capacity to outrage the more orthodox and conventional in the audience, most famously in 1907 when J. M. Synge's *The Playboy of the Western World* was produced. Some spectators objected to various words spoken in the play, such as the word 'shift' for a piece of women's clothing, and the general irreverence with which the Irish peasants were represented. Of the first night Lady Gregory wrote: 'The disturbance lasted to the end of the evening, not one word had been heard after the first ten minutes'; 'There was a battle of a week. Every night protestors with their trumpets came and raised a din.'[8] *Playboy* was greeted by riots in America when the Irish Players toured in 1911–12 – in New York for instance the first act was inaudible through the hullabaloo and had to be played again – and in Liverpool in 1913.

J. M. Synge, who sadly died in 1909 at the early age of 38, wrote only six plays, amongst them *Riders to the Sea* and *The Well of Saints*, but all are distinguished by their vivid dialogue, based upon the Aran peasants who provide their subject-matter. In his preface to *The Playboy of the Western World*, Synge recounted:

When I was writing *The Shadow of the Glen*, some years ago, I got more aid than any learning could have given me from a chink in the floor of the old Wicklow house where I was staying, that let me hear what was being said by the servant-girls in the kitchen. This matter, I think, is of importance, for in countries where the imagination of the people, and the language they use, is rich and living, it is possible for a writer to be rich and copious in his words, and at the same time to give the reality, which is the root of all poetry, in a comprehensive and natural form.

And it is this powerful and compelling language which most distinguishes the plays of the Abbey Theatre at that period from the rest of the British stage.

The Abbey faced enormous problems and obstacles. For one thing the theatre was only open three evenings each week and held less than 600 spectators, so that even if full it barely covered the running expenses. But more often, faced with this new and innovative 'folk-drama', the Dublin public simply stayed away, as Lady Gregory remembered: 'Often I have gone out by the stage door when the curtain was up, and come round into the auditorium by the front hall, hoping that in the dimness I might pass for a new arrival and so encourage the few scattered people in the stalls.'[9] A device that many in the alternative theatre might wish to have copied!

After the storm over *Playboy*, the more working-class Pit forgave and forgot, but 'the more expensive seats, the Stalls and Balcony, grew shy and the audiences in Dublin were meagre. Rigid economy and tours to England were necessary to induce ends to meet.'[10]

The influence of the Abbey Theatre was felt throughout Ireland, inspiring other societies such as the Ulster Literary Theatre and also trade union sponsorship of drama: from 1911 when Jim Larkin's Irish Transport and General Workers' Union took over Liberty Hall in Dublin, a full programme of plays and concerts was given, with Larkin's sister Delia founding a group called the Irish Workers' Dramatic Company.[11] The Abbey's impact was confirmed by its habit of playing in Dublin for four months and then touring the country, a practice which had enormous consequences, as the writer Sean O'Faolain has suggested. As a small boy of 15 he went to one of their performances in Cork in 1915:

Before that I had seen nothing but plays brought to Cork 'straight from the West End' (They never needed to add the words 'of London': where else could it be). The play, *Patriots* by Lennox Robinson, is not a great play; but to me it was a revealing and exciting experience, because it dealt not with adultery in St. John's Wood or Abbot's-Bedrock-Under-the-Hill, or with Gordon in Khartoum, or Sir Percy Blakeney playing rings around the revolutionary thugs of Paris under the Directorate, but with ordinary Irish peasants, small-town shopkeepers and farming folk any of whom could have been one of my uncles or aunts whom I had met during my summer holidays down in the country. The sight of them on the stage brought me strange and wonderful news – that the streets of my native Cork might also be full of unsuspected drama. When the final curtain fell in the Cork Opera House, that wet night in 1915, I was ready to explore, to respond to, for the first time to *see* the actuality of life in Ireland.[12]

The Abbey Theatre before the First World War offered the most important and realised example of just what an alternative and experimental theatre – alternative to the commercial and West End London stage – might be like. It managed to attract new writers and plays which drew upon legend and myth as well as incorporating such elements as masks and dance (Yeats later wrote *Plays for Dancers*). The lack of money meant that economy of staging was imperative, thus emphasising the importance of the words and language and restoring poetry to drama. The variety of entertainments put on, ranging from sausage-eating contests and broadest melodrama to the latest J. M. Synge play, proved an invigorating mix in contrast to the West End, where unity of style was paramount. Nor was the Abbey afraid to be adventurous: it was the first theatre to use the screens of Gordon Craig which, because of their two-way hinges and possible variation in both size and colour, could replace painted scenery. The theatre also combined the work of running a permanent base with frequent tours.

Above all, the strength and vigour of the Abbey emanated from its firm grounding within Irish culture and nationalism. As Allardyce Nicoll recognised:

The Irish theatre is in itself but the literary counterpart of that movement which brought Sinn Fein into birth, which gave an air of passionate idealism to the Easter Rebellion of 1916, and which has ended in the establishment of the Saorstat Eireann [the Republic of Eire]. The literary and political aspects of the movement cannot be separated.[13]

The person largely instrumental in the building of the Abbey Theatre, Annie Horniman, later withdrew her support from the venture in rather acrimonious circumstances, but she did not leave the theatre world altogether. In 1907, making use of the Court Theatre experiences of Barker and Vedrenne and the continued revulsion felt by some at the commercialism of the West End stage, Miss Horniman decided to establish a repertory theatre. Hoping at first to settle it in London, she found the rents and rates in the capital prohibitively expensive and decided instead on Manchester where the local cultural traditions had remained powerful.

Two major hopes animated her company at the Gaiety Theatre, Manchester. First of all, the theatre was to offer opportunities for new plays; there would be, in the words of Miss Horniman and the Gaiety's director B. Iden Payne, 'an especially wide open door to present-day British writers, who will not now need to sigh for a hearing, provided only that they have something to say worth listening to, and say it in an interesting and original manner'.[14]

The second principle upon which the theatre was run centred on the determination to be a repertory and not a long run company. A group of plays would be learnt by the company and then rotated at least twice a week, notwithstanding the success of any single production. This in turn required the maintenance of a permanent stock company which would function as an ensemble with the premium being placed on team work in order to lessen the strain on performers. The trappings of stardom were discouraged: 'No individual curtain calls were allowed, no names were printed larger than others on posters and programmes, all actors were under contract to play whatever parts they were given.'[15]

As regards the first aim, Miss Horniman was reasonably successful in calling forth new playwrights – unlike, say, the

Independent Theatre of the 1890s. Reading her way through the 40 manuscripts often sent in each week, Horniman gradually fostered what was dubbed, predictably enough, 'the Manchester School' of writers, amongst them Allan Monkhouse, Stanley Houghton and Harold Brighouse.

The best of the Gaiety plays were rooted in the specific detail and occurrences of everyday life, often located in a topical Lancashire setting, such as Houghton's one-act *The Dear Departed*, Brighouse's *Lonesome Like* with its dialect passages, and Frank's Rose's Lancashire fairy play *The Whispering Gallery*. Brighouse's *The Polygon* focused on the chronic housing problems of the Edwardian period, and two of the Gaiety's most famous plays dealt with the position of women in contemporary society. In St John Ervine's *Jane Clegg*, Jane leaves her husband rather than turning a conventional blind eye to his repeated infidelities. Most controversial of all was Stanley Houghton's play of 1912, *Hindle Wakes*, written by a young clerk in his spare time. Mill girl Fanny Hawthorn spends a weekend away with the factory owner's son. In usual theatrical terms such an episode could only have led to marriage. But not for Fanny who upends the stereotypes and rejects Alan's efforts to 'make an honest woman' of her:

> FANNY: You're a man, and I was your little fancy. Well, I'm a woman, and *you* were *my* little fancy. You wouldn't prevent a woman enjoying herself as well as a man, if she takes it into her head?

Hindle Wakes sparked off a storm both when it was put on at the Gaiety and then staged in London. The critic of the *Pall Mall Gazette* was of the opinion that the 'toleration of such a character [as Fanny] in a London play is one of the most sinister symptoms of social illness that have arisen in my lifetime'. The *Liverpool Post* asked: 'why select the pigsty as a theme when other subjects offer?' The Vice-Chancellor of Oxford University forbade his students from seeing the play.[16] That *Hindle Wakes* should arouse such responses – even if it was 'a suffrage play' in the view of the suffragette newspaper *Votes for Women*[17] – once again underlines the rigidities and conservatism surrounding the West End stage.

Sadly, Stanley Houghton died at the age of 32, but other members of the Manchester School went on to write some fine plays, such as Harold Brighouse and his *Hobson's Choice*. Apart from its own works, the Gaiety also staged plays by established authors, especially those by John Galsworthy, whose *Strife*, *The Silver Box* and *Justice* all made a great impression on Manchester audiences. The Gaiety's first manager, Ben Iden Payne, who had once worked at the Abbey, was responsible for some excellent productions, and in 1913 Lewis Casson's version of *Julius Caesar* was distinguished by its apron stage and its arches, pillars and steps which could be twisted around in order to form new sets. In all the Gaiety put on over two hundred plays between 1908 and 1917, many of which were new to the stage.

As for the hope of creating Britain's first repertory theatre, the Gaiety was handicapped from the start by the comparative smallness of its auditorium which held no more than 1200 spectators. Even with Miss Horniman's generous subsidy, the theatre needed to be three-quarters full at each performance to cover costs, an imperative which thus resulted in a conflict between financial caution and their proclaimed boldness in the choice and staging of plays, particularly as the latter was bound to alienate some of the more traditional theatre-goers. With only a small company possible, the original repertory ideal had to be replaced by a weekly change of play. However the co-operative qualities of the Gaiety acting style were apparent in the first few seasons.

Unfortunately Miss Horniman was never quite able to take her eyes off the London scene – sometimes plays were chosen with the possibility of a London transfer in mind – and seasons in the capital gradually led to the break-up of the original company and the subsequent decline in the unity of the acting. The setting up of two companies of which one spent most of its time on tour also reduced the early co-ordination of the Gaiety venture. Manchester audiences appreciated certain performers, such as Lewis Casson's wife Sybil Thorndike, and when they left the box office takings slumped. Finally, the strains and tensions entailed in running even a weekly repertory company were enormous: the most successful of the Gaiety's Managers, Iden Payne, left after four years because of physical exhaustion. In 1917 the company was finally disbanded.

The example of the Gaiety stimulated the founding of other repertory theatres up and down the country, all of which were rooted in the antagonism felt towards the commercial stage which had turned the provincial theatre, in the words of Cicely Hamilton, 'into a dramatic lodging-house for replicas'.[18] The Scottish Repertory Theatre was set up in Glasgow in 1909, the Liverpool Repertory Theatre in 1911 and Barry Jackson's Birmingham Repertory Theatre in 1913.

The stranglehold of the London theatre was especially galling in Scotland where it was not only dramatic companies touring West End successes that was all on offer, but English dramatic companies at that. In 1909 Alfred Wareing, who had once arranged a tour of the Abbey Theatre Players and previously worked with Miss Horniman – a demonstration of the personal links vital to the early repertory movement – issued a prospectus, the fourth aim of which was: 'To encourage the initiation and development of a purely Scottish Drama by providing a stage and an acting company which will be peculiarly adapted for the production of plays national in character, written by Scottish men and women of letters.'[19] Yet again the intended ensemble character of the acting was stressed.

Lacking a wealthy patron such as Miss Horniman the venture was financed by means of private subscriptions from individual members of the public, thereby encouraging a community identification with the playhouse. But the perennial problem as to just where the new plays were going to come from was never solved. Although one-third of the plays produced in the Scottish Repertory's five seasons were new, none went down as well as the old favourites by writers like Ibsen, Shaw and Galsworthy. In fact on some occasions the audience was so small that the spectators were invited to sit in the front stalls to get a better view. The first four seasons showed a financial loss, but the fifth a substantial profit of £790.[20] But by then, however, the outbreak of the First World War in 1914 had doomed the whole enterprise when members of the company joined up.

Liverpool in the early years of the twentieth century was a

relatively prosperous city with strong cultural traditions. Not surprisingly, a sizeable group of individuals began to campaign for the establishment of their own repertory theatre. Like Glasgow, the organisation was based upon shareholders, 900 people collecting an initial sum of £12 000. An old theatre called the Star was taken over and adapted, and in November 1911 the Liverpool Repertory Theatre opened its doors for the first time. Under the direction of Basil Dean, the company operated as a short-run theatre with weekly changes of play. Like the Abbey and the Scottish Repertory, Dean found that the more experimental plays tended to empty the middle-class stalls if not the pit or gallery, and this factor was bound to place some restrictions on the number of new plays that could be produced. The first historian of the Liverpool Repertory noted sadly in 1935 that 'no group of writers had grown up, as had been hoped, around the repertory theatre'.[21]

In Birmingham the Repertory Theatre was the brainchild of Barry Jackson, a wealthy man who came from a family of local merchants. For five years he ran an amateur company called the Pilgrim Players which presented more than 160 performances of 28 plays before he opened a permanent theatre in February 1913, the first to be built specifically as a repertory theatre. Jackson was utterly opposed to the commercial theatre of his day, stating that his company would 'serve an art instead of making that art serve a commercial purpose', and 'realize a higher ideal than a satisfactory commercial balance-sheet'.[22] The venture had only just begun to develop when war was declared.

All four repertory theatres were partially successful in establishing a tradition of theatre alternative to that of the West End – before the war disrupted their work. The major problem was that, apart from the Manchester Gaiety, none of them proved able to nurture their own plays and authors. Why was this? The answer to this question is tied up in the fact that there was a relatively small number of interested playgoers in each of the respective cities, not nearly large enough to support the theatres adequately and give them the scope for experimentation. For instance, one historian has written that 'The history of the Birmingham Repertory Theatre is the story of Barry Jackson versus Birmingham.'[23] The Abbey Theatre in

Dublin was not able to surmount this problem, and Charles Frohman's season of short-run plays at the Duke of York's in London in 1910 was not sufficiently well supported to make a continuation of the project viable.[24]

However enough was achieved by the above initiatives to have given a sense of the opportunities possible, especially when the Gaiety and the Liverpool Rep exchanged companies for several productions, and players from the Abbey visited the others, but the dominance of the West End both financially and in terms of prestige continually tempted away the most talented of the repertory personnel and also some of their productions.

The strain of the repertory or even the short-run system was massive: 'Only the young, the enthusiastic and the physically strong can bear it for more than a few years.'[25] Productions were often rushed jobs, overtaxing the performers' memories; one sympathetic observer has referred to 'those demands on the prompter which, in the days of weekly repertory, were too common'.[26] Like Iden Payne, Alfred Wareing also resigned after four years because of exhaustion. Some playwrights too were unenthusiastic, preferring the substantial royalties accruing from the long run to the small sums paid here and there by the repertory theatres. The short-run method was expensive, with additional costs in advertising, costumes and scenery if plays were to be rotated at frequent intervals; most significantly, audiences complained of 'chopping and changing'. Only at the Liverpool Repertory between 1914 and 1916 did a genuine repertory policy operate, and even that had to be given up on financial grounds.[27]

Furthermore if the repertory theatres were indeed a revolt against the commercial stage, then how were they to be financed? In Germany, for example, hundreds of municipal theatres were supported by the local authorities, but this was far from being the case in Britain, where the doctrine of laissez-faire still dominated the cultural field. Barry Jackson could indeed claim that 'Art has no possible relation to money', but not even the incomes of a Jackson and a Horniman could sustain a whole national movement. Without secure financial foundations, any attempts at creating alternative and experimental drama could only be fragile; as Harley Granville Barker wrote in 1922: 'The efforts to reform the theatre during the last fifteen or twenty years in English-speaking countries can roughly be split into two classes: those that have had enough capital and those that haven't; ten per cent, perhaps, have been of the first class and ninety of the second.'[28]

This problem was aggravated by the individualism of the non-commercial ventures which therefore tended to develop in splendid isolation away from each other; the playwright and critic St John Ervine noted that 'The Gaiety in Manchester was barely aware of the existence of the Playhouse in Liverpool, and was almost ignorant of the existence of the Repertory in Birmingham'.[29]

All the organisations discussed above were supported by interested theatre-goers antipathetic towards the values of the West End theatre, but other initiatives in the late nineteenth and early twentieth century drew upon alternative methods of aid. The upsurge of the labour movement in the 1880s and 1890s largely in response to the economic depression which had undermined Britain's position as 'The Workshop of the World', had led to the formation of several socialist bodies which stressed the importance of cultural activities. The most widespread was Robert Blatchford's Clarion movement which spawned such affiliated groups as the Cinderella Clubs for children, Clarion Scouts, Clarion Vans and Rambling Clubs, Clarion Debating Societies, the *Clarion* newspapers and Clarion Cycling Clubs, Clarion clubhouses and Clarion villages in New Zealand, and even an in-language called 'Clarionese'. Blatchford himself was interested in the theatre but his only known project a comic opera written with his colleague A. M. Thompson, was toured briefly and disastrously in 1891 at a cost to himself of £400.[30]

Several Clarion branches began theatre groups and a National Organisation of Clarion Dramatic Clubs was introduced in 1911 which supplied scripts and information. One of these affiliated groups, in Newcastle, had started as part of the local British Socialist Party (BSP). Members were preoccupied with raising money, prompting some individuals to ask whether, if 'money was needed to keep the wolf from the door of our faith, why not use the drama both to collect funds and to propagate our faith?'[31] They relied on the plays of George Bernard Shaw, setting themselves up as a membership organisation in 1911 in order to present his banned work. Other branches of the Clarion Players were also active, particularly that in Liverpool where Shaw's *Widowers' Houses* was put on to raise money for the bread and soup fund.[32] However the outbreak of the First World War sent the Clarion movement into terminal decline and most of the drama groups folded, although not the People's Theatre of Newcastle as they were now called: they continued to stage the plays of writers like Ibsen and Synge, and in December 1915 they moved into new premises which held 250 people, giving 59 performances over the next 4½ years. Another small group which flourished was that of the Gateshead Independent Labour Party, eventually becoming the Little Theatre, Gateshead.

But perhaps the best example of 'ethnic drama', and the more unusual because it was actually carried on within a few miles of the West End itself, was the Yiddish theatre of the East End of London. In this case its identity was protected by its geography – no drama critic ever ventured into such an area – and by its Yiddish language which excluded outsiders. Neglect then has been perpetuated down the years: none of the standard books about the Victorian and Edwardian theatre mention this important non-West End form of drama.

Yiddish drama, just like that of the Catholic Church in the Middle Ages, grew out of religious ritual and ceremony. The latter originated in the drama of the Mass and the desire to bring to life passages from the Bible; the former in the annual Jewish carnival called the Festival of Purim when dramatic representations of Biblical stories like 'The Sacrifice of Isaac' or the story of Esther were enacted. These Jewish playlets were peformed exclusively by men because the Talmud did not permit the presence of women at such entertainments.

London's Jewish community staged these plays from an early date, as the *Memoirs* of the famous East End boxer Daniel Mendoza suggest when he recalled of the year 1780: 'we resolved to be present at a dramatic performance, taken from scripture history, which was to be acted by some of our acquaintances (it being a common practice with the Jews to perform pieces of this kind during the festival). We accordingly went, and found them preparing for the performance of a drama founded on the History of Esther . . .'[33] A pub called the Green Dragon in Stepney was a well-known venue for these plays.

But the real story of Yiddish drama begins with the troupe of players set up by Abraham Goldfaden in Eastern Europe in 1876, performing not in the more high-class Hebrew but rather in Yiddish, a vernacular and mongrel dialect whose flexibility reflected its diverse origins and borrowings from other sources. As a result, the Yiddish theatre always faced unswerving hostility from the Rabbis.

Goldfaden's first theatre was at Jassy in Rumania and he used this playhouse as a base from which to tour the countryside before moving in 1878 to Odessa. A man of tremendous versatility who wrote his own plays and composed the music as well as painting the scenery, Goldfaden also adapted the works of Schiller, Shakespeare and Lessing. Before long other actor–managers were running companies, some of which included actresses. However in the 1880s a wave of pogroms against the Jews was launched in Russia and a determined effort was made to stamp out their way of life. Since 1835 they had already been confined to a particular area of the country known as the Pale but now the authorities' persecution was much fiercer, of such a magnitude that over two million Jews fled from Czarist Russia between 1881 and 1912. The Yiddish theatre was banned outright in 1883.

Many of those emigrating from Russia and Eastern Europe came to the East End of London, a district already suffering from the decline of the weaving and dock industries and the consequent unemployment. The only jobs available to the newcomers entailed long hours in 'sweatshops', and in any event the jobs were usually seasonal. Forced back into themselves, the Jewish people developed a range of cultural institutions largely as compensation and a defence, from the coffee shops where simple plays were produced to the lively Yiddish press. In 1872 the Jewish Working Men's Club was founded, moving to new buildings in Great Alie Street eleven years later which could hold over 1500 people, and amongst their activities was the presentation of Russian plays. One or two troupes started to perform in such clubs and at other

makeshift venues, the conditions resembling those of the penny
gaffs in which spectators perched on crowded, wooden benches
very close to the performers.

Although of course produced in a different language, the type
of play was similar to those at the English minors in so far as the
audience, desperate to enjoy themselves after labouring 12- or
14-hours days, hankered after melodrama. Music, song and
dance together with generous helpings of sentiment had been
features of Goldfaden's plays and were continued here, the
'anything goes' character of the entertainment matching the
haphazard and chaotic way in which it was staged, as one
eyewitness testifies:

> With a different play staged nightly, and invariably under-
> rehearsed or hastily cast – I have seen the distribution of
> parts undecided during the playing of the overture – the
> prompter was often the chief comedian. He was the most
> important personage on the stage: his head, poked through a
> trap-door, was visible to a good many of the audience, and
> his arms and snapping fingers – signals to the actors and
> conductor – appeared wildly every few minutes from behind
> the trap lid. It was marvellous how the artists managed to
> play their roles when they obviously knew not a line of their
> dialogue, but they did it amazingly well as a rule. Often
> there were interludes with the prompter – unconcealed
> altercations sometimes. Once, when a fist had been waved
> menacingly from behind the trap-door, an actor indignantly
> stamped his foot on the lid and banged it on the unfortunate
> prompter's head.[34]

But this observer goes on to praise the audience whose
imagination was equal to the task of filling up any gaps: 'Any
contretemps only added a zest to the performance and kept the
house on the tiptoes of expectancy.'

Not all the Yiddish companies were quite so hit and miss: one
of the troupes which came to London in 1883 as refugees from
Czarist persecution comprised nine adults and a child and was
led by Jacob Adler, who had already made a name for himself
as an expert actor. This highly professional and talented outfit
performed at first in local clubs and coffee shops, but in 1883 a

wealthy butcher called David Smith built a theatre for them in Prince's (now named Princelet) Street which contained an orchestra pit, a gallery, a library and could hold 300 spectators. Rooted in the local community – whenever the troupe was short of numbers it drew upon neighbouring inhabitants – Adler's company was far from parochial, as is clear from its repertoire which included the works of Shakespeare, Schiller, Goldfaden and adaptions of the contemporary English playwright H. A. Jones.

The Rabbis maintained their opposition towards dramatic performances partly because they were in Yiddish and included actresses, but also on the grounds that Adler's players lived as a commune and performed on hallowed Fridays. Financial inducements were offered to Adler and his company to migrate elsewhere – in 1884 for instance the Rabbis had actually organised a benefit night at the Holborn Theatre for Chaimovitch's troupe in order to speed them on their way to the United States – and American agents likewise were angling for them to come over, but with no success.

Then in January 1887 a tragedy occurred at the Prince's Street Theatre. A packed house of 300 was watching the operetta *Gypsy Girl* when someone yelled 'Fire!' There was a stampede for the exit; and when everything finally calmed down outside it was discovered that not only had it been a false alarm but that 17 people had perished in the crush.[35] Understandably the local population was superstitious about returning to the theatre in the following weeks, and in February Adler and the others left for New York, helped by a gift of £200 from the Rabbis.

The next group we know something about are the 'Jargon Players' described in Israel Zangwill's 1892 novel, *Children of the Ghetto*. This company eventually took over the Prince's Street theatre, and Zangwill recounts how they would try their hand at anything and everything with the inevitable result that 'they had the gift of improvisation more developed than memory'. Their current play, *The Hornet of Judah*, was being staged in front of so small an audience that the actors simply cancelled the third Act.[36]

By the turn of the century many of the East End's huge minor theatres were facing stiff competition from other entertainments such as the music hall and Bioscope shows, and many of them closed down altogether. Others, like the Standard in Shoreditch and the Pavilion in Whitechapel, desperately tried to survive by catering for local audiences and tastes – in this case, Yiddish drama. Once more it was great dollops of sentiment and melodrama that these audiences demanded and were given, as one writer later recalled of the Pavilion:

> Here, the Yiddish theatre flourished in all its sentimental glory, offering the romance-deprived audiences improbable slices of life where virtue always triumphed over vice. At predictable intervals during each performance the actors broke into ballads that wrung the hearts and brought tears to the eyes of the audience, already smarting from the pall of tobacco smoke that partially obscured the stage. Upstairs, in the overcrowded gallery, and looking amazingly like an animated Hogarth cartoon, were the mums and dads who watched the action and at the same time consumed gargantuan snacks of schmaltz herring, fish and chips, pieces of cold chicken, oranges, pineapple chunks and monkey nuts, all openly carried into the theatre in shopping baskets. The unconsumed portions of the repast were tossed over the rails onto the heads of the 'Capitalists' in the pit below. The remote verbal exchanges that followed the bombardment often provided better entertainment than the advertised play.[37]

Several of the Jewish clubs, such as the Jubilee Club set up in 1906, had a tradition of dealing with political topics, and some theatrical representations talked of the worsening situation around the immigrants because of the anti-semitism engendered by the economic decline in the years leading up to the First World War. Clubs also staged plays about 'labour themes' and strikes, and in 1912 for example performances were held as benefits for those involved in a tailors' dispute. The Yiddish theatre also dramatised one of the most burning issues of the day: 'An actor who played Major Esterhazy in a Captain Dreyfus play in the East End during the great agitation in France was not merely howled off the stage; he was threatened by a crowd at the stage-door for daring to represent the villain responsible for the Dreyfus infamy.'[38] The plays of authors like Moliere, Ibsen and Strindberg were also translated and produced, giving them a cutting edge derived from the audience's own experiences – as must have been the case when a version of Gogol's *The Government Inspector* was presented.

But the tide was running against Yiddish drama, exemplified by the fate of a theatre called 'The Temple' which was opened along the Commercial Road in March 1912. At its first night a Jewish opera *King Ahaz* was followed by a performance of *Rigoletto*:[39] 'Alas! – mistakes in planning, clashes in administration and poor judgment of the public's taste and its pocket brought the venture to an end after six months.'[40] That the Temple was turned into a cinema indicated the shape of the challenge still to undermine the prospects of non-commercial theatre.

But whatever its failings, the Yiddish drama with its emotion, passion and exuberant mix of music and dance – very different from the then West End where unity of style, balance and moderation were imperative – offered a startling contrast to mainstream theatre.

Chapter 5

Women in the Theatre: the Actresses' Franchise League

For centuries the position of women within the theatre has been fraught with innuendo because of men's persistent tendency to equate actresses with prostitutes – which was indeed the case in the Roman theatre. Apart from this prejudice, women have usually been allowed to perform only minor roles and steered away from the more influential jobs relating to the organisation and administration of drama. In the Middle Ages, for example, the male-dominated church and guilds ensured that the major parts were reserved for their own sex, although there were practical reasons for this in so far as women would have had difficulty in projecting their voices to thousands of people at open-air venues. Within the tradition of strolling entertainers, we get tantalising hints but no more of female minstrels in medieval times.

The public playhouses of the Elizabethan period were devoid of actresses, and when a mixed company from France played in London in 1629 the women were jeered and hissed off the stage – although both James I's and Charles I's queens participated in the private royal masques. In 1642 the Puritans closed the theatres and a pamphlet issued the next year complained that the boys trained to play female parts, 'ere we shall have liberties to acte againe, will be growne out of use, like crackt organ-pipes, and have faces as old as our flags'.[1] By 1660 when Charles II reopened the playhouses exactly such a process had

66

occurred, and in 1662 he sanctioned the appearance of actresses on the English stage:

> we do likewise permit and give leave that all the women's parts to be acted in either of the said two companies from this time to come may be performed by women, so long as these recreations, which by reason of the abuses aforesaid were scandalous and offensive, may by such reformation be esteemed not only harmless delights, but useful and instructive representations of human life, by such of our good subjects as shall resort to see the same.[2]

Working conditions for the Restoration actresses were dreadful: there was little space to change; wages were low; the strain of learning two or three plays a week unrelenting; and always the continual pestering of royal courtiers and parasites to ward off. As Pepys confided to his diary in October 1667 when he visited Nell Gwyn and her colleagues backstage: 'what base company of men comes among them, and how lewdly they talk . . .'[3] On stage the managers took the opportunity of inserting 'breeches parts' into plays which thereby called for the actresses to dress in men's clothes and show off their legs. Women-only plays were presented and some managers boasted of their indecency in the hope of attracting larger audiences.

Of the Restoration actresses themselves, it seems as if a kind of hierarchy of knowledge exists: the more murky and complicated their private lives the more we know (Nell Gwyn and Elizabeth Barry); the more respectable and conventional, the less information has come down to us (Mrs Betterton). It should however be noted that there was one prolific woman playwright of the time, Aphra Behn, who had 18 of her plays produced in the 1670s and 1680s, making her the first woman to support herself entirely through her writing. But her plays were very much in the mould of the comedy of intrigue then popular, and reveal meagre feminist leanings.

During the eighteenth century a German visitor judged that the English actresses 'support the honour of the theatres, by means of a nobleness and a dignity which charm the beholder'.[4] Certainly performers like Sarah Siddons were greatly admired and respected, but D'Archenholz was referring only to the London theatres. The majority of actresses worked for touring companies which patrolled the provinces, and there public opinion was much less sympathetic. A letter of 1730 addressed to the Lord Mayor spoke of 'stage-players and their constant attendants, lewd strumpets'; and William Hogarth's painting, *Strolling Actresses Dressing in a Barn* of 1737, underlined the stark living and working conditions. For whole swathes of respectable opinion, actresses remained little more than glorified prostitutes.

In the early nineteenth century this association was not helped by the clusters of prostitutes who stationed themselves around and inside the playhouses. Complaining of the 'hundreds of those unhappy women with whom London swarms', another German visitor wrote in the 1820s that: 'The evil goes to such an extent, that in the theatres it is often difficult to keep off these repulsive beings, especially when they are drunk, which is not seldom the case.'[5] One newspaper of the 1840s referred to the theatres as being 'great public brothels'.

During the course of the nineteenth century the status of acting as a profession began to rise, particularly with the advent of actor–managers like Squire Bancroft, Henry Irving and Beerbohm Tree who did their best to distance themselves from the memory of the Kean era. Their success was confirmed by the knighthood awarded to Irving in 1895. In 1904 Tree founded the Royal Academy of Dramatic Art (RADA), a further sign of the profession's newly acquired self-confidence. Hand in hand with this process, it proved impossible to set up an actors' trade union – both the Actors' Association of 1891 and the Actors' Union of 1905 lasted only a short time – as the most prestigious actors with their new status were deeply suspicious of such organisations.

Actresses too shared in the increased standing of their jobs, but they were bedevilled also by the problem of the spectators identifying them with their roles, a hazard not faced by actors. As Fanny Kemble wrote in 1835: 'Many actresses that I have known, in the performance of unvirtuous or unlovely characters . . . have thought it fit to impress the audience with the wide difference between their assumed and real disposition, by acting as ill, and looking as cross, as they possibly could.'[6]

Actresses were offered few substantial parts in the Victorian period. The melodrama for instance called only for conventional stereotypes: the wronged and none too bright heroine; the suffering mother; the old woman. Pantomime regarded actresses primarily as suitable chances for the display of the feminine form, and within the plays of the 'legitimate' stage women were expected to fill the role of contented wife and mother. Woe betide the straying woman, from eighteenth-century plays like *East Lynne* and *Lady Audley's Secret* to H. A. Jones' *The Case of Rebellious Susan* of 1894. Only in the music hall did female performers establish a sort of parity. In fact so few were the decent parts for actresses inside the commercial stage that when Pinero wrote his *The Second Mrs Tanqueray* in 1893 there was the spectacle of actresses jockeying for the role of Paula Tanqueray in a reactionary and stereotyped play. Many society drama plots at this time centred on the woman with a 'shameful past'.

Probably the only form of theatre in this period which sketched out even in passing the problems of women and in particular of the violence of men towards their wives, was the street theatre of the Salvation Army – a fact noted by George Bernard Shaw and drawn upon by him in *Major Barbara*. Shaw's biographer Hesketh Pearson explained:

> His street-corner work at the east end, where he often shared the best pitches with the Salvation Army, drew his attention to the dramatic talent of some of the Salvation Lassies in their songs describing the trials of 'saved' women married to brutal husbands, culminating, when they were expecting a savage kicking, in their rapturous happiness as they saw in the tyrant's transfigured face that he, too, had found salvation.[7]

In the second half of the nineteenth century the inferior position of women began to come under attack. There were legal changes such as the 1857 Matrimonial Causes Act which made divorce more widely available, and the Married Women's Property Act of 1870 that allowed a woman to retain ownership of her property whilst she lived with her husband. The opportunities for employment, whether as teachers after the 1870 Education Act or as shop assistants, also brought more women out of the home. In 1878 London University decided to allow women to attend on equal terms with men.

Actresses started to occupy more influential posts within the theatre. Madame Vestris had led the way with her managership of the Olympic from 1830, and she was followed by Marie Wilton at the Prince of Wales, and at the turn of the century by Lady Gregory at the Abbey, Annie Horniman, Lena Ashwell at the Kingsway, and Lilian Baylis, who took over from her aunt at the Old Vic. In part this process reflected the growing number of actresses: 'In 1861 there were well under 900 actresses on the regular stage, according to the census; over the next decade, however, this figure nearly doubled, and by 1881 actresses were beginning to outnumber actors for the first time.'[8]

Despite this change, the actor–managers, typically a chauvinist and patriarchal breed, remained hostile to greater parts for women whether as performers or as writers; as Cicely Hamilton recalled of her first efforts as a playwright in the early 1900s when a manager warned her that: 'it was advisable to conceal the sex of its author until after the notices were out, as plays which were known to be written by women were apt to get a bad press. My name, therefore, appeared on the programme in the indeterminate, abbreviated form, C. Hamilton.'[9] In similar vein the actress Lena Ashwell recounted in her autobiography that: 'Once when I went to see Tree I had in my hand a book called *The Soul of a Suffragette* by W. L. Courtney. Tree picked it up and with a magnificent gesture of contempt flung it into the far corner of the room.'[10]

It is therefore not surprising that the plays of Ibsen were taken up with such avidity in certain circles. Early articles on the Norwegian writer stressed Ibsen's call for equality between men and women and the transformation of the marriage relationship. Plays such as *A Doll's House* carefully dissected a sterile marriage and, uniquely at that time, interpreted it from the woman's point of view. As Nora says to her husband: 'We must come to a final settlement, Torvald. During eight whole years . . . we have never exchanged one serious word about serious things.' She finally decides to leave her husband. In *Hedda Gabler* too the usual representation of women was turned on its head. But as we saw in Chapter Three, few productions of Ibsen's plays were staged in England before the First World War. The successive Examiners of Plays were antagonistic and theatre managers either more so or else completely uncomprehending – *The Master Builder* was thought by many of them to be unintelligible, which meant that this work could only be performed privately.

At these productions the audience was often assailed by the press in hysterical terms, indicating both the chauvinism which pervaded the West End theatre and the threat that Ibsen's plays seemed to mount; *Truth* described the spectators at *Ghosts* as being 'The unwomanly woman, the unsexed females, the whole array of unprepossessing cranks in petticoats.'[11] In the next few years occasional productions of Ibsen's plays, notably *Ghosts*, were sometimes put on in order to raise money for the women's movement.

The growth of regional and nationalist theatres at the turn of the twentieth century, expressing as they did dissatisfaction with the West End stage and exploring less hidebound and more imaginative forms of drama, widened the opportunities available for actresses as well as challenging conventional assumptions. One Scottish woman who later became an active suffragette, Helen Crawfurd, traced her own and others' development back to the activities of the Glasgow and Dublin theatres: 'The Glasgow Repertory and the Abbey Theatre, Dublin were alive and vital, dealing with the real problems of the people struggling either for National Independence or against sex inequality and the insubordinate position of women. There can be no doubt whatever of the value of the educational work of these companies.'[12]

But the major assault on the male-dominated stage of the day came from an organisation called the Actresses' Franchise League (AFL), formed in December 1908. The AFL put on plays and pageants, encouraged new women writers and organised a Women's Theatre season. Despite these wide-ranging initiatives, it is only in the last few years that any research has been undertaken on the AFL, and standard works on the Edwardian theatre offer no assistance at all.

In 1903 the Pankhurst family founded the Women's Social and Political Union (WSPU) to campaign for votes for women

– which no woman at this time, or until 1918, possessed. The
WSPU engendered a whole range of cultural bodies, although
the claim sometimes made that it was the first political
agitation to organise the arts in its aid was incorrect in view of
the work of the Clarion movement. One such was the Women
Writers' Suffrage League of 1908 which hoped to advance the
suffrage cause by 'the means proper to writers – the use of the
pen'. The women writers were responsible for issuing their own
publications and launching letter writing campaigns to the
press. A prominent member was Elizabeth Robins, whose
play *Votes for Women* had been staged with some success by
the Barker–Vedrenne regime at the Court Theatre in April
1907.

The AFL was set up in December 1908 and its membership
included many distinguished actresses: Mrs Forbes-Robertson
was a founder, Mrs Kendal was President, Lillie Langtry
Vice-President, and both Ellen Terry and Sybil Thorndike
were members. Its stated objective was to 'convince members
of the theatrical profession of the necessity of extending the
franchise to women', and the AFL soon expanded into a
propaganda body by putting on plays, meetings and lectures.
One of the AFL's leaders claimed that because of their
dramatic nature the suffrage plays attracted the undecided:
'They get hold of nice frivolous people who would die sooner
than go in cold blood to meetings. But they see the plays, and
get interested, and then we can rope them in for meetings.'[13]

At first the AFL relied on the old stalwart G. B. Shaw for
plays, but then his new work *Press Cuttings* fell foul of the
Examiner of Plays. Coupled with the realisation that many of
his works were unsuitable in terms of their length and casting,
several women began to write plays themselves. Easy to
produce, and most popular, were a series of monologues in
which a woman hostile to the idea of votes for women is
gradually convinced of the error of her ways, as in *A Chat with
Mrs Chicky* by Evelyn Glover, where charwoman Mrs Chicky
meets and ingenuously converts Mrs Holbrook, an anti-
suffrage canvasser. Another in this vein was Glover's *Miss
Appleyard's Awakening*, which centres on the arguments between
Miss Appleyard and yet another anti-suffrage caller Mrs
Crabtree.

CRABTREE: This – this is beyond everything! You consider yourself capable of forming a political opinion?

APPLEYARD: Well – shall we say at least as capable as the gentlemen who's going to vote for Mr Holland because his own wife's a Dutchwoman!

CRABTREE: You don't think that a woman's place is the home?

APPLEYARD: Place – certainly. Prison – no. You might as well say that a man's place is his office and blame him for coming home in an evening or taking an interest in his wife's duties or his children's lessons!

The AFL's plays were bound to reflect their times in style and approach, particularly as there were no forerunners or models from which to learn. Most of them were, like the West End society dramas, set in drawing-rooms and the servants therefore are allocated only walk-on parts: it is aristocratic women who are being converted, as in another popular monologue by Beatrice Harraden called *Lady Geraldine's Speech*. Some AFL plays are now very dated – *The Reforming of Augustus* is full of lines like 'Augustus, you are found guilty of having been a cad to your sister', and platitudes suggesting that it is the poor people who get more of the real things of life – but several are still lively to read, and have recently been staged.

There were some important exceptions to the general drawing-room settings. One was a short play by Margaret Nevinson, *In the Workhouse*. Nevinson had been a Poor Law Guardian and was quite sure of the purpose of her play, as the preface brings out:

In this little play I have attempted to illustrate from life some of the hardships of the law to an unrepresented sex, the cruel punishment meted out to women, and to women only, for any breach of traditional morality, the ruin of the girl, the absolute immunity of the male, the brutality that attacks an idiot, the slavery of the married woman . . .[14]

If all this sounds rather dull and predictable, in fact the seven characters – all women – do succeed in coming to life. In her autobiography Nevinson recalled that many critics were apparently shocked by the 'plain speaking' of the play: the

Referee refused to print either Nevinson's name or those of the seven actresses who appeared in 'this disgusting drama'.[15]

Another play which broke out of the conventional confines was the musical comedy *The Suffrage Girl*; written by some female employees of Selfridges, it was presented at the Court Theatre in 1911.[16] A third was Gertrude Vaughan's *The Woman with the Pack* which, although full of heavy symbolism, does represent scenes of sweated labour and of prostitution, pointing out the economic reasons for such evils. Finally, the AFL also adapted in dramatic form Olive Schreiner's novel, *The Story of an African Farm*. First published in 1883 under the pseudonym Ralph Iron, one of the heroines is an unmarried mother and there are numerous passages arguing for equality between the sexes.[17]

The AFL tried not to be just an exclusively London-based organisation: in 1909 a tour of *Press Cuttings* was arranged (the Examiner granted the play a licence after changes had been made), and the Secretary's Report for 1909–10 shows that performances of suffrage plays took place at Saffron Walden, Sevenoaks, Southampton and Glasgow. In the following years Nottingham, Colchester and Northampton were visited by a touring company, and of the four permanent provincial branches Edinburgh was the most active. Men's Leagues for Women's Suffrage also conducted active programmes outside London which included the performance of plays.

Intriguingly, the AFL also formed an East End section in 1910 with the somewhat patronising intention of holding meetings in the East End 'for the poor working men whose lives contain so little pleasure', and the annual report related that thanks to the help of the local Labour politician George Lansbury, splendid (and free) meetings were held in Bow and Poplar: the programme included 'suffrage recitations and songs'. However the Secretary's Report for 1911–12 spoke of problems, indicating the restricted social background of the AFL: 'We are still continuing our meetings in the poor districts of London, as far as Stratford in the East and North Kensington in the West. Latterly we have found the question of working them up a difficulty, as we must necessarily get in touch with people on the spot, who can help this way.' Matters were not helped by incidents at a WSPU rally in Victoria Park in May

1913 when the AFL's platform was 'singled out for attention by a band of rowdies, and the speakers were not given a hearing'.[18]

The suffragettes also pioneered forms of street theatre. The Pankhursts had always been aware of the value of publicity, which they often tried to attract by means of outdoor events. There were weekly poster parades, huge meetings such as that in Hyde Park in June 1908 which numbered some 300 000 people, and also a Women's March in 1912. Such demonstrations were usually led by the WSPU Drum and Fife Band, supplemented by banners and streamers supplied by the Artists' Suffrage League, and in the variety theatres short films notified the audiences of forthcoming events. Even the more famous episodes such as the chaining of suffragettes to railings, the stoning of West End shop windows, the wheeling of the ill Mrs Pankhurst onto stages in a wheelchair, Emily Davison's fatal leap in front of the King's horse during the 1913 Derby – all of these were planned and executed in a deliberately theatrical manner. The AFL also supplied disguises which enabled the WSPU's leaders to slip away undetected by the police at the end of meetings often held in theatres. Their most notable open-air production was the panorama *The Pageant of Famous Women* which highlighted the life and times of famous women down the ages. It was the success of this pageant which allowed the AFL to finance the opening of five regional offices.

The AFL arranged debates and meetings which discussed questions other than women's suffrage: members were polled as to their views on the abolition of theatre censorship (there was a small majority against such a move), and in February 1911 a meeting overwhelmingly passed a resolution which stated that 'an interest in politics was of vital necessity for the truthful interpretation of the drama of life'.[19] Unfortunately there is no evidence that the AFL ever tackled or was interested in such issues as the role of the actor–manager, state support for the arts, the dominance of the long-run system or even the music hall.

The AFL's membership had carried on rising steadily, from 360 in 1910, to 550 in 1911, 700 in 1912, and 760 by June 1913. The Secretary of the Play Department struggled to keep up with the pace of activity: 'The services of our members have been requisitioned for all manner of entertainments, and the response had been so great that it has been quite impossible to keep a record, which is in any sense adequate to the extent of service rendered to the various Societies.' Self-confidence had also risen, encouraging the AFL to embark upon its most ambitious project: the establishment of a 'Woman's Theatre'.

Votes for Women of 23 May 1913 carried an article by Inez Bensusan of the AFL's Play Department, explaining that the Coronet Theatre in London had been leased for a week at the end of October in order to present previously unperformed plays: 'I want it to be run entirely for women. The whole business management and control will be in the hands of women.' If successful a longer season was planned, but even the initial first week required an outlay of £450. A few months later it was suggested that 'the idea of the whole scheme is that it should be a preliminary to a permanent theatre managed by women in the interest of the woman's movement, which shall be established on a sound commercial basis'.[20] The setting up of a 'Women's Theatrical Agency' was also mooted.

The week finally took place in December 1913, with the main play being Brieux's *La Femme Seule*, translated by Mrs Bernard Shaw. The venture proved to be a huge success, securing a net profit of £442. The Annual Report justifiably took pride in this demonstration that women could run a theatre quite capably and announced a similar event for 1914 on a profit-sharing basis. Throughout that year preparations were under way for a week's season at the Court Theatre in October, the play chosen for performance being *The Sphinx*, which 'purports to present in symbolism the mystery underlying the sex problem'. But on the outbreak of the war in August 1914 it was decided to defer the season.

Instead the AFL threw its energies into arranging War Relief matinees in London and variety programmes for the troops in France under the title of the Woman's Theatre Camps Entertainments. By October 1916 over 634 such entertainments had been given and between six and eight concerts were organised a week. But, as Julie Holledge has observed: 'After their years of struggle before the war to represent the reality of women's lives, the actresses were back in their timeworn role – an image of beauty like a china tea-cup with sexual overtones.'[21] The AFL was not resurrected after the war.

The AFL reflected wider trends beginning to permeate Edwardian society. We have already seen that two of the Gaiety's most popular productions, *Jane Clegg* and *Hindle Wakes*, dealt with the question of female emancipation. Other established writers also tackled these issues: J. M. Barrie's *The Twelve-Pound Look* of 1910 for instance was about the greedy materialism motivating a man and which prompts his wife to leave him. Barrie's play was often presented over the next few years, especially by amateur groups.

Women during this period were also not afraid to object to representations of them on stage. In the spring of 1914 a Merseyside trade unionist called James Sexton wrote and had performed at the Liverpool Repertory Theatre *The Riot Act*, based upon the Liverpool strikes of 1911. The play aroused much hostility: 'His most determined critics were the suffragettes. The one woman character lied, was disloyal, had a "past", made open love to her employer, – and was a suffragette. Here, it was alleged, was an attack on the whole movement. So suffragettes rose in the stalls, protested and were forcibly ejected; or they addressed the audience from the boxes and were ejected from there.'[22]

The AFL's activities had been wide-ranging and valuable: the East End section, the tours, the plays dealing explicitly with political issues, the street theatre, the downplaying of the distinction between amateur and professional, the Woman's Theatre season which might have developed as intended into a permanent repertory theatre – these were all projects created outside of the West End, despite the fact that several of its members were employed there. Perhaps most encouraging of all, it has been estimated that some 400 women playwrights were active between 1900 and 1920.[23]

But unfortunately even the AFL provoked no fundamental changes with the commercial theatre. For example, figures for RADA graduates between 1910 and 1914 showed that men stood nearly twice as much chance as women of getting a West End engagement. In the inter-war period a few women did contribute significantly, such as Lilian Baylis at the

Old Vic, Mary Kelly and the Village Drama movement, the Lena Ashwell Players, whilst other innovative spirits like Edith Craig, who had run the Pioneer Players, found theatrical openings non-existent. Not until the 1970s did the question of women's theatre surface once more.

Chapter 6

Between the Wars: the 'Little Theatre Movement'

The First World War accelerated the changes which had been taking place within the commercial theatre. Rents in London quadrupled during the four years, and when combined with the escalating costs of productions it resulted in the ousting of the old Victorian and Edwardian actor–managers – many of whom had retired or died by 1918 – by business conglomerates to whom the drama was just one among many of their concerns. Whatever the failings of the actor–managers they did at the very least bring a personal touch to the running of their playhouses.

The fact that no new theatres were built between 1914 and 1918 increased the competition for those that remained, ensuring that few managements were prepared to take risks either with their choice of plays or with their methods of production. Further, the theatrical boom of the war years, which had been caused by the understandable enthusiasm of military men for escapist entertainment, had confirmed the two key foundations of the West End against which the pre-war reps had battered in vain: the long run and the star system.

The 'splendid isolation' of the West End stage between the wars was reinforced by its expensive seat prices, certainly as compared with the new cinemas springing up all over the country: an average of 9s a seat as against the cinema's 2s 6d to 4s 6d. And already by 1914 there had been over 3500 cinemas in Britain.[1] The Entertainments Tax also struck at the theatre's finances: when the Birmingham Rep secured exemption from this tax in 1934, it was estimated to be worth £2000 a year to it.

In such circumstances it was hardly surprising that naturalism – stage action as the representation of 'real', i.e. middle-class, life – should dominate the West End or that the experiments and innovations current elsewhere in mainstream European theatre should pass the British commercial theatre by. Although the odd 'serious' play was a success, such as R. C. Sherriff's *Journey's End* of 1928, which attacked the suffering of war (though even then this play had started as a Sunday night production for the Stage Society), most popular was the endless diet of musicals or historical period pieces like *The Barretts of Wimpole Street*. Censorship also made certain that nothing provoking or controversial should be staged: the 1930s was overshadowed by the rise of fascism on the continent, but as late as 1939 a Herbert Farjeon lyric was forbidden because it began:

> Even Hitler had a mother
> Even Musso had a ma.[2]

The respected commentator Allardyce Nicoll, writing in 1936, complained that 'a darkness of now outworn tradition hangs over the greater part of the professional theatre . . . the English theatre, lacking the spirit for experimentation, is artistically and mentally moribund.'[3] Unfortunately the influence of the West End theatre percolated down into other dramatic circles.

Amateur theatricals had been for many years a pleasant way of passing an hour or so. Jane Austen's *Mansfield Park* (1814) describes the performance of a play – 'We mean nothing but a little amusement among ourselves, just to vary the scene, and exercise our powers in something new' – and Charles Dickens was renowned for the energy with which he threw himself into productions. Amateur clubs were founded at the universities of Oxford and Cambridge in the nineteenth century, and many plays were published in order to meet the demands of the numerous play-reading groups throughout the country.

The real growth of amateur theatre in British occurred after 1919 when Geoffrey Whitworth formed the British Drama League (BDL). Its objects were defined as broadly as possible – 'the encouragement of the art of the Theatre, both for its own sake and as a means of intelligent recreation among all classes of the community' – and on this basis more than 360 societies had affiliated to the League by 1923.[4] Headquarters in London were acquired, plays published, an extensive library built up and a periodical called *Drama* issued. In 1927 the League inaugurated its own annual National Festival competition as well as offering lectures, drama schools and postal courses in play-writing. During the 1930s the BDL continued to stimulate a marked expansion of the amateur theatre: by 1939 there were some 30 000 amateur groups playing to approximately five million people each year.[5] In Scotland the Scottish Community Drama Association was formed in 1926 and by 1937 Scotland boasted over 1000 amateur clubs.[6]

However the BDL and its affiliated groups were never able to sever their overwhelming dependence on the West End stage as a guide and arbiter of taste. L. du Garde Peach, founder and director of the Village Players, castigated societies in 1936 for their continued bad productions of recent London shows,[7] and one of the BDL's own organisers was quoted as saying that 'to a great extent the amateur movement is still content to tread the beaten track of out-worn West End successes, or machine-made one-act plays, and is satisfied with clumsy production and stereotyped acting, but then,' she added, 'could not exactly the same be said of, say, 60 per cent of the professional theatre?'[8]

The one playwright of enormous potential revealed by the amateur movement was the ex miner from Fife, Joe Corrie. He had begun his Bowhill Village Players in 1926 in order to raise money for starving miners and their families, and his play *In Time Of Strife*, which toured widely, presented a tough and gritty portrayal of mining life. Sadly, however, Corrie's skills were largely dissipated during the 1930s by his trying to satisfy that insatiable amateur demand for lightweight one-act dramas. Another weakness of the amateur movement was that there were simply too many groups and societies, thus spreading the available talent much too thinly. It was not that the BDL was completely insular or unadventurous in its ideas – for example, it sponsored trips to the Moscow Theatre Festival between 1934 and 1936 – but that the influence of the West End was bound to be overpowering in the absence of a strong tradition of 'alternative theatre'.

But if the hold of the West End theatre continued, then its

very pervasiveness provoked a significant counter-reaction amongst the 'little theatres'. These were usually run on a shoestring and supported by a single wealthy individual, but they displayed a spirit of experiment the commercial stage often lacked. Some, such as the Abbey, the Liverpool and Birmingham Reps, the Yiddish theatre and the Old Vic, were continuations of pre-1914 initiatives, whilst others like the Maddermarket in Norwich , the Cambridge Festival Theatre, the Gate and Group Theatres were new. The more political alternative theatre will be discussed in the next chapter.

The Abbey Theatre in Dublin teetered on the edge of financial disaster in the immediate post-war years but in 1924 the new Eire government granted it a subsidy of £850 per annum, making the Abbey the first publicly-supported theatre in the English-speaking world. Even then the Abbey owed its further existence to a new playwright whose works aroused as much passion and controversy as had those of J. M. Synge twenty years before – Sean O'Casey.

His works plunged deep into topical issues: *The Shadow of a Gunman* was about slum-dwellers during the Black and Tan war in Ireland, *Juno and the Paycock* examined the civil war of 1922, and *The Plough and the Stars* dealt with the 1916 insurrection. When the last play was first performed in 1926, the stage was invaded by a group of spectators objecting to the carrying of the Irish Republican flag into a pub as a slur on their nation.[9] Apart from O'Casey's willingness to dramatise recent history – again, in marked contrast to the West End with its supervision by the censor – he also mixed various ingredients into his works such as song and dance, thus flying in the face of literary dictates as to unity of style. The Abbey's capacity for continued growth was demonstrated by the opening of an Experimental Theatre in 1937.

The Birmingham Repertory Theatre had also kept going during the war. Its most controversial production was J. M. Synge's *The Tinker's Wedding*, which in 1917 sparked off considerable uproar: 'Boos, hisses, shouts, and songs prevented a single word of the play from being heard, so the curtain was dropped and the lights turned up.' Protests at the representation of a Catholic priest in a supposedly unfavourable light had started the riot. A debate then took place on stage between the leader of the protesters and a member of the theatre staff, but with no clear-cut result. The play then proceeded to its end, accompanied by missiles and further noise.[10]

In 1918 the Birmingham Rep presented John Drinkwater's *Abraham Lincoln* with such success that it transferred to London – testifying once again to the tendency for provincial hits to transfer to the metropolitan theatre. Furthermore some of the company remained in London after the play had come off. Back in Birmingham Barry Jackson was still struggling against the local public's indifference. When in late 1923 the average audience at a production of Shaw's *Back to Methuselah* was 109, less than that involved in the performance and administration of the play, Jackson closed the theatre down. He reopened it seven months later only after receiving promises of much greater local support. By 1935 Jackson had spent over £100 000 of his own money on the venture – the continual drain on his resources ensuring that the introduction of both a School of Opera in 1922 and genuine repertory in 1931 had to be discontinued on financial grounds. In 1935 Jackson transferred the Birmingham Rep to a local trust.

The Liverpool Repertory Theatre was re-named the Liverpool Playhouse in 1917, but yet again financial problems continued to work against opportunities for experimentation. In 1921–2 alone the theatre lost nearly £4000, which meant that few new plays were staged and the most successful, such as Brighouse's *Hobson's Choice*, ran for seven weeks, thereby raising the spectre of the 'long run' against which such theatres as the Liverpool Rep had originally rebelled. In 1922 William Armstrong, who had trained at the Glasgow Rep, took over as Director and quickly established a favourable reputation with a judicious mix of old and new plays. But the influence of London was still in evidence, as the theatre's historian noted in 1935: 'much of the theatre's work consists of selecting the best of the London drama and re-presenting it in Liverpool for the benefit of the Liverpool public.'[11] This was true of most of the repertory theatres.

The Old Vic in Waterloo, London, was run first by Emma Cons and then by her niece Lilian Baylis, who managed to build up a local following. Opera had been introduced from

1889, a pioneer picture palace operated before the First World War with an average attendance of 2000 people a show, and then in 1914 Baylis began the Shakespearean productions for which the Old Vic became famous. During the war the shortage of men meant that many of their parts were played by women, an interesting reversal of the Elizabethan practice of boys playing the women's roles, and the comparatively low prices attracted a non-West End clientele.[12] That there was little difference in price or comfort between the stalls and the gallery created a certain unity of character among the spectators.

After the war Baylis continued with her Shakespearean programme – by 1923 all of his plays had been seen at least once at the theatre – and in 1931 she also took over the Sadler's Wells Theatre as a home for opera and ballet. Here Ninette de Valois established her dance company which later transformed the state of English dance. Both Baylis's theatres offered a comprehensive repertoire which included plays, ballet and opera and stood in contrast to the West End. But the Old Vic's financial difficulties, which were always so pressing that Baylis acquired a reputation for meanness, led in the 1930s to the growing use of the Old Vic as a shop window in which established stars could recuperate for a season or two, leaving it to function less as an alternative than as a supplement to the commercial stage.[13]

Another group surviving from before the war was the People's Theatre of Newcastle, so named from 1921. Their move into new premises in 1915 and the need to sustain a building which held 250 people resulted in them playing down their earlier political affiliations. The plays of Shaw remained their perennial stand-by, but several of their productions incorporated local elements, notably in Hauptmann's *The Beaver Coat* where Tyneside idiom was employed for the dialect passages. The People's also put on a number of operas, but inevitably they were hampered by the smallness of their amateur company and the lack of resources and time; as their leader put it, 'our crying sin was under-rehearsal'.[14] In 1928 they moved once more into new premises, a converted church which held 300 people.

After the First World War much of the dynamism behind

Yiddish culture was gradually dissipated, particularly when many immigrants returned to Russia after the 1917 Revolutions – the Worker's Circle, for example, lost nearly one-half of its members. A visiting group of Yiddish actors from Poland, the Vilna Troupe, came to London between 1922 and 1924, impressing all with their histrionic skills; but there was not a large enough audience to support a permanent venture. The Standard became the Shoreditch Olympia cinema in 1926 and was then pulled down. The Pavilion closed in 1934.

At the end of the 1930s another attempt was made to establish a Yiddish theatre. The actress Fanny Waxman, who had performed at the Standard in the 1890s, opened her Jewish National Theatre in a converted dance hall in Adler Street just off Commercial Road. At the same time the Yiddish Folks Theatre was started in the Grand Palais, Commercial Road. Both theatres were small, holding less than 400 spectators, but they managed to support professional companies playing repertory for ten months of the year. Unlike the commercial stage with its emphasis on star names and the long run, these theatres presented a different play nearly every night – and consequently one observer wrote of 'the perpetual rumble of the prompter's voice' – with the actors and actresses in full emotional flood, eyes wild and arms waving.[15] But the Second World War ended both these theatres and also other Yiddish drama groups such as that attached to the Workers' Circle cultural organisation.

There were several reasons behind the decline of Yiddish theatre. The language itself was dying out, as was inevitable with the integration of Jewish children into the English educational system, a process of assimilation similar to that which had overtaken the Jewish labour movement. The 'ghetto' of the East End faded away as families moved northwards to the suburbs of London. The car aided mobility and broke up communities, and in any case the flow of immigration had virtually ceased. The Yiddish press had also disappeared, while Hebrew retained its pivotal position in religious life with the support of the Rabbis.

But if as the above accounts show, the ventures which had survived from before the war into the 1920s and 1930s suffered mixed fortunes, several new initiatives were undertaken which demonstrated the possibilities still open for creating a tradition of alternative and experimental theatre in Britain. One such enterprise was the Maddermarket Theatre in Norwich, set up by Nugent Monck, who had trained at the Royal Academy of Music. He had once been employed as a producer at the Abbey Theatre, Dublin, and then managed one of its American tours.

Monck was hostile to the concept of the picture-frame proscenium arch stage then largely taken for granted, and when in 1921 his Norwich Players took over what had once been a Roman Catholic chapel and a baking powder factory, he subsequently converted it into an open plan stage without a proscenium and with a gallery at the back. The theatre held only 220 spectators, which meant that, in Monck's words, 'The stage does not extend sufficiently into the audience, but we could not afford to lose a row of seats.'[16] Monck regarded the Abbey Theatre as the parent of the Maddermarket, and it was therefore appropriate that W. B. Yeats should write and deliver the opening address in September 1921.

Slowly building up a local following, Monck's choice of plays was often adventurous, including Japanese Noh and Indian works, puppet shows, music recitals and dance performances by visiting companies such as that run by Ninette de Valois. Monck specialised in Shakespearean productions, insisting – like William Poel (who had once employed Monck as his stage-manager) and Granville Barker – that speed and pace of performance was imperative. But it should be noted that of the 280 plays Monck staged at the Maddermarket between 1921 and 1952, the high number of 40 were receiving their premieres in this country. Monck was also unusual in not letting the names of the amateur company's players appear in print and in not allowing them to take a curtain call, thus retaining the Norwich Players' ensemble quality.[17] It was a policy continued after Monck's death in 1958 and it is still observed today.[18]

Perhaps the most important of all the experimental theatre projects between the wars was that based at the Festival Theatre in Cambridge, set up by Terence Gray in 1926. Gray was a man of private means who had used his wealth to explore a myriad of interests and he was fully aware of the latest theatrical work on the continent, especially as regards expressionism. Gray's internationalism was a quality which few others within alternative theatre at this time displayed.

Like Gordon Craig and W. B. Yeats, Gray hoped to restore the elements of mime and dance to modern drama; his book *Dance-Drama*, published in 1926, attacked the West End stage for its 'commercial exploitation', arguing that it had established a 'tyranny of words': 'the use of the human body rather than the intellectualised spoken words is the medium that is most essential for dramatic art.'[19] Unlike Craig, who shied away from the mechanics of actually producing plays as opposed to theorising about how they should be presented, Gray took over the Barnwell Theatre in 1926, a playhouse a few miles outside Cambridge which had once been used by strolling players when visiting Stourbridge Fair in the early nineteenth century and since then had enjoyed a patchy existence as, amongst other things, a Mission Hall and a Boys' Club.

Gray proceeded to rebuild the theatre along the lines he wanted, scrapping the proscenium arch in favour of an open stage with multiple levels, installing a revolve and also an advanced lighting system costing over £2000 which was manned by his colleague Harold Ridge. The use of the forestage and of movable screens meant that the playing space was highly flexible; as Gray wrote: 'I myself would rather produce Shakespeare in a barn, a cellar, a church, a concert hall, a boxing ring, a public square, or any architectural structure than in a traditional theatre.'[20]

Insisting that the Festival Theatre should be – as playhouses had once been – places offering a wide range of entertainments, Gray opened an excellent restaurant inside the theatre. The programme, called the *Festival Theatre Review*, was of a high standard, including articles on British and European developments. Gray tried to involve the audience by such means as awarding prizes for the best criticism of each weekly production.[21]

Gray operated a genuine repertory system, paralleling the life of the university town by presenting three eight-week seasons with a new production each Monday. He also ensured that the Festival Theatre was distinguished by the ensemble character of the acting, despite the presence in various plays of such powerful performers as Flora Robson, Robert Donat and

Robert Morley. In 15 seasons Gray put on over 150 plays, including more than 30 verse plays, an indication of his enormous energy.

Perhaps even more notable were Gray's sustained powers of invention: a Victorian *The Merchant of Venice*; the expressionist *The Adding Machine* by Elmer Rice; one vaudeville-style production; Greek plays in which whole scenes were played amongst the audience; taking off the wings so that the spectators could see the stage-hands at work; a *Richard III* making effective use of a variety of levels; performances by de Valois' dance troupe; the use of masks: these were just a few of Gray's experiments. In order to get over the problem of presenting Shakespeare with only a small company he used cardboard cut-outs for the minor characters, and after having clashed with the Examiner of Plays over Ernest Toller's *Hoppla!*, Gray bawled out the censored passages from the wings through a megaphone![22]

Gray once asserted that 'the exploiters [of theatre] tend to perpetuate old forms which they know will be universally understood rather than to encourage the new developments which must at first, owing to their strangeness, puzzle the thoughtless who are satisfied with what is familiar and seek nothing but that to which they are accustomed.'[23] As this statement suggests, Gray was often some way in advance of his audience, with the consequence that the ordinary theatre-goers of Cambridge tended to shun the Festival Theatre. Gray survived because of the students, but every three years this population of the university changed and he had to 'train up' another batch. In any case the theatre itself had less than 400 people and a full house brought in no more than £62.

The strain of weekly repertory was immense, and Gray realised that if his theatre was to survive he needed to join forces with other pioneering groups. He tried to create a circuit together with the Oxford Playhouse run by J. B. Fagan and Peter Godfrey's Gate Theatre. A site in Covent Garden was purchased, but as Gray later recalled, 'the local authorities in Oxford would not let us do what was necessary for my kind of stage (in terms of building alterations), the London Gate Theatre was minute and a club and the international financial crisis of the time rendered the financing of a new

London theatre unrealisable.'[24] That even Gray with all his drive and administrative flair was unable to set up an embryonic alternative theatre circuit emphasises the organisational problems always undermining the development of a non-commercial drama in Britain.

By 1933 Gray had had enough and he left the Festival Theatre, never to return to the stage – another talent which the British theatre had failed to make use of. The Festival Theatre staggered on for a few more years in the face of competition from the new Arts Theatre in the centre of Cambridge but finally closed down during the war. It is now a storeroom for Arts Theatre costumes.

The little London theatre mentioned above, the Gate, had been opened by Peter Godfrey and his wife Molly Veness in Floral Street, Covent Garden, in the autumn of 1925. It was tiny, holding less than 100 people, but Godfrey turned the lack of money and resources into a virtue by dispensing with solid and realistic scenery, as one observer described:

> From the beginning, his method had been to use a permanent black background, indicating the locale of the scene by the minimum of properties and furniture, relying for atmosphere and effect purely on unrealistic lighting. Even his favourite method of opening a play by drawing the curtains on a pitch dark stage and then gradually bringing up the lights had a practical origin. The theatre could not afford curtains of a material heavy enough to be impenetrable by light.[25]

Like Gray, Godfrey was aware of the European traditions of drama and his first season alone included plays by Hauptmann, Toller, Evreinoff and Capek amongst the 23 others on show. As the Gate was a club theatre Godfrey did not have to trouble about the Lord Chamberlain and the Examiner of Plays. In 1927 the Gate moved to a new theatre in Villiers Street, Charing Cross, a building which had formerly been a skittle alley and was so small that spectators in the front row could rest their feet on the 18-inch-high stage. Godfrey put on more than 350 plays in his nine years at the Gate, expanding the membership to over 1200, but by 1934 and after the failure of the proposed scheme with Terence Gray of the Cambridge

Festival Theatre he was exhausted and sold the theatre to Norman Marshall.

Marshall managed to raise £2500 from his family in order to buy the Gate and refurbish it. In such a small working environment – the performers often had to bring the props and furniture on with them, and the two boxes were reached by ladders – the production of plays could only be totally different from that in the West End: in particular the proximity of the spectators to the actors recalled both the Elizabethan playhouses and the Victorian music hall.[26] Salaries were meagre, but at least everyone was paid the same. In the early months the Gate nearly went under, and in desperation Marshall hit upon the idea of staging a revue. The success of the Gate revues which became an annual event raised a familiar problem facing fringe theatre: shows transferred to the West End, revitalising the commercial stage but undermining the little theatres from which they had emerged. The 1939 revue, for instance, notched up 449 performances at the Ambassadors' Theatre that year, forcing Marshall to search and try to build up another company.

Because of its club status Marshall could put on plays which had run foul of the censorship, such as Lillian Hellman's *The Children's Hour* and historical plays like *Victoria Regina* and *Parnell*. The latter two transferred, as did *Oscar Wilde* with Robert Morley in the title role. Ironically enough, by September 1939 when war was declared, Marshall had become, indirectly, a man vital to the well-being of the West End theatre. In the spring of 1941 the Gate Theatre was bombed out of existence.

The Cambridge Festival Theatre and the Gate were both run by individuals trying to shake the British theatre out of its insularity and introduce European innovations, whether they were 'unrealistic' scenery and staging, plays which eschewed naturalism in favour of expressionism, or works which dealt with political themes. But two other enterprises of the inter-war years sought to rediscover and make use of elements once an integral part of the British dramatic tradition.

The first was at the Lyric Theatre, Hammersmith. In 1918 the actor Nigel Playfair was hoping to find a London playhouse in which to start his own company; but on finding that theatres which before the war had cost £90 a week to rent were now in the region of £300–£400, Playfair was on the verge of giving up his ambition when he stumbled across the Lyric, known locally as the 'Blood-and-Flea-Pit'.[27] Being some distance away from the inflated theatre rents of the West End, the Lyric like the Old Vic was able to offer an exciting and varied programme 'because the suburbs are cheaper than Aldwych or Shaftesbury Avenue – and the new line of policy can be given fair trial, not scrapped in a panic at the end of the first bad week'.[28]

Playfair's first major change was that his performers did not ignore the audience but instead made them a partner, seemingly a minor alteration but in fact flying in the face of the 'Fourth Wall' convention of naturalism. He also stressed the importance of stage design and was fortunate to have the artist Lovat Fraser working for him (sadly Fraser died at an early age). Finally, Playfair was always attracted by the plays of the eighteenth century, and his biggest success was a revival of John Gay's *The Beggar's Opera* of 1728 in which the importance of the music and dance – again refugees from the 'well-made play' – was underlined. The play ran for three years. Playfair's revue *Riverside Nights* also went down well.

But the Lyric was very much a one-man organisation; as Playfair's son wrote: 'He intended to have a theatre in which he could amuse himself by producing plays of his own choice and in his own way.'[29] The drawback with this was that when the one man tires, as Playfair inevitably did, then the whole venture soon collapses. By the late 1920s Playfair's perilous financial situation meant that long runs were a necessity and in 1932, voicing the usual complaint that no new decent plays were being written, Playfair ended his association with the Lyric.

The second enterprise which drew upon parts of a wider dramatic approach, in this instance the popular tradition of circus, music hall and pantomime, was the Group Theatre of the 1930s. Founded by the dancer Rupert Doone in 1932, the Group espoused the rather vague aim that 'Art should serve life',[30] but it soon attracted a wide range of painters, musicians and writers who began to experiment with types of drama excluded from the West End stage, such as masques and cabaret.

In 1934, for example, Auden's *The Dance of Death* made use of circus, revue, music hall and melodrama. Auden went on to collaborate with Christopher Isherwood in writing *The Dog Beneath the Skin*, *The Ascent of F.6* and *On the Frontier*. Most commentators when examining these works are preoccupied by the influence of German cabaret and early Brechtian techniques, but Auden himself has written that 'the real influence were the English Mystery and Miracle plays of the middle ages'.[31] Perhaps the best known of the Group's plays was also one of the least experimental. Stephen Spender's *Trial of a Judge* was first performed in 1938 and reflects the growing menace of fascism by portraying the dilemma of a man of liberal conscience caught up in a fascist state where there is no middle way. Apart from *Trial of a Judge*, Group productions played up the roles of dance and music: when Nugent Monck produced *Timon of Athens* in 1935 the music was provided by a young Benjamin Britten.

Doone always hoped to establish a permanent repertory company, realising that lack of resources and rehearsal time was hampering their work. A blunt note by W. H. Auden in the 1936 programme for *The Agamemnon of Aeschylus* asked: 'Are You Dissatisfied With This Performance? Quite possibly. The chorus have rehearsed altogether about three times. Why? Because the actors have had to go to paid engagements.' He went on to lament the problem of 'too little cash', pointing out that the art of theatre is 'extremely expensive' and calling for patrons to make it a permanent theatre.[32]

The Group Theatre was certainly hampered by the friction arising from the formidable egos involved in the project. The painter Robert Medley has written of Auden and Isherwood that: 'They found it difficult, to say the least, to subordinate themselves to the imperatives of co-operative production. . . . It was simply another activity in the promotion of their own careers, to which they were prepared to give only as much attention as they thought necessary.'[33] Not the first or the last time in which this has occurred within alternative theatre.

The major failing of the Group Theatre was that it was never able to build up a public large enough to sustain an expanded range of activities, although it did its best with lectures, classes, exhibitions, debates and even a film group. Partly this was because of its lack of business sense – the administration was always chaotic – and partly because of its reliance on the use of the Westminster Theatre, lent to it on Sundays by its manager Anmer Hall. No thought seems to have been given to the idea of finding and performing in alternative theatre spaces as Unity Theatre was doing at that time.[34] In 1935 the perennial conflict between fringe and commercialism came to a head when a six-week season was staged at the Westminster. The need to attract a substantial audience led the company to such lengths that they even put on a drawing-room comedy called *Lady Patricia*. Not surprisingly in view of such opportunism the season was a failure and Anmer Hall lost around £10 000. The company never recovered from this blow and had faded away by 1938.

The British Drama League, O'Casey at the Abbey, the rep theatres at Birmingham and Liverpool, the Old Vic and the People's Theatre of Newcastle, Yiddish drama, the Maddermarket, Terence Gray at the Cambridge Festival Theatre, the Gate, the Lyric, the Group Theatre – these organisations gave an indication of just what achievements and successes experimental theatre could create. There were other initiatives, too, such as the Scottish National Players which performed and toured 131 plays between 1921 and 1932, one-half of which were new; the Everyman Theatre in Hampstead under Norman Macdermott; Ashley Duke's Mercury Theatre in London, where his wife Marie Rambert began to revolutionise British dance; and also Michel Saint-Denis' London Theatre Studio of 1936 where methods of acting very different from the formalism dominating the West End stage were pioneered, classes including the study of improvisation and pantomime.

But by 1939 several of the ventures had come to an end or were virtually moribund, such as the Lyric, the Festival and Group Theatres, and Yiddish drama, and it was generally accepted that the 75 reps in existence by then were, with only a handful of exceptions, secondhand exhibitions of old West End successes. Why was this?

Several reasons have already been mentioned, including the West End habit of creaming off fringe productions and personnel, and the experimental theatres' small seating capacities which meant that they lunged from one financial crisis to another. Often, too, in an attempt to stay afloat they found themselves relying on long runs of popular productions and the importation of star names. Allied to this was the distinct lack of coordination within the non-commercial theatre. As early as 1924 commentators like St John Ervine were arguing that the quality of the reps could only rise if they pooled their talents: in *The Organised Theatre* Ervine called for the linking of companies into groups, but nothing happened.[35] It is also indicative to note that if one looks back through this chapter few new British plays were even considered for production.

However the major reason accounting for the little theatres' inability to establish secure foundations between the wars lay in their failure to attract a substantial enough audience. Not since the days of stage melodrama in the early nineteenth century had theatre-going been a popular activity, and by the 1930s the West End stage, let alone non-commercial theatres, faced enormous challenges, notably from the spread of rival and much-frequented forms of entertainment. By 1931, for instance, one family in three owned a radio set, a figure which by the end of the decade had risen to three out of every four families. More than this, by 1937 20 million people each week were going to the country's nearly 5000 cinemas.[36] Throughout this period theatres were being closed completely or turned into cinemas: Scotland had possessed 53 theatres in 1910, one-third of which shut down over the next thirty years, and Birmingham's five theatres and five music halls of 1913 had dwindled to two theatres and one music hall by 1948 – but the city did have 90 cinemas. It was an international trend: the 1500 theatres in the United States of 1920 had dwindled to 500 by 1930 and then 200 by 1940.[37] These statistics are worth bearing in mind when reading the next chapter.

In his history of experimental theatre between the wars, Norman Marshall pointed out that an important problem for groups was obtaining theatre buildings in which to perform. But neither Marshall nor the organisations discussed in this chapter ever seem to have considered seriously the possibility of using 'other spaces'. Gray might have declared in a rhetorical flourish that he would rather produce Shakespeare in a boxing ring or a public square than in a traditional theatre, but nobody followed up such a suggestion. It is not just hindsight to criticise the little theatres for this shortsightedness: the British documentary film movement of the 1930s was exploring 'non-cinema' venues, and John Grierson coined the phrase that there were more seats outside cinemas than inside them. Only the political groups of the 1920s and 1930s raised and tried to solve this question of widening the social basis and habits of theatre-going.

Chapter 7

Between the Wars: the Political Theatre Groups

The growing strength of the British labour movement between the wars was demonstrated by the election of two Labour governments in 1924 and 1929 under Ramsay MacDonald. Although the second in particular ended in disaster with a divided Labour Party and a huge National, or Conservative, majority at the election of 1931, the fact was that the Labour Party had replaced the Liberals as the Conservative Party's major rival.

However the mainstream labour movement remained uninterested in cultural matters, unlike its counterparts abroad which sponsored scores of newspapers, periodicals, film and theatre groups, and publishing houses. In fact, the only venture with which the Trades Union Congress (TUC) was involved proved to be a success – but nothing came out of it. The centenary of the trial of the Tolpuddle Martyrs who had tried to form a trade union in Dorset was in 1934. The TUC commissioned a play, *Six Men of Dorset*, from Miles Malleson and Harvey Brooks. Malleson especially had for many years been writing works which dealt with topical issues, often provoking predictable responses from the authorities: his two war time plays, *D Company* and *Black Hell*, had been banned by the Lord Chamberlain but were still performed secretly.[1]

Six Men of Dorset consists of two acts and a prologue, and Malleson and Brooks based much of the dialogue on contemporary accounts of the trial and on the letters and speeches of George Loveless, one of the Tolpuddle labourers.[2] Largely because of this approach, *Six Men of Dorset* contains several well-rounded characters and also moments of humour, making its political points in an indirect yet powerful way, as in this exchange between George and his wife Betsy:

GEORGE: What's come over you, Betsy? You didn't say 'Amen' when I spoke the blessing.

BETSY: And why should I?

GEORGE: It was the Lord I was thanking.

BETSY: And what for?

GEORGE: Betsy!! 'Twas a bad example for the children, showing a rebellious and discontented spirit.

BETSY: Maybe that's the best thing I can gie 'em. I can gie 'em little else.

GEORGE: You've never said things like this before! What ails you?

BETSY: What should ail me? And me out in the fields and the blindin' rain, all day and every day and day after day, with my body bent double, pickin' stones and with another child movin' in me . . . for three shillings a week! They do say the Lord sends the babies, why He'd do that, without sending the vittles for 'em, is more'n I know!

GEORGE: That be blasphemous talk!

BETSY: Be it!! And that's more'n I know, too! Maybe it's a blasphemy for you to stand there askin' a blessing, when the children go to bed with their bellies empty, and lie crying for hunger in the night.

GEORGE: You shouldna say that. You know my heart aches that I can't do better for 'em; you know that. Every night I pray –

BETSY: Aye, you may pray! And read your Book!

GEORGE: Betsy!!

BETSY: And did you get comfort out of it this night? About the children asking their father for bread, and he give 'em a stone! What do you give yours? Taties! And not enough o' them!

GEORGE: Be fair, Betsy! I only mean, for myself, I do try to be content with my lot and accept in a humble spirit what the Lord sends.

BETSY: What the Lord sends! Do the Lord send that you and
I, and the likes of us, should slave all our lives, from the
cradle to the grave – and live worse than beasts; and
others live on the fat o' the land. That bain't God's
Goodness, George Loveless, that be Man's Wickedness.
That be the real blasphemy, putting *that* on the Lord!

After several performances in 1934, three years later the
TUC paid for a touring version of *Six Men of Dorset*. A company
led by Sybil Thorndike and her husband Lewis Casson
presented the play during 1937, visiting Wolverhampton,
Southport, Birmingham, Manchester and Norwich, among
other places. Revealingly, the company played at traditional
venues, mainly in the commercial theatres of these cities, but on
one occasion at least a more original setting was used, as one
member of the company has recalled of their trip to Harworth
in Nottinghamshire:

The whole village turned out to meet the company, which
was headed by Sybil Thorndike and Lewis Casson. After a
meeting in the local cinema, we repaired to the village green,
where we performed the central scene from the play. Only
with difficulty and after joining hands to sing *The Red Flag* did
our hosts allow us to climb into our bus and depart.[3]

The tour proved a success, with the play being seen by
between 30 000 and 50 000 people.[4] Other plays were offered to
the TUC which was urged to establish a more permanent
theatrical organisation. But to no avail, and the TUC never
again involved itself in such an enterprise.

The Co-operative movement also spawned a number of local
dramatic societies, with at least 49 active groups by 1937. The
list of plays supplied by headquarters as recommended
material was solid if not particularly exciting or innovative:
John Galsworthy, J. B. Priestley, 'all G. B. Shaw's plays', and
Miles Malleson.[5] Nationally the Co-op sponsored a huge
pageant at Wembley in 1938 which dealt with the history and
traditions of the labour movement. One participant has
referred to the sequence of action as rather like 'living pictures'.

The producer, André van Gyseghem, was one of those who tried to get the London Co-op to establish 'a permanent co-operative workers' theatre':

> We did not succeed. The Co-op had the money, but was not interested in using it in that way. It had spent a lot on the Wembley pageant, of course; but it could have gone on to start a real professional socialist theatre then. I had made a whole list of actors ready to work with us for a moderate wage in a theatre which had social realism and played with a social conscience. But the Co-op refused; it did not feel it was its task.[6]

Apart from other assorted ventures such as the London Labour Dramatic Federation under Herbert Morrison, which put on four performances of *The Insect Play* by the Capek brothers at the New Scala Theatre in 1925 and lost £100, it can be seen that the official labour movement evinced little interest in social drama in the 1920s and 1930s, concentrating instead on 'bread and butter' issues. It was left therefore to groups such as the Workers' Theatre Movement, the Rebel Players, Unity Theatre and the Left Book Club Theatre Guild – often associated with political groups to the left of the Labour Party and the TUC – to address themselves to a range of problems largely ignored by the experimental organisations discussed in the last chapter: notably the relationship between politics and drama, the possibility of reaching new audiences by going outside of the traditional theatrical venues, and finally of restoring the 'lost, public world' to plays which had been missing since the work of Ibsen.

Of the two political organisations involved, the Independent Labour Party (ILP) and the Communist Party, the former was the least important. Like the Clarion movement, the ILP stressed the importance of 'ethical socialism', holding out to its members a vision of a better world. Drama played a significant part in these hopes, and in 1922 the ILP set up its Arts Guild which brought together older societies like the Liverpool ILP Dramatic Society that had existed since 1917 and also sparked off the formation of new groups: within three years 50 such bodies were active, with 9 in London alone.[7] The Strand

Theatre in the middle of London was sometimes used for fund-raising theatrical events, and in 1926 during the General Strike groups of ILP Players toured the country performing and raising money for the miners. Unfortunately information is lacking as to the detail of their activities: apart from the ubiquitous Shaw plays, we know little about their productions.[8]

However the ILP dramatic movement did provide a platform for the actor and writer Miles Malleson who, as we saw earlier, was responsible in the 1930s for *Six Men of Dorset*. Malleson's banned *D Company* and *Black Hell* had been marked by their voicing of the rank and file's feelings about the war in the trenches. One vivid example comes from *Black Hell* where the hero of the play describes how he has been within earshot of the German lines:

> It's all a bloody muddle! . . . If you'd heard them. There was a man there, a Socialist or something, I suppose, talking against the war . . . and the way they all sat on him. They got furious with him. They talked just like you . . . how they were afraid of Russia and France and England all against them, and how nobody wanted the war; and how, now it had come, they must all protect their wives and their children, and their homes and their country . . . That man in their trenches – he'd had enough . . . he said he was going to refuse to kill any more, and they called him traitor and pro-English and they've probably shot him by now . . . Well you can shoot me . . . because I'm not going back . . . I'm going to stop at home and say it's all mad. I'm going to keep on saying it . . . somebody's got to stop sometime . . . somebody's got to get sane again . . . I won't go back . . . and I won't, I won't . . . I won't.

This was powerful and dangerous material to be written in the middle of a war.

In 1925 Malleson wrote the play *Conflict* for the ILP groups, and it clearly brings out the virtues and failings of this movement. Mirroring the West End stage, the action takes place almost entirely within the mansion of a Lord Bellingdon. There is one highly articulate socialist in the play who spends most of the time lashing the corrupt society he sees around him. The only working-class characters shown in *Conflict*, and then briefly, are a butler, a footman and a landlady. And yet right at the end of the piece, in Malleson's closing stage-direction, he hints of a world outside of theatrical drawing-rooms:

> Outside someone begins singing the 'Red Flag', which is taken up in chorus, and howled down. Someone begins singing 'God Save the King', which is taken up in chorus. Cheers and howls and countercheers . . .[9]

This seeming inability of the ILP to work out just what it was they were trying to do – present more socially aware middle-class plays or build up a circuit of venues and audiences who shied away from traditional theatre-going? – was witnessed by the fate of the Masses' Stage and Film Guild which replaced the ILP Arts Guild in 1919. As well as presenting films, often the latest production from the Soviet Union, the new Guild planned to organise a full dramatic programme. They had three aims:

1. Present modern plays and films of social significance.
2. Utilise the services of some of the best known actors and actresses of the time.
3. Charge for seats at rates within the reach of working-class families.[10]

They began with the American writer Upton Sinclair's play *Singing Jailbirds*, presenting it at a West End theatre on a Sunday evening – and immediately the contradictions of the Guild were revealed. It was impossible to hire such a theatre without paying large sums of money, which meant high admission prices, which in turn kept away working-class families, even if they were prepared to venture into the West End anyway.

And what plays were to be staged? One of the organisers breezily wrote that 'Much of the Society's choosing will probably be among German and middle-European plays', which thus involved problems of translation.[11] In any case few such playwrights were known in Britain even among those familiar with the modern drama. The Guild soon had to abandon its aspirations of forming a 'People's Theatre'.

The political body most involved in the development of alternative theatre between the wars was the Communist Party. Founded in 1920, although it never claimed more than a few thousand members, the Party exercised a disproportionate influence because of the energy and commitment of its rank and file. Predictably enough, the Party and its sympathisers were opposed to the development of the commercial stage, often attacking it in highly moralistic terms and concentrating on what they saw as its decline since 1918: 'Vice, immorality, licentiousness, and ribaldry took the stage. . . . Barely dressed actresses vied with each other in showing the most of their persons; filthy jokes and suggestive songs ruled the theatre.'[12]

In August 1926 the Communist Party's leading theorist, Palme Dutt, discussed the question of 'The Workers' Theatre' in an article in *Labour Monthly*. He criticised the repertory theatre companies – 'It is impossible to escape the atmosphere of liberal philanthropy that runs through the greater part of the work' – and the ILP drama groups, arguing that it was obvious that 'the full development to a workers' theatre can only take place after the conquest of power, because only then are the objective conditions – control of economic resources – available, and the social consciousness of the workers widely awakened.' Dutt also suggested that the repertoire of the embryonic proletarian theatre should focus on 'the stories of the workers' struggle, and particularly from vivid episodes in English working-class history or from current events'.[13]

In 1924 a Guild of Proletarian Art was formed and two years later the first Workers' Theatre Movement came into existence, both of them supposedly national organisations. However neither functioned effectively and the running was made by a local group in Hackney called the People's Players. At first they were confronted by the familiar problem of the lack of plays available, and one of their first productions, Upton Sinclair's *Singing Jailbirds*, was attacked as being 'too defeatist' because the gaoled activists remained in prison at the end of the play. Shaw was another early influence, as one leading member of the Workers' Theatre Movement (WTM) has recalled: 'we always had to go and see his plays; queue up for the gallery, that was, you know essential – *Man and Superman*, with the revolutionists' handbook at the back of it.'[14] The People's Players put on *Mrs Warren's Profession*.

The lack of suitable material was undoubtedly the major difficulty holding back the WTM. Even Shaw's plays called for a depth of acting ability that few of their groups could attain. The ILP Arts Guild, for instance, had reported that 'The majority of letters from local groups ask for advice in choice of plays.'[15] Writing in 1926 Ness Edwards in *Workers' Theatre* listed several works of 'Bourgeois Drama' which workers' groups could perform – plays by Shaw, Stanley Houghton, Harold Brighouse and Miles Malleson – but barely any 'Workers' Drama'. The only lasting attempt to fill this vacuum was the series called *Plays for the People* which issued 3 full-length and 16 short plays between 1920 and 1929. They also published Monica Ewer's *Play Production for Everyone* which had an introduction by Sybil Thorndike. Although rather better than nothing, few of the plays seem to have received good reviews even from friendly organisations, and it was not an area likely to attract commercial publishers. It is a sign too of the general immaturity of the WTM and other bodies that more was not written about the General Strike other than Joe Corrie's *In Time of Strife*, especially when Corrie's play was successfully toured around Scotland.

However in 1927 Tom Thomas, the leader of the People's Players in Hackney, hit upon the idea of adapting Robert Tressell's novel *The Ragged Trousered Philanthropists*. Tressell's book about a group of house painters in Hastings had never been published in its entirety and was available only in a mutilated form, but even then its characters and passion jumped off the page at the reader. Requiring few props or costumes, Thomas's version kept the earthiness of the original:

> The Lord Chamberlain objected to the number of 'bloodys' in the text – 31. I pointed out that Shaw had broken the ice with a single and celebrated 'bloody' in *Pygmalion* and that I had already been guilty of misrepresenting the vocabulary of the building workers by leaving out all the numerous and then completely unprintable words with which their language was embellished. We finally compromised: 15

'bloodys' would be licenced, 16 or over, not. I agreed but left an all important question unanswered because unasked – namely – who would count the 'bloodys'.[16]

The play ended with the resolution that 'socialism is the only remedy for unemployment and poverty' and invariably the audience would respond with a great shout of 'Aye!' – a technique of participation which would be repeated often in the years to come. Ideal for small groups because the play needed only a few performers, Thomas's *The Ragged Trousered Philantropists* was presented over 100 times by the Hackney organisation, and sometimes in dramatic circumstances: a production at the Manor Hall, Hackney, was interrupted when some Hunger Marchers arrived in the middle of the performance. Seats were given up to the men and the play begun again.[17] The People's Players did not restrict their shows to London, as one member has testified:

> I shall never forget the show we did at Braintree – we rolled up to the Town Hall in a coach provided by the Labour Town Council, who gave us a right royal welcome and incidentally a high tea, and then we all paraded the town with bell, book and candle, with leaflets and posters and the audience literally crammed the hall. I have a sneaking fancy we were not the main attraction – the weird and wonderful wigs and battered hats, the red noses of their usually staid and respectable Town Councillors (twelve Pied Pipers and how they piped!) cannot be overlooked as a powerful persuader. But although the audience came to gape, they stayed to listen and admire – us! We got home at five the next morning owing to fog, but for all that, it was a bracing experience.[18]

Although *The Ragged Trousered Philanthropists* was published by the Labour Publishing Company in 1928, other plays were required. In 1926 the pages of the *Sunday Worker* had contained a discussion as to the type of material which workers' groups should produce; several correspondents suggested the idea of revues, preferably incorporating contemporary satire. Although nothing came of these proposals for a year or two, mainly because of severe financial and organisational deficiencies – an appeal for £500 in 1927 for the WTM was not met, and only Hackney of the seven other London companies maintained a steady level of work – by 1929 Thomas had written a twenty-minute sketch called *Malice in Plunderland*, a playlet representing a significant departure from the naturalistic tradition of British theatre.

Making use of the trial scene in *Alice in Wonderland*, the characters were dressed as playing cards, each of them being a prominent political figure of the time, such as Stanley Baldwin and Winston Churchill. The Press formed the jury and the Knave of Hearts the defendant, charged with organising a secret society named the Labour Party. The dialogue was staccato and rapid and the sketch was full of topical satire.[19] The same year Thomas wrote a revue called *Strike Up!* which was supposed to parody Hollywood and included a 'leg-show' and six chorus girls. Not surprisingly the production provoked a storm of protest, the reviewer in the *Daily Worker* claiming that it was 'an example of what the WTM should not do'.[20] The attempt to draw upon aspects of popular culture in order to reach wider audiences was also condemned at a WTM weekend school in the summer of 1930 by a member of the German movement, then the most powerful and prestigious in Western Europe, who denigrated efforts to 'wed decadent and erotic jazz tunes to the revolutionary message'.[21]

Instead the emphasis was to be on what was called 'agit-prop' (agitation and propaganda), a form which fitted in with the general orientation of the international communist movement. In 1928 the Communist International had adopted a 'Class versus Class' policy, which in ordinary language meant that the Communist Parties were seen as the only true embodiment of the working-class and that the other Labour and trade union leaders were in fact a part of the establishment and should therefore be attacked as 'social fascists'. In cultural terms this expressed itself as a rejection of all forms of 'bourgeois art'. The correct approach was that of agit-prop which had been introduced into Russia after the October Revolution as a method of spreading the latest news to a largely illiterate peasantry. Without props, scenery or costumes, the performers simply conveyed the bare outline of events in cartoon-like simplicity and directness. There were as many as 24 000 theatre groups in Soviet Russia in 1927.

At the first Conference of the International Workers' Theatre Organisation in Moscow in 1930, it was laid down that art only had validity in so far as it exposed the evils of capitalism and propagated Communism. In Germany agit-prop skits were used in election campaigns. Characterisation, complexity, plot, dialogue, costumes, make-up, the curtain – these were all jettisoned, together with any notion of entertainment, in favour of a didactic and sloganising style which presented issues in a clear, black and white fashion. The German Red Blouses group put it thus:

So long as men are condemned to hunger,
So long will we know no aesthetic principles,
So long there will be for us no art form,
So long will we be only a purpose theatre.[22]

Translated into an English context, such an approach dismissed naturalistic theatre for not disclosing 'the reality' which lies beneath the surface of everyday life. Harking back to medieval theatre, the agit-prop plays were to be staged outside, often by means of 'lorry tours', and usually dealt with local and topical events. The WTM also rejected the 'Fourth Wall' convention ignoring spectators as well as G. B. Shaw's 'discussion plays'. At its root, of course, agit-prop theatre was concerned with politics rather than drama, as Ness Edwards underlined: 'The object of the workers' drama is to organise the working class for the conquest of power, to justify this conquest of power, and arouse the feelings of the workers to intensify this struggle.'

As a necessary consequence many WTM groups involved themselves directly in current political struggles. In Lancashire for instance the textile strikes of 1932 attracted the Red Megaphones of Salford:

If we were due, say, to go to Wigan, in the bus on the way up, we'd write the sketch, and we'd try it out for about half an hour, and then put it on at the market-place, by the stalls. We'd maybe be there for ten minutes before the police arrived in a van, and we'd scarper, say, to the steps of the public baths, and put it on there. Or we'd go to a factory, and occasionally we'd manage to get through a short play – certainly through a few satirical songs – outside the factory gate before the police came and moved us on . . . One day in Burnley we played to a crowd of a hundred and fifty thousand strikers, many of whom had travelled for a couple of days over the moors, and perhaps had fights on the way with police.[23]

Other plays dealing with contemporary issues included *The Sailors' Strike* about the Invergordon Mutiny of 1931, and a drama highlighting the perils of a miner's job, *Murder in the Coalfields*. Once when this last play was being performed in the Rhondda, news came through of a terrible disaster at Llwynpia in which eleven miners lost their lives. One of the WTM groups, Proltet, was purely Yiddish-speaking, performing in the East End of London between 1932 and 1934. For their play *Strike!*, 'actors were dispersed among the audience to shout Strike, strike! rhythmically to those on stage, and were often indignantly shushed by those not in the know.'[24] The WTM published its own plays such as *The Fight Goes On* about a Durham mining village, as well as the magazine *Red Stage*, which between 1931 and 1933 kept groups in touch with other.

The problem with the sectarianism of the WTM – one of the London branches was called simply the Hammer and Sickle Group – was that it inhibited contact with Labour Party drama societies and prevented thought being given to forms of theatre other than the explicitly didactic, such as the native traditions of music hall and variety which Tom Thomas had utilised in his controversial *Strike Up!* Potential supporters and recruits were put off by the strident sloganising. A Welsh tour undertaken by leading figures in the movement lasted 16 days and saw them holding 29 meetings before a total audience of 17 000; but it was judged only partially successful primarily because the material spoke only to 'the converted' and was useless in front of 'non-political' spectators. The influential German theorist Erwin Piscator had observed in 1929 that 'A revolutionary theatre is absurd without its most vital element, the

revolutionary public' and this was certainly lacking in
Britain.[25]

A further difficulty for the British WTM was that the value of
its work was often doubted. The Plebs League was a working-
class educational organisation with branches all over the
country, some of whom presented short plays, but
correspondents in its journal *Plebs* frequently expressed such
opinions as 'working-class resources are not large enough to
enable us to deal before the revolution with culture in all its
branches', and that drama attracted middle-class dilettantes
who were more of a hindrance than a help.[26] If theatre was
viewed purely in political terms then it was indeed a diversion;
one veteran of the WTM has recorded the general feeling:

> there were definitely Party people, proper Party people, who
> looked on this as not proper Party work, just an excuse to get
> out of selling the *Daily Worker* at Tottenham Court Road tube
> station. No, there was not support from the Party as such – it
> was rather frowned upon. Bit odd. The idea that it could be
> used as a method of putting propaganda across was just not
> on.[27]

By early 1933 the WTM's twenty groups were suffering from
a crisis of confidence: fewer meetings were being held and many
shows found themselves facing strong criticism for their
incompetence. That year a group of twenty members from the
Red Players and the Red Front went to a Workers' Theatre
Olympiad in Moscow where the crude caricatures of their plays
were castigated for being 'unbelievably primitive'. Just as the
international communist movement was beginning to soften its
sectarian position in the light of Hitler having come to power in
Germany – the Volksbuehne with its half-million members was
taken over by the Nazis – theatrical policy started to move away
from the simplicity of agit-prop. Gorki's plays of the 1930s, to
take one significant example, contain portayals of individual
characters. The International Workers' Dramatic Union was
now also based in Moscow rather than in Germany.[28]

The British WTM, chastened after its Moscow experiences,
was less scornful of accepting advice from professional theatre

people and tentatively widened its range of contacts. A number of groups were amalgamated, forming five in all in London and five in the provinces. The most important was again based in Hackney, the Rebel Players. A newspaper report of the time indicated the far-reaching changes which had occurred: 'This group, under a professional producer, will work on a curtained stage and will concentrate on attracting those who will go to see a performance in a hall, but will not listen to a "dramatised newspaper" shouted at them from a street corner.' Comprising some thirty people in all, the Rebel Players began to rehearse plays which required props, scenery and an indoor performance. The Rebel Players specified that they would not be acting outside and also made clear that membership was open to 'non-party' (i.e. non-Communist Party) individuals. It was not that the Players now contradicted their former belief in the political basis of all art – their motto of October 1935 still claimed that 'Art is a Weapon of the Masses' – but that they realised that something more than direct propaganda was needed.[29]

Elsewhere in Britain, under the impact of the Depression, widespread unemployment, the means test and the rise of European fascism, other theatre workers were striving to develop forms of theatre which at the very least reflected current events rather than ignoring it like the greater part of the West End's productions. One such was André van Gyseghem, the professional producer who was involved with The Rebel Players. He worked at the Embassy Theatre in London and together with Ronald Adams had introduced a club membership which permitted them to stage more ambitious plays than those ordinarily sanctioned by the Lord Chamberlain. One such was *Miracle at Verdun* which depicted the carnage of the First World War and others were Eugene O'Neill's *All God's Chillun Got Wings*, and also *Stevedore* by Peters and Sklar, both of which included the fine American Negro actor Paul Robeson. The latter production of May 1935 called for a large black cast and showed Negro characters fighting for their rights.[30] Membership of the Embassy increased to over 2000 and plays like *Age of Plenty* – an ironical title because the play focused on the human consequences of the Depression –

provoked a furore: 'We received a lot of publicity from the national press, mostly hostile and indignant, complaining about the left bursting into the theatre, disrupting it and using it as a weapon of propaganda. Thus the play had its effect, bringing the attention of a great many serious people to the problem of what was missing in the theatre.'[31] That this play caused such a storm indicates how insulated the West End and its critics were from the realities of everyday life for millions of people.

But the strains of the Embassy's methods of working, of producing a play a fortnight, took its toll and in 1934 van Gyseghem left this theatre to set up his own company which failed. Again, however, it is revealing to note that the Embassy provided the West End theatre with 28 transferred productions during Ronald Adams' 7 years in charge.[32]

One new organisation comprised sympathetic professionals working within the commercial theatre. Left Theatre began giving guidance to workers' theatre groups from January 1934 before embarking upon its own programme of productions. Starting with Frederick Wolf's *Sailors of Catarro*, a play about the mutiny of some Austrian sailors, Left Theatre soon encountered the familiar problem of the threadbare repertoire: 'there is one comment that nearly all our Left Theatre audiences make: "We want English plays".'[33]

To this end a play-writing competition was held, and the winning entry out of the 46 submitted was Montagu Slater's *Easter 1916*, concerning the Easter Rising in Dublin. Successfully staged, this play was followed by Slater's mining drama, *Stay Down Miner*, a title which was later changed to *New Way Wins*.[34] It is worth spending a little time on this work as it sums up many of the virtues and vices of political theatre at that time. Written for a cast of only eight, it was first staged in May 1936 with music by Benjamin Britten. It represents a Welsh mining village during a strike and the attempt to stop a 'blackleg' train from getting through. On several occasions the audience is appealed to directly, once as potential blacklegs:

GWEVERIL: You don't look like miners. You're not miners.
      You can't bear being looked at. Ay, swear, but you're

frightened when you're swearing. You'll be dizzy going down the pit-shaft. Your stomachs will be staying up here with us, and you down at pit bottom.

At another point voices in the orchestra pit and the auditorium begin to repeat 'Stop the ghost train'. The play ends rather weakly with another appeal to the spectators telling them to 'join Wales'. Although there are some strong passages – and the suggested backdrop was a pit-head, very different from the West End – *New Way Wins* was and is unlikely to attract anyone who is not already a committed socialist.

Left Theatre also introduced the revue, a form which combined humour, music and satire; and in all the range of their productions makes an impressive list. But their major dilemma was, as one friendly commentator suggested, 'to find an audience. . . . More of this Sunday night business in the West End, or play-acting in Hampstead drawing-rooms, is simply futile if propaganda is the object. . . . It is no use complaining that West Ham will not go to the theatre unless you have taken the theatre to West Ham.'[35]

The organisation did its best: its plays were indeed first presented in a West End theatre, often the Phoenix or the Westminster, but then taken to the East End. However almost everyone involved in the venture had full-time jobs elsewhere which meant that some productions were thrown together, as one critic revealed in what was meant to be a favourable notice:

> It would be possible to complain that the curtain rose three quarters of an hour late on the second house of the Left Theatre Revue; that two of the main items had to be omitted; that most of the sketches were under-rehearsed; that curtains and lights and microphones failed to act properly; that the most ambitious item was a fiasco. All these are true, all of them are important and should be put right. Yet with its many faults this revue is far brighter and livelier than most West End shows, and far better sense.[36]

Left Theatre's hope was to establish a permanent repertory theatre in a working-class theatre, an objective which required a substantial sum of money. Strong links were formed with the

labour movement and over 40 trade union branches affiliated
to the company, but an appeal for £2500 failed to reach its
target by a long way. The TUC did not respond and by 1939
this initially promising project had faded away.

In September 1935 a meeting confirmed the shift which had
transformed 'workers' theatre', deciding that the description
'Social Drama' was preferable to 'Revolutionary Drama'. In
November the Workers' Theatre Movement was officially
disbanded and prominent individuals within it such as Tom
Thomas were quietly asked to find other extra-mural
activities.[37] At the same time the Rebel Players, which had
given 54 indoor shows in the first two years of its existence,
began to discuss the idea of setting up a permanent theatre. It
possessed firm foundations in the shape of its 60 active
members and 300 associates, and the first question to be settled
was the name of the new enterprise: 'of course, there were the
usual political diehards: Theatre of the Revolution was one
suggestion. I said, "No. Let's stick to an abstract name so that
people we want to attract to us won't be put off." Someone
suggested Unity and everyone agreed.'[38] Its success in enticing
a broad range of support was illustrated by the composition of
Unity's General Council, which included such figures as actor
Lewis Casson, politician Sir Stafford Cripps, producers Michel
Saint-Denis and Tyrone Guthrie, publisher Victor Gollancz
who was to run the Left Book Club, playwrights Miles
Malleson and Sean O'Casey, and the actor and singer Paul
Robeson.

A small hall in Britannia Street, King's Cross, was thought
suitable as Unity's headquarters. After building alterations
costing £600 it could hold 100. Unity stressed that it would be
determined to portray 'the realities of life' as opposed to the
escapism of the commercial stage, and the *Rules* spoke of
creating 'new forms of dramatic art'. But yet again there was an
acute shortage of plays thought suitable for this new theatre.
Fortunately for Unity the radical theatre movement in America
had brought forth Clifford Odets' *Waiting for Lefty*.

Originally a writer for radio, Odets entered his play in a
one-act competition, which therefore meant that *Lefty* was
short and relatively easy to produce. The action centres around
a meeting of New York taxicab drivers who are debating the

pros and cons of going on strike. They come from very different backgrounds, which gives Odets the opportunity to sketch out the effects of the Depression; lacking any kind of trade union experience, they are waiting for their leader Lefty before coming to a final decision. But Lefty, like Godot, never appears, and when news is brought of his murder at the hands of the corrupt union boss Harry Fatt the drivers take up the cry of 'Strike! Strike!' – whereupon a sympathetic audience usually joined in the chorus.

It is hard today to convey the excitement which the play normally induced, but one indication of its force was that when the stage fight began in the audience during Unity's production, concerned spectators hurried off to call the police. In Glasgow spectators threatened to attack the actors in the auditorium who were deliberately interrupting, and at the People's Theatre in Newcastle they warmed to their task with such zeal that the audience lost interest in what was happening on stage.[39] Certainly *Lefty*'s impact was crucial, as Vernon Beste recalled later:

> This one play carried the workers' theatre movement both here and in America off the streets and into halls. It was exactly what was required in order that this step could be made: it had clear if unsubtle characters; it required not brilliant technique but sincerity and fervour from its actors; it needed only the barest staging; one spotlight and the table and chairs which could be found in every Union Hall . . . it was twice as effective in the kind of draughty school hall that can be hired for union meetings than it ever was in a fully equipped theatre.[40]

In the first half of 1936 Unity played 130 London shows, prompting some members to complain that the permanent venue had blunted the company's sense of attack as well as inhibiting its mobility. In fact Unity had continued with its tours, visiting Durham for a week in September 1936. Nineteen people went on the tour, playing to more than 3000 spectators in all, but the problems of having to arrange such a crowded itinerary in order to fit in with the job demands of what was an entirely amateur company were evident: 'Unity now realises that one show a night in towns entails too much work and does not draw in enough of their potential audience. Alternatively, future tours must be better organised and advertised.'[41] The tour cost £80.

Unity's repertoire depended heavily on *Waiting for Lefty*, of which they gave 300 performances in 1936 and 1937 alone. Financially they could not afford to stop playing it – and it was *Lefty* which got the theatre through the difficult summer months of 1937. But it was a reliance which eventually became unhealthy and stultifying, as Honor Arundel has pointed out:

> I remember, too, working in Unity Theatre's Play Department, being dogged by demands to find a play we referred to as 'the English Lefty' which was to be an exact replica of Clifford Odets' brilliant piece of dramatic journalism *Waiting for Lefty*. Play after play was criticised or turned down, not on the basis of its own merits or de-merits but because it did not follow the master recipe.[42]

It was not a problem confined to this country. In the United States 'left' companies were going out of existence by the autumn of 1936 because of the lack of plays. In desperation the head of the New Theatre League was advising members to put on productions of Ibsen, Gorki and Chekhov.

However Unity did manage to develop several very different types of play from that on offer in the West End. One was the political comedy, which sprang out of the discovery of a play called *Where's That Bomb?*, written by the London taxi-driver Herbert Hodge. As he recounts in his autobiography, Hodge's play was presented in a mood of sheer desperation after the negotiations with agents for another American play fell through; but it soon became a favourite with audiences, especially as its humour relieved some of *Lefty*'s intensity.[43]

Where's That Bomb? relates the experiences of an engine fitter called Joe Dexter who is fired from his job when his boss finds out that a left-wing newspaper has published some of his revolutionary poems. He is then visited by a gentleman from the British Patriots' Propaganda Association who reveals that their new plan is to infiltrate lavatories with right-wing writings:

GENTLEMAN [triumphantly]: This! Rolls supplied free to all patriotic employers. And sold at a specially cheap rate in the shops, so that the working-classes will be certain to buy 'em. On every sheet will be a verse or a little story so designed to instil into the mind of the worker his duty to his employer, his duty to his country, and above all, the dreadful danger of attempting to think for himself. Not dryly, you know, not dryly. But beautifully, poetically, romantically.

JOE: You clever devils!

GENTLEMAN: Oh, that's only the start. We are already in touch with one of the gramaphone companies, and by the time the written matter is ready, we hope to have a special holder. Every time a sheet is pulled off, it will play the national anthem.

JOE: H'm, it'll be a bit awkward for patriots, won't it?

GENTLEMAN: I'm sure all *true* patriots will rise to the occasion.

Harassed by debts, Joe agrees to write such material, but the characters – the Hero, the Hero's Mother, the Boss's Daughter, the Bolshy – come to life and make him ashamed of himself. The two-act play ends with the Hire Purchase Collectors carting away Joe's possessions and him laughing in the face of the gentleman:

JOE [exploding at Gentleman's puzzlement]: Oh, you fool! Why come to me for your toilet-paper propaganda – why come to *me*? Go to the Press Lords of Fleet Street. They've been printing the workers' toilet-paper for years.

At the time *Where's That Bomb?* was hailed as Britain's 'first proletarian play', but today it does little more than raise a smile.[44] Predictably, the Lord Chamberlain found it subversive enough to ban from public performance. Hodge's play did indicate that Unity had recognised the importance of humour in drawing crowds, and, as the producer of *Bomb*, John Allen, wrote, 'unless you succeed in getting people into your theatre, you thunder against capitalism in vain.' And the review of one

critic who on the face of it was not prejudiced in Unity's favour,
hinted at the force of *Lefty* and *Bomb* as a double bill:

> It suffices to say that both plays were performed with an
> extreme vivacity which carried all before it. Whatever one
> thinks of the propaganda, one is forced to admit that here
> were a band of amateurs who stood out head and shoulders
> above the majority of their peers. It is not untrue to say that
> many amateur actors lack the passion which the experienced
> professional is able to assume imaginatively. This lack was
> supplied in the case of the Unity Theatre Players by a
> passion which was real and not assumed. They were the
> mouthpiece of a doctrine which thrilled them, and they were
> able to convey their emotion to the audience since they had
> obviously undergone a lengthy and obedient training under
> a producer who knew his job.[45]

Herbert Hodge followed *Bomb* with a new play called
Cannibal Carnival, first performed in the summer of 1937. It
deals with an industrialist named Crabbe, a Bishop and a
policeman, who are shipwrecked and washed ashore on a
remote island where they immediately try to 'civilise' the native
Egbert. Some of the exchanges are witty and deft, but the play
did not go down so well with audiences, mainly because it
lasted over two hours.

Other than the political comedy, Unity in London also
pioneered the 'mass declamation'. The writer Jack Lindsay
had issued a pamphlet entitled *Who are the English?* which Unity
asked him to turn into dramatic form. More importantly,
Lindsay published another piece, *On Guard for Spain*, which
celebrated the Republican cause in the Spanish Civil War that
had broken out in the summer of 1936. Even critics hostile to
its political stance have admitted that it possessed 'a fresh,
vigorous style, redolent of the style of the eighteenth-century
periodical broadsheets, which, if recited by the trained person,
might make even the substance of the poem palatable'.[46] Over
the next three years *On Guard for Spain* was often recited at
political meetings, frequently by Unity's special mass-
declamation group, on one occasion from the plinth of Nelson's
Column in Trafalgar Square. The Drama Group attached to

the Jewish Workers' Circle even performed mass declamations in Yiddish.'[47]

By mid-1937 Unity's expansion enabled them to employ a paid staff of six people as well as to run three separate companies and it was clear that a larger building was needed. A derelict Methodist chapel built in 1850 and situated in Goldington Street near King's Cross was chosen – ironically enough Unity bought the building just before the British Union of Fascists could do likewise. It was estimated that the job of converting it into a 320-seat theatre would take six months and cost between £3000 and £4000; in fact, 300 volunteers threw themselves into the work with such vigour that the building with its two dressing rooms, library, offices and advanced lighting system was ready to open within nine weeks and at a third of the original financial estimate.[48] The new Unity Theatre was opened on 25 November 1937 by the publisher Victor Gollancz.

Unity tried to strengthen its links with members by organising a series of weekly discussions after performances and also by summer schools, night classes, acting and playwriting clinics, film shows, a School of Dramatic Studies and a monthy publication *New Theatre*. Within the productions themselves the distinction between player and spectator was as far as possible reduced: on one occasion the producer André van Gyseghem led the cast in applause of the audience, pointing out that they were an integral part of the performance and had been especially sharp and perceptive that evening.[49] The whole of the building was sometimes used, as in Irwin Shaw's anti-war play *Bury the Dead*, when the returned soldiers marched down into the auditorium at the end of the play, through the spectators and out of the theatre. Both Margaret Barr's Dance Drama Group and the Workers' Music Association often performed at the Unity, and a mobile unit maintained contacts outside London by working in miners' halls, working men's clubs and public rooms.

But two problems continued to haunt the company. The first was entirely familiar; as one committee member, Tom Foster, expressed it: 'Our own work has consisted of sending our speakers, publishing plays, reading hundreds of manuscripts and answering innumerable letters. But, in spite of our efforts, it is still absence of plays that is still one of the most serious difficulties our movement has to face.'[50]

Secondly, the financial demands of Goldington Street and the wages bill meant that it was imperative that all Unity's shows were well patronised, and their own publication *New Theatre* complained in the March–April 1938 issue that 'At present there are far too many empty seats'. In view of this complaint it is unclear how successful Unity was in attracting this ultimate goal of all alternative drama: the 'non-theatrical' audience. Certainly it had become fashionable among the Bloomsbury set to visit Unity from time to time for a welcome change from the West End experience, but these were not the kind of people for which Unity had been established.[51] Although Unity was not directly controlled by the Communist Party, it is possible that even in the Popular Front era of the late 1930s when the onus was on cooperation within the labour movement the fact that the bulk of Unity members belonged to the Communist Party proved alienating and intimidating for potential recruits.

Many of the plays produced at Unity emanated from the United States where the progressive theatre movement was on a more substantial scale than in Britain, resulting in several valuable plays other than *Lefty*. There was Odets' *Till the Day I Die* about communists in Germany and *Awake and Sing!* portraying the Jewish lower middle-classes; Albert Maltz's *Private Hicks*, Irwin Shaw's *Bury the Dead* and Ben Bengal's *Plant in the Sun* – all of them grappled with topical issues such as pacifism and anti-militarism in a provocative and thoughtful way. Their influence on groups as far apart as the Glasgow Workers' Theatre Group and Bristol Unity Players was crucial. Later, however, the supply of suitable material began to dry up when Odets, John Howard Lawson and other writers departed to Hollywood.

The Americans were helped too by the introduction of the Federal Theatre, a project which grew out of President Roosevelt's New Deal programme. Between 1935 and 1937 Federal Theatre was granted $46 million and at its peak employed 12 000 people. In its four seasons 830 plays were produced and performed before a total audience of around 30 million, and its Negro Unit alone presented 75 plays. In June

1939 Congress ended the Federal Theatre scheme because of its progressive political (but not socialist, let alone communist) associations. Not all of the Federal Theatre's programme was different or unusual but it did inspire one new form: the 'Living Newspaper'. This involved basing a documentary-style play on a current and contentious issue; for example *Power* discussed the electrification of America's rural areas and the various vested interests concerned. The force of Living Newspapers derived from their speed and pace, similar in many respects to the *March of Time* newsreels then being shown in cinemas all over the world.

Unity Theatre in London made use of the Living Newspaper technique with their *Busmen*, a production which dealt with the rank and file strike of London busmen in the summer of 1937, and also with *Crisis*, which was performed at the time of the Munich crisis when Prime Minister Neville Chamberlain flew off to meet and 'appease' Adolf Hitler. *Crisis* was written and staged within 72 hours and then continuously rewritten: 'We rehearsed for three days ending up usually about one o'clock in the morning. As the headlines changed we changed the script, going on with the scripts in our hands.'[52] Inevitably there were running battles with the Lord Chamberlain's office over *Crisis*.

Unity always tried to maintain an interest in the European stage and developments. For instance, they premiered Brecht's short play *Senora Carrar's Rifles*, showing what happened to a Spanish woman caught up in the Civil War and the painful dilemmas which she has to face up to and overcome. Some indication of the generally recognised quality of Unity's productions is given by the review in *The Times* of this performance: 'It is well acted and gives a natural and convincing picture of a peasant family waiting in suspense not far behind the front.'[53]

Another political theatre organisation active in the 1930s was the Left Book Club Theatre Guild, an adjunct of the Left Book Club which had been founded in 1936. The Club provided members with radical books at relatively cheap prices, proving so successful that within months most towns contained readers' groups which in turn prompted a range of cultural activities and events. From April 1937 the Left Book

Club Theatre Guild encouraged the formation of local groups, of which there were over 250 by September 1938, to read and perform plays. The Guild also published its own magazine, *Theatre for the People*, which was of a very high standard: the June/July 1939 issue for example contained articles on 'How to get a new audience', Ibsen, mass recitations, open air theatre, producing a play, Stanislavski and Mayakovski, book reviews, letters and news of groups' activities.

The Guild published a few short plays, including one about a rent strike written by Simon Blumenfeld. The Sunderland Guild adapted it to local conditions where a rent strike was actually taking place:

> Last Friday we went down to Sunderland and performed the play twice, once on each estate where they are striking. At the first one they had built us a platform on the estate's field nearby and assembled in their hundreds to hear the play. We were late in getting there (we couldn't find the place), but the crowd waited patiently for three-quarters of an hour and gave us a rousing reception. . . . Lots of the first audience followed us a mile to the next estate, where we performed again, and not one of the crowd left until the play was finished at 10.40 pm.[54]

Although some groups wrote their own material, such as the Glasgow Workers' Theatre Group, and there are tantalising hints and asides (the Guild's organiser John Allen once wrote that 'we have a first-rate play on Trade Unionism with an all-women cast'[55]), the Guild soon found itself scraping around for suitable plays. John Allen lamented: 'But where are the plays? . . . The plays we have so far received have frankly not been good enough. They have varied between two kinds: the political pamphlet in dialogue form, and the magazine story peppered with a few lines showing an awareness of social disparities. This is not good enough.'[56] Groups relied heavily on the faithful three – *Waiting for Lefty*, *On Guard for Spain*, and *Where's That Bomb?* – and once they had performed them the cupboard was largely bare.

One other form which was sometimes used was the pageant. Apart from the London Co-op's Wembley Pageant, one was produced in South Wales where the show was put on at three places at the same time in front of 6000 people; and another was organised by the London District of the Communist Party, welcoming back those British volunteers who had fought for the Republicans in Spain. The obvious drawback where pageants were concerned was that they required substantial resources and commitment.

The success of Unity Theatre in London was derived primarily from its teamwork and ensemble acting. Like the Maddermarket in Norwich, programmes did not print the names of the actors and actresses, and training was continuous. The usually insurmountable gap between amateur and professional was ignored: in 1938 Paul Robeson joined the theatre for its production of Ben Bengal's *Plant in the Sun*, and he was treated as just another member of the cast. Robeson had turned down the offer of lucrative work in the West End because he was attracted by the enthusiasm of this little theatre and its company.

Apart from the handful of paid staff at Unity, almost everyone mentioned in this chapter undertook their theatrical work after their daytime jobs – if, that is, they had jobs in the Britain of the 1930s. It ensured that all involved gave their labour out of love and enthusiasm, a quality that gave so many productions their vigour and excitement. But there were problems too: the membership inevitably changed and fluctuated. The Yiddish group Proltet disbanded in 1934 when it was found impossible to continue: 'Its members were dispersing, some to other countries; some, through marriage and the setting up of new homes, to distant parts of London; and some, through pressure of other political tasks as fascism grew more threatening.'[57]

It was a similar story, too, with the Bristol Unity Players who had given more than 150 shows between 1936 and 1938: 'there was a high turnover in membership. Members working long hours on the factory floor, with distances to travel and homes to mind tended to be ready only for occasional shows and infrequent rehearsals. They were unwilling to cope with long committee meetings when attendance was casual, unpunctual and irregular.'[58]

Unity Theatre in London also presented more conventional,

naturalistic plays: there was Pogodin's *Aristocrats* about the building of the White Sea Canal in the Soviet Union; J. L. Hodson's *Harvest in the North*, for which the members of the case went up to Rochdale in order to study at first hand the experience of work within the textile mills; and Geoffrey Trease's *Colony*, which focused on a Negro slave revolt.

But the play for which Unity is perhaps best remembered at this time was its 'political pantomime' *Babes in the Wood*, a full-length satire on Neville Chamberlain's appeasement of Hitler and Mussolini. Not since the days of Fielding in the 1730s had the English stage seen such a biting attack on a well-known politician, and in many ways it anticipated the 'satire boom' of the 1960s and 1970s. *Babes in the Wood* drew on the traditions of popular theatre – music, song, dance and all – as well as being influenced by a similar production then playing in New York called *Pins and Needles*. *Babes* ran from November 1938 to May 1939. Its range of targets was wide, as this song indicates:

> Love on the Dole,
> That's a luxury we can't afford,
> For they don't approve of love on the dole
> On the Unemployed Assistance Board.
> We've no room of our own,
> There's nothing but the benches in the park;
> Where we can sit alone and hold our hands,
> And whisper in the dark.
> We can't do the things
> That other lovers do,
> And it's hard to live on nothing but dreams
> When the things you dream can never come true.
> There's not much sense in life for us it seems:
> Funny romance, though we love each other body and soul,
> In our hearts we know we haven't a chance,
> For there's no such thing as love on the dole.

It was not an easy production to stage: the fact that Unity's actors were amateurs meant that two casts were needed, a total of 72 performers in all. Yet it came off triumphantly. In all, 162 shows of *Babes* were given to some 40 000 people, and by the time it was withdrawn Unity's individual membership had risen to 7000.[59] The profits were ploughed back into a Film Unit and the periodical *New Theatre*, and plans were well advanced for a full-time professional repertory company at the Kingsway Theatre in London together with a suburban theatre where musicals would be presented.[60]

The latter plans sparked off a considerable amount of friction. Unity had performed once before in a West End theatre, in May 1937 when a show raised £125 for the Republicans in Spain; but this was much more substantial. Some members of Unity had always been worried about the stultifying effects of having a permanent theatre anyway – 'Personally I still felt our real function was touring, and that the theatre was a white elephant. It was nothing but committees'[61] – and there was hostility to the idea of a professional company under the producer Herbert Marshall as undermining the group and egalitarian methods which Unity had always used.[62] Another bone of contention lay in the hold of the Communist Party on Unity: most members were in the Party too, and occasionally there were conflicts between the political and the artistic.

In the summer of 1939 Unity's momentum, which had seemed to be so strong, was destroyed. Much of the Popular Front good will which had surrounded political theatre groups in the late 1930s had been rooted in the seeming benevolence of the Soviet Union – the Moscow Trials notwithstanding – but in August 1939 Nazi Germany and the Soviet Union signed a non-aggression pact. Organisations like the Left Book Club were torn apart by bitter dissension and the Theatre Guild dissolved. Unity's plans for a repertory theatre could only be shelved when war was declared in September 1939. But although initially the outbreak of the Second World War threatened to demolish the achievements and gains which had been accomplished by the political theatre groups of the 1930s, in fact it led to many new projects and successes.

Chapter 8

The War Years

Together with its ally France, Britain declared war on Nazi Germany on 3 September 1939. After a brief campaign during which Poland was defeated, the Germans settled down to build up their military machine undisturbed, biding their time until the spring of 1940, when they suddenly launched an attack on Belgium, Holland and France.

Although the period between September 1939 and May 1940 saw Britain engaged in no major campaigns or battles – leading some to talk of the Phoney or 'Bore War' – the social changes induced by the war were already making themselves felt. It was clear that this could only be a 'Total War' because of its enormous requirements, entailing the conscription of both the military and civilian populations. Economic demands ensured a huge expansion of the government's activities as well as the need for it to exhort its people to accept severe deprivations. But if this was to be the case, then it was recognised that the morale of the nation was all-important and the process could not be one-sided – especially when the unfulfilled promises bandied around after the First World War were recalled. The government had to give something too, and the series of White Papers issued towards the end of the war laid the foundations of the welfare state later introduced by the Attlee administration. It was a dislocation of traditional and conservative attitudes which also affected the role and provision of theatre during the war.

The introduction of the blackout from September 1939, and more importantly the start of the Blitz in London a year later, led to massive disruption of the entertainment industry in general and the theatrical world in particular: overnight, theatres closed down, several of them never to reopen. Shaftesbury Avenue was thrown into chaos. Two theatres started up again when restrictions were eased in the middle of September 1939 after ten days. One was the Windmill, just off Shaftesbury Avenue, which offered a programme of humour, music, 'legshows' and immobile nudes; it boasted 'We never closed', and it is sometimes claimed that it was the only London theatre never to do so at this time. This is wrong: Unity Theatre likewise rapidly reopened, putting on a revue entitled *Sandbag Follies*, which had been written, rehearsed and produced within 48 hours. That Unity was so quickly in action proved symbolic of the changes which were to transform British theatre over the next few years.

This transformation revolved around two trends which contradicted the general trajectory of recent theatre history. The first was a move away from the traditional venues, which people were understandably reluctant to visit when the bombing began, and a shift towards touring and mobile companies entertaining audiences at makeshift 'non-theatrical' locations: evacuation centres, war hostels, factory canteens, army camps, gun sites, tube shelters. These were places at which the 'Shaftesbury Avenue' values of proscenium arch and evening dress were obviously completely absent.

The second change followed on from the first and flew in the face of what we have seen was the growing dominance of the London West End stage since the nineteenth century. The provinces now came to the fore, especially in view of the large-scale evacuation from London. In December 1940, for example, Equity reported that of its 1500 members usually at work in London, only 26 were now employed there.[1] The veteran critic W. A. Darlington observed that 'London ceased, for the first time in her history, to be the headquarters of the English stage': 'She became a place to which theatre companies might pay fleeting visits when either the lightening of the German attacks, or the hours of performance, permitted. In stage terms, London had become a "touring date"; and not until after the last severe bombing raid, on 10 May 1941, did she become once more the home of the long run.'[2]

An additional factor lay in the general rise in the standard of living during the war, resulting from the full employment which it brought. Real wages rose steadily, and with the shortage of consumer and luxury goods extra money was available for the cultural activities regarded in peacetime as no more than the icing on the cake. It would be wrong to exaggerate this picture of the thriving culture stimulated by the 'People's War'; but it is undeniable that interest in the arts expanded enormously: expenditure on books doubled during the war, educational bodies found their membership numbers going up by leaps and bounds, and performers and artists in all fields were surprised and excited by the size and quality of their audiences.

As the role and scope of government intervention grew massively, so did the old shibboleths concerning the importance of laissez-faire within the area of culture become discredited and fade away. Just as Roosevelt's New Deal in the United States had led to the Federal Theatre, so did the coalition government initiate a programme of subsidies and grants to the arts. At first it shied away from creating new institutions but instead gave a small sum of money amounting to £25 000 to the Pilgrim Trust, a private organisation headed by Dr Thomas Jones, its energetic secretary. The Trust was also given an office and the use of one of its secretaries by the Board of Education.

Disturbed by the widespread unemployment of artists and musicians arising from the outbreak of war, the Pilgrim Trust introduced the idea of 'Music Travellers': violinists, pianists and singers who were sent out to entertain listeners in temporary settings, rather like the medieval minstrels. Both performers and spectators were sceptical at first – the former having been advised to keep their programmes simple and not to annoy the irretrievably debased taste of listeners conditioned to jazz and film music, the latter suspicious that these entertainments were simply another aspect of official propaganda and doled out with the intention of 'keeping the workers happy'.

Sometimes the concerts were not a success, one musician finding that an audience which was labouring twelve hours a day, seven days a week, was apathetic. But then s/he went on to note:

If it is necessary to balance the rather drab picture I have given of C.E.M.A. [Council for the Encouragement of Music and the Arts] concerts, let it be said that four concerts during the tour, organized publicly in mining villages, met with tremendous success and appreciation, which showed that there really is a keen and widespread demand for music among the working people of this country. My complaint is that C.E.M.A. is not really adequate in its scope or arrangement to cover one small part of this demand.[3]

The government too recognised this problem of insufficient funding and in April 1940 CEMA was established on a permanent basis and given more money on the understanding that the government would contribute, up to £50 000, a pound for every pound donated by private sources. This turned out to be a last attempt to marry the public and private ownership of art and proved unsuccessful: in April 1942 CEMA became wholly government-financed.[4] It was also reorganised so that there were Regional Offices all over the country as well as paid directorates of music, art and drama and audition panels for local talent. This last feature was especially significant: CEMA played down the normally rigid distinction separating professionals from amateurs.

CEMA continued to organise factory concerts – to such an extent that 4500 of them were put on in 1943 alone – but also began to widen its range of activities. In 1940 the Old Vic requested assistance in organising two tours of South Wales and County Durham, and it was the success which attended them that encouraged CEMA to support dramatic companies. The Old Vic had already transferred its headquarters away from London to Burnley ('Burnley, where's Burnley?' many of the smart London set were heard to ask), and then in 1942 they established a permanent repertory company at the Liverpool Playhouse. They also embarked upon a series of tours, deliberately visiting places ignored by the commercial drama: when the Old Vic played *Othello* in Wigan it staged that town's first straight play for twenty years.

The touring Old Vic companies had no option but to travel light; the opera company for instance had only one piano as accompaniment. But somehow this did not seem to matter. The tour to South Wales was led by Sybil Thorndike and Lewis Casson and the company's meagre scenery and costumes were transported in a single lorry with everyone travelling by bus. In such circumstances their productions had to dispense with the grandiose and formal requirements of West End shows. The major play presented during this Welsh tour was *Macbeth*, which was preceded by a 'plain-clothes prologue' written in order to emphasise the contemporary nature of Shakespeare's drama with its themes of power and dictatorship. The down-to-earth and unpompous character of setting and performances achieved magnificent results, as Sybil Thorndike described in a letter of the time: 'We've never played to such audiences. None of them moved a muscle while we're playing, but at the end they go wild and lift the roof with their clapping. This is the theatre that we liked best – getting right in amongst people. Afterwards they all come round and talk to us.'[5]

Other plays toured by the Old Vic included *The Merchant of Venice*, *Medea* and Shaw's *Candida*. The ballet company could now boast two pianos when it toured and the opera company two violins, a clarinet and a violincello.[6] By 1944 the bombing of London had largely subsided, allowing the Old Vic Repertory Company to take over the New Theatre in London. In one respect of course this was a reversion to type – the pull of London – but the Old Vic's tours had demonstrated just what could be accomplished, and the group organisation of the company's travelling plays lived on in the repertory basis of their new home. Furthermore the achievements of the Old Vic's tours prompted CEMA to fund more touring theatre companies: 14 in all by October 1942.

Another body which by and large benefited from wartime events and moods was Unity Theatre in London. After its *Sandbag Follies* revue of September 1939, which was revised and went through three editions, the theatre then produced another revue, *Turn Up the Lights*, which ran from December 1939 to February 1940. Both revues were critical of the Chamberlain government, inspiring a Unity fund-raising pamphlet to claim that 'We are the first theatre to attack the war policy of a government in war time since Euripides' *Trojan Women* was performed in Athens in 415 BC.'[7]

In March 1940 Unity demonstrated its continuing ambition

by mounting the first production of Sean O'Casey's *The Star Turned Red*. It did not confine its work to its base in Goldington Street, London, but created an Outside Shows Group during the Blitz which specialised in performing before audiences at tube shelters and bomb sites. One of its organisers, Ann Davies, described the conditions surrounding one of the first shows, at a shelter in Belsize Park underground:

> We had to ask people to squash even closer together and allow us to pile up on their rugs and coats. They very readily did this and off we went. Swanee River, John Brown's Body, Roll out the Barrel, etc., got them interested . . . prepared the way for a couple of sketches, solos, songs and jokes. Ten minutes at one end of the platform, and ten the other, the same thing on another platform, and finally a show at each end of the liftshafts. Even when these items had to be done sideways on, with occasional trains roaring through, they went over big, and the crowd was almost as pleased as we were.[8]

The Outside Shows Group mixed straight plays with music hall and variety entertainment, finding a gratifying measure of audience participation. In all, Unity put on over 1000 outside performances during the war. Early in 1944 they even ran an all-women troupe called the Amazons Company who likewise organised outside shows drawing upon revue material – although sadly little information has survived relating to this group, the first since the Actresses' Franchise League to perform 'women only' plays.[9]

But not everything went well for Unity. The outbreak of war and the consequent introduction of conscription had led to the disintegration of the experienced collective formed during the late 1930s; the theatre was hit four times by bombs, on one occasion blowing the roof off; and in 1941, 1942 and 1943 the lack of writers and performers resulted in the staging of some rather poor productions. In 1943 it was decided to jettison the principle of anonymity in the hope that individual recognition might attract more talented recruits. Later that year the company turned the corner, putting on Lope de Vega's *Fuente Ovejuna*, a play never seen before in London, and a music-hall history called *Winkles and Champagne*. Membership began to climb again, passing the figure of 5000.

Other Unity theatres sprang up, most notably that in Glasgow which was formed in January 1941. Five groups amalgamated to create Glasgow Unity, the variety of their names indicating the comparatively healthy dramatic tradition still existing in Scotland: the Workers' Theatre Group, the Clarion Players, the Glasgow Players, the Transport Players and the Jewish Institute Players. Like its London counterpart, Glasgow Unity tried to escape from the conventional repertoire of plays and put on Odets' *Golden Boy* and *Till the Day I Die* and some Scottish plays, including James Barke's *Major Operation*, which dealt with a group of Clyde shipyard workers. They also had one section concentrating on full-length plays and another specialising in outside performances.[10] Another of the most active groups was Merseyside Unity based in Liverpool, and by 1942 there were over 25 amateur Unity theatres in existence. A National Federation was set up that year in order to encourage contacts and the sharing of experiences.

Older organisations such as the British Drama League found that their number of affiliated amateur groups surged upwards, reaching a record 5000 in the winter of 1943–4. New enterprises included the People's Entertainment Society, sponsored by the Co-op, which toured a play called *The Rochdale Pioneers* about the founding of the Co-op, published other works under the title *People's Plays*, and hoped to finance the actual ownership of its own theatre. Another new organisation was ENSA (Entertainments National Service Association) which was set up by Basil Dean and catered primarily for troops stationed overseas, putting on cabaret and music-hall type performances which did incorporate some drama. In all, ENSA arranged 2½ million shows during the war in front of a total audience estimated at over 300 million people.[11]

Plays presented to the troops were often staged in highly unlikely settings; Bernard Miles once performed in the Orkneys in 1943: 'playing on a rough platform slung between the destroyers *Orwell* and *Opportune*, with five hundred sailors surrounding the stage and hanging on to every available projection of the two ships.[12] Donald Wolfit organised a six-week tour of *Twelfth Night* to garrison theatres and army camps, evoking tremendous enthusiasm: 'Based at hostels, we travelled to four and sometimes five camps in a week, returning at night to the luxury of ENSA beds with seemed to be made of teak.' On only one occasion were there disturbances, when American soldiers greeted Viola with cries of 'Hello Blondie' and punctuated the performance with such remarks as 'Sez You' and 'Jesus, I don't take this at all'. Wolfit complained and the next evening the audience made not a sound. On asking for an explanation of this reversal, the commanding officer told Wolfit that he had had a talk with the men, 'and in case there was any further trouble to-night I had the military police parading the aisles with their revolvers out of their holsters'.[13]

One of the most interesting developments within non-commercial theatre during the war was also aimed primarily at the troops. By 1941 the War Office was alarmed at the succession of reports revealing the low morale and boredom of the troops, most of whom had been stationed in Britain after the evacuation from Dunkirk. All too aware that this mood included widespread antagonism towards 'Blimps' and the 'officer' in general, the War Office tentatively made arrangements for lectures and talks to be part of the military routine, establishing a body called ABCA (the Army Bureau of Current Affairs) in September 1941. Certainly those in command laid down stringent guidelines, censoring pamphlets and posters and stipulating that the discussions were to be conducted by regimental officers, but nevertheless by the winter of 1943–4 over 110 000 courses, lectures and classes were taking place.

Several groups of soldiers began to organise dramatic activities: 'Penny Readings' were popular, play-reading was widespread, army groups affiliated to the British Drama League (280 had done so by July 1943), Scottish Command put on its own festival, and the garrison on the Orkneys even built its own theatre.[14] It was revealing, too, that the selection of plays by these groups indicated that light West End comedies were being ousted in favour of more serious productions: the Army Education Syllabus actually recommended Odets' *Waiting for Lefty* and some O'Casey plays as suitable material.[15] In June 1944 a more specialised organisation called the ABCA

Play Unit was formed in order to dramatise the ideas and topics discussed in the ABCA pamphlets.

The personnel of the Play Unit demonstrated just how many of the wartime dramatic experiments were built upon initiatives of the 1930s: Michael Macowan, Stephen Murray, Bridget Boland, Miles Tomalin, André van Gyseghem, Jack Lindsay and Ted Willis had all been involved in non-commercial theatre projects before the war, the last three having worked extensively with Unity Theatre in London. The Unit operated as a collective of 18 with everyone contributing suggestions and proposals for the content of the plays as well as being expected to help out wth the carpentry, stage design, paperwork and other chores. As one of the members has said: 'Everyone took a turn at acting, or on the switchboard or carting rostrums or scene shifting. It was understood these jobs were done in rotation.'[16] Unit members also gave readings and lectures and held courses for the troops on all aspects of drama.

The crucial factor influencing the work of the Unit was that it performed in a variety of 'non-theatrical' locations – nissan huts, gun sites, factory canteens – and in front of audiences the majority of whom had never been inside a theatre. In these circumstances the traditional proscenium barrier separating performers from spectators in most theatres simply did not exist and the Unit had to develop an approach which recognised this fact. It came up with a form of presentation that was almost cinematic in the speed and excitement by which it continually surprised audiences – for instance, there were speakers placed in the auditorium and even staged fights, as in *Who are the Germans?*, as well as innovative lighting effects which directed the spectators' attention towards one spot and then another.

The documentary style kept scenery and costumes to a minimum, ensuring maximum concentration on the essentials of the plays, and the themes dealt with focused on contemporary issues. The ABCA Play Unit drew upon the 'Living Newspaper' format pioneered in America in the 1930s and taken up by Unity in London, but whereas Living Newspapers often became little more than 'dead history' the shock tactics used by the Unit and their willingness to combine both naturalistic and expressionistic forms continually challenged and startled the audience. As Michael Macowan wrote in January 1945: 'We have given the troops verse at two o'clock in the afternoon and heard them applaud it to the echo; we have made them leap in their seats with realistic dive-bombing and listen, hushed, to a Japanese cradle song. We are still learning, and, we hope, still shaking them.'[17]

It is curious how some seasoned observers missed the significance of the novel work that the ABCA Play Unit was doing. J. B. Priestley, for example, wrote a play for the Unit called *Desert Highway*, which, whatever the merits of the piece itself, was quite unsuitable for the venue and spectators where the Unit performed. In fact *Desert Highway* was later a success on the West End stage.

The two main protagonists behind the writing of the Unit's shows were Jack Lindsay and Ted Willis, and their plays grappled with immediate and concrete issues. In Jack Lindsay's words, 'the plays were not at all socialist. . . . Anything looking remotely like party politics we excised', but in the radical context of the war years their plays chimed with the undercurrents which resulted in the substantial Labour Party victory at the 1945 election.[18] Their first production was given at the Garrison Theatre in Aldershot in July 1944 before an audience of hundreds: *It Started as Lend-Lease* looked at the effects and implications of American aid to this country. *Where Do We Go From Here?* delved into the problem of post-war reconstruction.

The influential Indian novelist Mulk Raj Anand was responsible for *Famine*, and *Who are the Germans?* and *The Japanese Way* explored the nature of fascism in both these countries, but always in a way that was clear and comprehensible to the audience. The topicality of the latter play in exposing the hero-worship of the Emperor was forcibly brought home when Churchill himself ordered the play to be withdrawn. Fearing the possible political outcome of a crushing Japanese defeat, Churchill had decided that the Emperor would after all have a part to play in the post-war world. In their first six months alone the Unit gave 58 performances to a total audience of around 20 000 people, and one experienced observer noted that 'they were as responsive as any audience I have ever seen . . .'[19]. In May 1945 the ABCA Play unit played at the Arts Theatre, London, for four very successful nights.

This upsurge of non-commercial drama continued throughout the war. All the groups and organisations were characterised by their enormous commitment and enthusiasm, bolstered by the optimism engendered by an anti-fascist war. For all these individuals the theatre was indeed a weapon in helping to bring about a more just post-war society. A typical example of this energy was that of the Bristol Unity Players, as one participant has recalled: 'I cannot remember a single week without one, two and – at times – three or four rehearsals and meetings, as well as regular monthly general members' meetings.'[20] Several of their plays were written by members themselves and their most ambitious project was a pageant performed on May Day 1944, *Now is the Day!*, recounting the lives and times of the Bristol labour movement from 1864 to 1944.

Longstanding repertory theatres were stimulated to new efforts by the prevailing mood. Birmingham Rep, for example, despite losing all its costumes as a result of an incendiary bomb, began performing in the city's parks from 1941, a project financially guaranteed by CEMA. They continued with this outside programme every year, attracting large crowds – the 1942 season alone was seen by over 35 000.[21] Even a smaller rep company such as that in York was notching up weekly audiences of 10 000 people.[22]

CEMA was still sending touring productions around the country, each play going through an eight-week cycle. The most popular of all was Ibsen's *Hedda Gabler*, and, springing out of these visits, play-reading groups at the hostels were often set up which developed into fully-fledged drama societies. CEMA also took a few hesitant steps into the minefield of theatre ownership, managing the Lyric at Hammersmith and the Theatre Royal, Bristol; the latter in particular achieved substantial financial success. Just as crucial, CEMA was involved in the founding of the Citizens' Theatre, Glasgow, in 1943 under the chairmanship of the Scottish playwright James Bridie. As its director stated, 'it was due to CEMA's backing that this theatre was able to be started, and although their guarantee has not been touched, without such backing the whole theatre would probably not have come into existence.'[23]

Older organisations thrived. The Unity Theatre of London reported that its individual membership was nearing 7000 and the Merseyside Unity was able to expand into new premises in the heart of Liverpool in 1944 as well as maintain their outdoor shows. The Co-op formed a National Association of Drama Associations. The membership of the British Drama League was now over 50 000 and by 1945 the BDL was able to claim that 5000 societies were affiliated. The People's Theatre in Newcastle experienced a wave of enthusiasm for its productions; Toynbee Hall in London formed a touring company; and other groups giving shows included the Shelter Players and the Pilgrim Players. These were but a few of the developments taking place all over the country.[24]

This public interest in live theatre – to which ENSA contributed a great deal, giving on its own 3000 performances each week by 1943 – was quite oblivious to the conventions and customs covering West End theatre-going behaviour and expectations, and it was a change which eventually began to be felt within London itself. Just as Dame Myra Hess's lunchtime recitals at the National Gallery were hugely popular, attracting around 800 000 people during the war despite (or because of) the makeshift surroundings, performers like Donald Wolfit began to present plays stripped bare of the usual production values thought necessary to their staging. Wolfit's 'Lunch Time Shakespeare' began in October 1940 at the Strand Theatre in London; he put on excerpts from Shakespeare's plays, songs, sonnets and prologues between one o'clock and two o'clock, changing the programme at least three times a week and continuing even when the theatre had been badly bombed. Edith Evans was another performer who presented solo shows.

In general, it was noticeable that the overall quality of the West End theatre was much higher than it had been in the First World War. Although, naturally, musical comedies remained popular, many more thoughtful productions were staged. Amongst them were Terence Rattigan's *Flarepath*, Peter Ustinov's satirical portayal of the military caste, *The Banbury*

Nose, Emlyn Williams' *The Morning Star* and *Watch on the Rhine*, and J. B. Priestley's *Desert Highway* and *They Came To a City*. John Gielgud also produced a highly influential series of Shakespearean plays at the Haymarket, London. With a lack of backroom staff and the normal financial trappings, the West End during the war was forced to discard many of its conventions and get closer to its audiences – a change which benefited them both. Together with this, managements such as H. M. Tennent sent companies out on tour, helped by imaginative fiscal laws which allowed such initiatives to avoid Entertainments Tax as long as they were non-profitmaking. Even the government got in on the act by issuing in 1945 its White Paper on *Community Centres*, an important blueprint which testified to the recognised achievements of the less formal theatrical activities of the war.

As can be seen from the above, the Second World War provided a tremendous boost for non-commercial drama, especially when it is borne in mind that a League of Audiences survey of 1939 revealed that 92 per cent of the British people had never been to the theatre. Many of the assumptions and conventions supported by the West End theatre – the barrier between amateur and professional and performer and spectator, the select audiences, the formalised settings, the emphasis on expensive production values, the restricted subject-matter of plays – had been challenged and weakened. For the first time since the Elizabethans, this country possessed what was virtually a national drama.

It would be wrong to overestimate the solidity of these successes. For instance, it was entirely foreseeable that the new audiences would disperse at the end of the war and that many of the novel locations such as hostels, garrisons and gun sites would close down. It was also true that few new forms of drama had emerged: instead it was older forms like variety, music hall and the 'Living Newspaper' which were used. ENSA was criticised for having no artistic policy.[25] Finally, it was significant that most of the productions seen during the war were of the classics – Shaw, Shakespeare, Ibsen – and there were few opportunities for new writers, although few in fact displayed startling talent: when the Arts Theatre Club held a new play competition in 1943, none of the 500 entries were judged to be of merit. But despite these reservations, it is clear that the war years saw an unprecedented growth in the size and vigour of alternative and experimental theatre in Britain. The question was whether this expansion would continue in the post-war world.

Chapter 9

After 1945

The Germans surrendered in May 1945 and in the British general election of July a Labour government was returned to office with a majority of more than 150 seats: Labour had 393 MPs compared with the Conservatives' 213. It seemed as if the electorate wanted radical change, to see whole areas of British life transformed by a new administration which would build upon the questioning of conventional beliefs and attitudes induced by the war. But in fact, as one commentator has observed, 'Far from introducing a "social revolution" the overwhelming Labour victory of 1945 brought about the greatest restoration of traditional social values since 1660.'[1] Did the 'old order' reestablish once again in the field of the theatre?

Within the commercial theatre the war had doubled the rent of properties as well as bringing about a reduction in the number of West End theatres: German bombing had destroyed almost one in five such buildings. Fewer theatres meant increased competition for those which remained, resulting in the squeezing out of the less powerful managements and proprietors by wealthy companies to whom the theatre was often only one sideline amongst many other business activities. The biggest of them all was nicknamed 'the Group' and led by Prince Littler: 'By the late 1940s, the Prince Littler Consolidated Trust directly owned with its affiliated companies 18 out of 42 functioning West End theatres and 57 (70 per cent) of the main out-of-London touring theatres. If we consider simply the Number 1 touring circuit, which then consisted of 53 theatres, 34 were owned by The Group.'[2]

The sameness of management led to a depressing sameness

of play, centred on the star system and the long run. As the critic Kenneth Tynan commented in the *Observer*: 'Joys and sorrows are giggles and whimpers: the crash of denunciation dwindles into "Oh, stuff, Mummy!" and "Oh, really, Daddy!" And so grim is the continuity of these things that the foregoing might have been written at any time during the last thirty years.'[3]

But although the mainstream theatre carried on oblivious in its own self-satisfied fashion, it did not necessarily rule out a strong alternative theatre movement, especially after the achievements of the war. But the new Labour government closed down ABCA, the Play Unit and all, and it was clear that strong institutions would be needed to counterbalance the weight and prestige of the West End stage. Many hoped that the trade unions with their influence and membership greatly expanded as a result of the war would step in to provide the necessary backing, and indeed in May 1946 the Amalgamated Engineering Union, celebrating its centenary, sponsored a week-long venture at the Scale Theatre in London.

Called Theatre '46, the season was based around Montagu Slater's play *A Century for George*, together with a comedy about the Home Guard by Bernard Miles, *Let Tyrants Tremble!*, and Jack Lindsay and Bert Coombes' drama-documentary *The Face of Coal*. Intriguingly enough, the next project was to have been a dramatised version of *Pilgrim's Progress*. However Theatre '46 was not a success. The Scala was a rather gloomy and dim venue, and situated in the West End it failed to attract either the 'non-theatrical' audiences of the war or trade unionists and it scared off those regular theatre-goers who liked their entertainment 'non-political'.

Even sympathetic critics criticised the lifeless acting as well as Slater's play; Ted Willis wrote in *New Theatre* that 'the central story was not that of the engineers, but an unreal love story of the washy magazine type, and the play finished on as tedious a bedroom scene as it has been my lot to see in the theatre.'[4] Not surprisingly in view of the failure of Theatre '46 no other trade union rushed forward in order to get involved in theatrical ventures, and the Co-op movement's interest had also waned.

But of course there were still those societies which had emerged in good shape after the war, particularly the Unity

Theatre movement which boasted more than 36 branches, and two of their companies seized the opportunity to turn professional. Unity Theatre in London was led by Ted Willis, playwright and drama critic for the *Daily Worker*, who had written and produced several plays for the company during the war under the name John Bishop. Individual membership was still increasing and had reached the figure of 9000, the Mobile Group was active and possessed a fulltime organiser and a film-making section called Crescent Films had been set up which was planning a three-reeler based on their war success *Winkles and Champagne*.[5] Willis had also started to experiment with popular forms too; his *God Bless The Guvnor* was 'A moral melodrama in Three Acts in which the Twin Evils of Trades Unionism and Strong Drink are Exposed'. In these encouraging circumstances plans for establishing a fulltime and professional company were pushed ahead. Writing in the *New Statesman* of December 1945, Ted Willis claimed that 'All our actors will be given continuity of employment for a term of two to three years, and at the end of that time it is hoped that conditions will have so altered that it will be possible for us to move into a larger and finer theatre.'[6] In February 1946 a professional company was formed which although under the direction of Willis remained a collective in so far as the plays were discussed by the whole company before and during production. It was planned to be a repertory venture, performing a play each month.

Unity began with Eugene O'Neill's *All God's Chillun Got Wings*, a production which included the superb black actor Robert Adams. This was followed by four more plays, all of them directed by Ted Willis, but disappointingly the company was finding that the number of spectators at their Goldington Street premises had remained static. None of the plays ran for more than six weeks (the repertory aspirations soon appear to have been shelved), a sufficient length of time when the company was composed mainly of amateurs but not for professionals. Its own *Theatre Newsletter* commented that Unity was slipping back. In September 1946 the company took Odets' *Golden Boy* to South Wales for a series of 65 one-night stands, supported by the Miners' Welfare Organisation; although this tour was justified in demonstrating that Unity was not to be a purely London-based organisation, it hardly helped their financial situation. By now economic factors were beginning to dominate Unity's work: they could not call on any forms of subsidy and certain productions proved to be disastrous flops – *Pardon my Greek* ran for barely more than one night at Goldington Street in December 1946.[7] As a tacit admission of failure the professional company actually began to rely on old favourites in an attempt to woo audiences, cobbling them together as *Star Parade*. Early in 1947 Unity performed a Living Newspaper about the coal industry, *Black Magic* by John Collier, but the once promising project was on the rocks. In May 1947 the professionals dispersed, leaving behind them debts of £2500 – a sum which forever handicapped Unity's future work and also punctured the organisation's self-confidence which had been acquired by such hard work since 1936.[8]

Many people did, and still do, blame Ted Willis for this debacle, and certainly it does not require hindsight to see that a professional enterprise was beyond Unity's resources. But the causes must lie deeper than the faults or otherwise of a single individual. The wartime mood had largely evaporated, especially with the introduction of Marshall Aid from the summer of 1947 and the increasing freeze of the Cold War. Any organisation associated with the Communist Party, as Unity was, was bound to suffer from the deteriorating international situation and the growing anti-Soviet sentiments. Even a socialist drama critic like Richard Findlater could dismissively refer to Unity as 'a minority theatre concerned with the specific manipulation of social facts to fit a party-line'.[9] Labour movement support was bound to be meagre. Nor did Unity manage to bring forth any new writers or new plays of lasting merit.

The other Unity Theatre which turned professional was that in Glasgow. In the spring of 1945 Glasgow Unity had taken over the Athenaeum Theatre for a season, playing on Thursday, Friday and Saturday nights. They had a full-time director in Robert Mitchell who had been heavily involved in London Unity during the 1930s, particularly the *Babes in the Wood* pantomime, and their repertoire was substantial: productions of Gorki's *The Lower Depths*, for instance, Odet's

Awake and Sing! and O'Casey's *Juno and the Paycock*. However Glasgow Unity was well aware of the need to develop and explore Scottish themes; 'Unity aims at a theatre indigenous to the people of Glasgow in particular, and Scotland in general. . . . What we try to create is a native theatre, something which is essentially reflecting the lives of ordinary people of Scotland.'[10]

Their production of *The Lower Depths* was performed to good reviews in London, and no doubt prompted by the example of London Unity the company turned professional in April 1946 with a performance of Sean O'Casey's *Purple Dust*. Glasgow Unity remained a collective: 'Unity believes in the group ideal. Each play is thoroughly discussed by the producer and players before it goes on the floor. There are no stars – only co-workers co-operating towards the idea of the production worked out as a collective of which the producer is the leader.'[11] The company's deliberate policy of building up Scottish writers meant that at first, as Robert Mitchell recognised, 'we should have to start with sub-standard plays',[12] but it certainly paid off. Works by such playwrights as James Barke (*Major Operation* and *The Night of the Great Blitz*) and Robert McLellan (*The Laird o' Torwatletie* and *Jamie the Saxt* – although the latter had first been produced in 1937) were staged. There were also the plays of Ena Lamont Stewart who sent in by post *Starched Aprons* and *Men Should Weep*, which dealt with the issues of domestic life from a woman's viewpoint. In view of their topicality, directness and humour it is no surprise that several of these plays have been rediscovered in the 1980s.

But perhaps Glasgow Unity's most famous production was Robert McLeish's *The Gorbals Story*, first performed in September 1946. McLeish was a cartoonist on a local newspaper, and he originally wrote a short 40-minute playlet which realistically portrayed the shortage of housing in Glasgow after the war, a problem aggravated by German bombing, and the squatting to which this gave rise. This was successfully shown to groups at various army camps and McLeish expanded it to deal with the lives of eight families who shared a slum dwelling in the Gorbals. The company threw themselves into the production with great vigour, making suggestions and revising the script as they went along, their commitment enhanced by their firsthand knowledge of such conditions:

PEGGIE: Ye'd think the Government would dae something about these people – trailin' about lookin' for rooms, I think it must have been the blitz that caused it.

HECTOR: It was before the blitz – it was bad before the war.

PEGGIE: It's a funny thing tae me – a'thae sodgers that came here – nane o' them had to go about looking for a room.

HECTOR: That was different, Peggie.

PEGGIE: Was it? – the people's war, and only the sodgers get hooses.

HECTOR: Ye know Peggie, there's always something refreshing about a woman's logic.

PEGGIE: That's awld-fashioned patter, Hector – men just talk about logic. They condemn honest folk to live three or four in a room. They gie a burglar a room tae himsel'. Hunners o' sodgers came here frae Canada and Australia an' Poland an' America – what wey can they no fix up their own folk. You mark my words, Hector, aye, you're laughin' – women chained themselves onto lamposts to get the vote. Its coming, you mark my words, some o' these days a woman will chain herself onto an empty house.

The Gorbals Story succeeded in attracting a wide, often working-class, audience. The play took over £4000 from its Glasgow run alone and by April 1947 had been seen by over 100 000 people.[13] The production toured widely. And yet *The Gorbals Story* was also to prove an important part of Glasgow Unity's downfall: just like London Unity's dependence on *Waiting for Lefty* before the war, Glasgow Unity was never able to escape from beneath the shadow of *The Gorbals Story*.

Not everyone at Glasgow Unity was professional; an amateur company continued and in fact was often more ambitious than its senior, not being restricted by the imperative requirement of financial success. It premiered new Scottish plays such as McLeish's *A Piece of Milarky*.

But by 1948 Glasgow Unity was finding that certain difficulties and weaknesses were threatening the whole venture.

Resources were lacking: once during a production of George Munro's excellent play *Gold In His Boots* about the effects of professional football on a working-class youth, a supposedly Cup Final team emerged from the Wembley tunnel onto the stage all wearing different jerseys. Very little trade union support was provided by the trade union and labour movement – again, as with London Unity, the company was daubed as 'pro-Communist' and therefore to be avoided. There was also, as one member of the company has recalled, 'organisational inexperience and naiveté', together with 'the failure to establish a permanent base, a bricks-and-mortar Unity Theatre, where an audience could have been built up, gains consolidated, activities extended, and the future planned for confidently. Over a period of years, this was a central dialogue within the theatre; but nothing ever came of it.'[14] Without such a base Glasgow Unity had to hire various theatres on an ad hoc footing.

Early in 1948 the impresario Jack Hylton offered the company a London theatre, the Garrick, which they accepted; of course *The Gorbals Story* was the major production chosen to be performed. With a permanent staff of 35 to support, Glasgow Unity needed the commercial success which only London seemed to offer. But if they stayed there, then what about their commitment to building up a native Scottish dramatic tradition? Much of 1948 was spent in London, although the professional company did tour Scotland in the summer. But cut off from their roots, with several performers joining London theatres in which the financial rewards were much higher and with a general air of gloom enveloping the company, Glasgow Unity disintegrated by 1950 – both the professional and amateur sections.

The history of London and Glasgow Unity's efforts to establish professional and repertory companies in the late 1940s, and their subsequent failure, brings out yet again the difficulties involved in creating a firm footing for alternative theatre. Lacking new plays, new writers or large enough audiences, both enterprises lurched from crisis to crisis, although being responsible for enough exciting and innovative productions to suggest what might have been possible. Neither possessed sufficient resources to sustain a fulltime, professional company. All over the country the amateur Unity theatres collapsed: in Bristol, for example, membership fell off drastically after the war and a key figure had had to resign because of health problems. Merseyside Unity kept going but found the political situation very different from the war years – Liverpool City Council banned the organisation from its halls because of its former Communist Party links.[15]

Another initiative which foundered after the war was Yiddish theatre. Determined efforts had been made to revive it. A New Yiddish Theatre was founded which had a permanent cast of 20 and a weekly budget of £350, and it produced a noted staging of *The Merchant of Venice*, even though the producer Robert Atkins could not speak Yiddish. The company published its own magazine, *Theatre World*, briefly obtained Arts Council support and planned to build a new theatre costing £70 000.[16] But nothing came of it: Arts Council assistance was terminated and the company disintegrated. As a sign of the times, interjections at the Grand Palais in the East End of London were now voiced in English,[17] and this theatre closed in 1961. Too many social and economic changes were working against the existence of a Yiddish drama.

It was not that Jewish culture found itself buried and forgotten but that – an important feature running throughout the development of alternative theatre – it was incorporated into the mainstream. One observer pointed out in 1961: 'Since 1945 there has been a veritable wave of Anglo–Jewish writers. Some of the best known are Arnold Wesker, Alexander Baron, Gerda Charles, Frederic Raphael, Wolf Mankowitz and Harold Pinter, all of whom have been understood and accepted by the non-Jewish public as well as the Jews, a significant fact which underlines the break-up of Jewish separatism in England.'[18]

In discussing these groups very little has needed to be said about the Arts Council, although in the immediate aftermath of the war some had hoped that this would be the organisation which provided a counterweight to the hold of the West End stage. CEMA had been renamed as the Arts Council in 1945 and its first head turned out to be Sir Ernest Pooley, a career civil servant whose tastes not unsurprisingly inclined towards the traditional. Before long, the Arts Council began to switch

its interest away from the CEMA emphasis on community
centres and the amateur towards the mainstream – a policy
summed up in the phrase 'few, but roses'. Thus by 1948–9 one
quarter of the Arts Council's entire budget was being spent on
the provision of opera at Covent Garden whilst its regional
offices were being quietly closed down and the factory concerts
ended. The plans for arts centres were shelved. In any event the
Arts Council was budgeting only £61 000 for drama in 1947
and its Drama Panel was dominated by figures from the West
End establishment.[19] In hindsight one can see that the Arts
Council, certainly in terms of its drama programme, acted as a
useful supplement to the commercial theatre but did not in any
way challenge or develop, as CEMA had done during the war,
alternatives to it.

However it would be wrong to pin too much blame on the
Arts Council: Glasgow Unity was aided for a few months from
May 1946 until the time of the first Edinburgh Festival to be
held in August 1947. No Scottish representation was planned
by the Festival organisers and Glasgow Unity decided along
with several other groups to hold a three-week season to
coincide with the main event – the origin of the Edinburgh
Fringe Festival. In the subsequent furore the Arts Council
withdrew its grant from Glasgow Unity on the grounds that it
did not boast 'high enough artistic standards'. In some respects
the Arts Council did try to sustain wartime initiatives, but the
cultural climate had undoubtedly changed. In 1949–50 the
Arts Council funded the three theatres which it managed, the
Arts Theatre Company of Salisbury, the Midland Theatre
Company and the Swansea Repertory, on tours of the mining
districts of Wales, Northumberland and the Midlands. The
results were disappointing: 'The council concluded that its
directly provided pioneer tours, so successful during the war
and immediate post-war years, had developed no firm roots.'[20]

Although the Labour government's welfare state necessitated   widespread   intervention,   the   Attlee   administration was loath to intervene with legislation affecting
the cinema or theatre. In August 1947 the Chancellor of the
Exchequer, Hugh Dalton, did impose a swingeing 75 per cent
customs duty on the value of all imported films. Hollywood
responded with a blockade and the refusal to send over any new

films, a decisive ploy which eventually forced the government to back down in March 1948 and lift the duty. With such an example behind it, the fate of the last major attempt to change the structures and patterns of British theatre was predictable.

One of the most influential figures within British theatre after the war was the writer J. B. Priestley, whose novels, plays and radio broadcasts had all proved highly popular. As a socialist Priestley was concerned by what he saw as the baneful consequences of the increasing commercialisation influencing the stage and in a series of books and pamphlets published in the latter half of the 1940s he put forward various remedies. In *Theatre Outlook* of 1947 he pointed out that the level of theatre rents had doubled since 1939 and expressed the view that 'What is wrong is that there is no public control over the ownership and letting of theatres', arguing for the creation of a Theatre Authority.[21]

In a lecture and pamphlet called *The Arts Under Socialism*, also of 1947, Priestley continued to inveigh against the domination of 'small powerful groups of theatre owners, whose monopoly cannot be challenged while new theatres cannot be built.' He called for what was in effect the nationalisation of the theatre by means of this new 'National Theatre Authority: 'All playhouses should be regarded as part of the public amenities and not as anybody's private property, and their use should be controlled for the public benefit.' However Priestley did add one final caveat: 'Many of the worst evils of our Theatre – the gambling and muddle and waste of commercial managements, the actor's feeling of insecurity, the playwright's feeling of helplessness, the lack of national organisation, cannot be remedied by the Government, but only by the combined action of theatre workers themselves.'[22] In view of the poor record in the past of British theatre workers organising themselves – Equity was not founded until December 1929 – this was a significant rider.

In February 1948 an important Theatre Conference was convened at the Caxton Hall in London, chaired by J. B. Priestley, which attracted most of the leading personalities within British drama – but, revealingly, the West End theatre managers were not represented nor were more than a handful of trade unions, despite countless invitations. Delegate after delegate criticised the inadequacy of Arts Council resources, the need to decentralise its activities and the pernicious hold of 'The Group': by contrast in France one management was not able to control more than two theatres, nor could a theatre be let to anyone other than a producing management, thus cutting out the interminable process of sub-letting within the West End theatre which, apart from anything else, increased production costs – thereby encouraging a 'play safe' attitude.[23] Sir Stafford Cripps, the new Chancellor of the Exchequer, attended the last day of the conference and heard it pass unanimously the following resolution: 'All existing theatre buildings shall be brought under the control of a public authority for the purpose of: (a) ensuring their continued use as theatres, and (b) of controlling their rents under a Rent Restriction Act.'[24]

The Theatre Conference did seem to have an influence on Cripps in so far as he halved the level of Entertainments Tax on live theatre and lifted it altogether from rural places with a population of 2000 or less and on audiences of less than 200 spectators; but little else emerged. By 1948 and the coming of the Labour government's austerity measures, a new National Theatre Authority was not feasible, as the West End theatre managers for one had realised by boycotting the conference. Desperate attempts to involve them failed – why should they welcome or work for drastic change when the old system suited them very profitably? The failure of the conference also demonstrated that even a reforming Labour government would never seriously interfere with the structures of British theatre.

Almost as palliatives, the Attlee administration did pass the National Theatre Act in 1949 (although this particular drama had several years yet to run before anything more substantial than the laying of a foundation stone on the South Bank in 1951 was accomplished) and the Local Government Act 1948, section 132 of which allowed local authorities to spend up to a 6d annual rate on entertainments, although few even approached this figure. However several repertory companies were given grants. By 1948 132 repertory theatres were in operation, playing before audiences of up to half a million each week. Unfortunately, as Norman Marshall put it, 'many repertory managements are far more purely commercial concerns than most of the much abused London managements'.[25] As always, the reps functioned as testing grounds for performers, directors and writers, the most promising of whom could then be given West End engagements.

One of the few reps which did pursue a more ambitious policy was the Citizens' Theatre in Glasgow which aimed to 'present plays that would not otherwise be seen in Glasgow', and 'to encourage native Scots dramatists, actors and technicians'. Unlike Glasgow Unity the Citizens had their own home and did achieve considerable success. But it is important to note that they were forced to drop their genuine repertory programme; the audience did not accept the constant chopping and changing, the staff found it exhausting and there were further expenses regarding costumes and advertising: switching to a series of short runs saved nearly £100 a week.[26]

Thus by the early 1950s with the demise of most Unity theatres, the collapse of Yiddish drama and Theatre '46, and the inability of the reps, the Arts Council or the Theatre Conference to provide viable alternatives, many of the wartime gains seemed to have vanished. The prospects for alternative and experimental theatre looked bleak – even leaving to one side the growing impact of television – as indeed they were.

London Unity staggered on. It was nearly closed for good at the end of 1952 but a diet of revue and pantomime staved off the crisis – until, that is, May 1954 when four out of the seven paid staff were dismissed. In 1956 a Living Newspaper about the Soviet invasion of Hungary, *World on Edge*, sparked off fights amongst Communists in the audience. One of those who had been involved for many years with Unity, Bram Bootman, called a conference of trade unionists at Unity in 1956 and was told: 'We do not want plays that deal with working class lives and the struggle of the working people. Our wives won't come. They say, "We know that already." Put on old-time music hall, and we will bring you block bookings galore.'[27] This longstanding problem – that the elusive 'non-theatrical' audience did not seem to want progressive and radical drama, preferring instead the escapism of, say, melodrama which had satisfied Victorian spectators – was one which plagued alternative theatre over the next thirty years.

By the end of the 1950s London Unity was in a state of almost

permanent financial collapse with just one paid employee
remaining, and only a series of appeals kept the theatre alive.
However as a testimony to the theatre's influence it should be
noted that the 1962 appeal included as sponsors John Osborne,
Alec Guinness and the director Lindsay Anderson. But if
London Unity was in terminal decline, there was one
alternative and experimental group active in these otherwise
barren 1950s and early 1960s which produced work possessing
a flair and range usually missing from the West End stage: Joan
Littlewood's Theatre Workshop.

Its origins went back to the 1930s when Ewan MacColl had
been active in the Workers' Theatre Movement in Lancashire,
performing short agit-prop sketches which sought to intervene
directly in current political and industrial struggles. In 1933
Joan Littlewood arrived in Manchester on her way to America
via Liverpool, having just left RADA (the Royal Academy of
Dramatic Art) somewhat abruptly in disgust at that
institution's stereotyping, West End perspective. The next year
MacColl and Littlewood formed the Theatre of Action in
Manchester, drawn by that city's cultural foundations which
had also attracted Annie Horniman thirty years before; the
name alone suggested the group's mobility and break from
traditional forms of theatre.

MacColl and Littlewood's Theatre of Action had no money
and relied on the dedication and hard work of the amateurs
who joined them, rehearsing until late at night having finished
their daytime jobs. Perhaps what distinguished the group was
its interest in and knowledge of European developments such
as the German expressionist movement and the theories of
Adolphe Appia, who stressed the importance of stage lighting.
Stanislavski's *An Actor Prepares* was their Bible. Only Terence
Gray at the Cambridge Festival Theatre in the early 1930s
possessed such broad horizons, and like Gray Joan Littlewood
and Ewan MacColl insisted that members should be familiar
with rather more than just straight acting and trained them
therefore in mime and ballet.

Renamed Theatre Union in 1936, they were also heavily
influenced by the political controversies of the time, especially
the Civil War in Spain. They put on a Living Newspaper called
Last Edition which dealt with Chamberlain's appeasement of

Hitler at Munich, staging it as a gangster movie and incorporating songs and the use of film. Although holding playwriting competitions, they also produced works by foreign dramatists, including Lope de Vega's *Fuente Ovejuna*, Aristophanes' *Lysistrata* and a version of *The Good Soldier Schweik*, all of them emphasising the role of music within the productions. Like Unity Theatre in London, Theatre Union's work was now largely inside enclosed spaces.

On the outbreak of war the still amateur company broke up but members resolved to keep in touch, agreeing to specialise in various aspects of theatre history and send their findings to each other. Joan Littlewood worked for BBC Radio. In 1945 the company came together once more, although several members had been killed, and re-formed as Theatre Workshop.

Relying once more on sympathisers for food and shelter, the company embarked on extended tours of Britain, performing at a variety of venues from working men's clubs to Butlin's holiday camps to the Edinburgh Fringe Festival. Having to travel light, Theatre Workshop boasted few props or costumes but, like the Shakespearean strollers, they were taking theatre back to the people. Salaries when paid at all were meagre and sometimes the audience was pitifully small, but often too their innovative productions, amongst them Ewan MacColl's *Johnny Noble* about a young merchant sailor and *Uranium 235* which examined the role of nuclear energy, drew out fresh responses from their audiences. The company made no concessions to their lack of resources, as Howard Goorney has recalled:

My abiding memory of *Uranium 235* is of the costume changes. There were fifteen scenes and fifty-seven characters, played by a company of twelve. I played eight parts, and quick changing, always in the wings, became an art in itself. Everyone found a space to pile up their clothes in precise order of use. Wing space was usually very limited and speed was of the essence, and as entrances were made to music cues, they had to be on time.[28]

By 1953 the rigours of life on the road were beginning to take their toll and Littlewood and Theatre Workshop's manager Gerry Raffles started to look for a permanent base. They found a rundown old theatre in Stratford, East London, called the Theatre Royal, originally built in 1884 but which like so many Victorian theatres had suffered from the rival competition of the cinema: although it still offered live theatre, just – the last show before Theatre Workshop took over was Paul Raymond's *Jane Comes to Town*. However it was a home for the company and members virtually moved in whilst doing it up, sleeping there at night. It meant that for the first time the technical staff could plan ahead, experimenting with lighting effects. The company's designer was John Bury, later a key figure at both the Royal Shakespeare Company and the National Theatre.

However some members of the company were not happy about the move, notably Ewan McColl:

> There was a feeling that it was time we settled down in a place where we could get the attention of the national theatre critics. I felt from the beginning that this was a mistake, and a number of other people did too. We felt that to suddenly change our policy in mid-stream was to abandon all the experiences and all the gains of those six years' hard work. Before this, the level of discussion had been 'What are we doing wrong when we take a play about mining to the Welsh coal villages and the miners don't care?' This is a perfectly valid question, and by answering it we could formulate a way of dealing with the situation. But the new questions were going to be, 'How are we going to get Harold Hobson (critic of the *Sunday Times*)? What is he going to think of us?' I don't think anybody at that particular time realised what was involved in trying to make the critics happy.[29]

As we have seen, this tension between touring and having a fixed base was not a new problem and it was to recur over the following years inside groups other than Theatre Workshop.

The company retained many distinctive characteristics which marked it off from the commercial theatre. First of all it was an ensemble – or in Oscar Tapper's words 'a commune, with a common interest, which not only worked together, but ate and lived together'[30] – which had been forged over many difficult years since the 1930s. Several members, like Howard Goorney, Rosalie Williams, John Bury, Gerry Raffles and of

course Joan Littlewood herself, had virtually grown up with
each other, and the strong group tradition meant that relative
newcomers such as Harry Corbett and George Cooper were
quickly assimilated. Decisions were arrived at collectively after
discussion: there were no 'stars'. Roles were swapped around
and everyone received the same salary and was expected to
'muck in' – it was as if Laurence Olivier at the Old Vic was
called upon to hump the scenery as well as sell programmes
before the curtain went up. Training was continuous: as
Littlewood pointed out, artists and musicians practised each
day for long periods so why should not actors? It was a point
which Harley Granville Barker had made in his *The Exemplary
Theatre* published over thirty years before.

Joan Littlewood's methods of rehearsing were her own, as
one of the company recalled of Brendan Behan's *The Quare
Fellow*:

For the first week of rehearsals of *The Quare Fellow* we had no
scripts. None of us had even read the play. We knew it was
about prison life in Dublin, and that was enough for Joan.
None of us had ever been in prison, and although we could all
half-imagine what it was like, Joan set out to tell us more –
the narrow world of steel of stone, high windows and
clanging doors, the love-hate between warder and prisoner,
the gossip, the jealousy, and the tragedy – all the things that
make up the fascination of dreariness. She took us onto the
roof of the Theatre Royal. All the grimy slate and stone made
it easy to believe we were in a prison yard. We formed up in a
circle, and imagined we were prisoners out on exercise.
Round and round we trudged for what seemed like hours –
breaking now and then for a quick smoke and furtive
conversation. Although it was just a kind of game, the
boredom and meanness of it all was brought home. Next, the
'game' was extended – the whole dreary routine of washing
out your cell, standing to attention, sucking up to the screws,
trading tobacco, was improvised and developed. It began to
seem less and less like a game, and more like real. By degrees
the plot and the script were introduced, although some of us
never knew which parts we were playing until halfway
through the rehearsals. The interesting thing was that when

she gave us the scripts we found that many of the situations we had improvised actually occurred in the play. All we had to do was learn the author's words.[31]

Similarly with Shelagh Delaney's *A Taste of Honey*, Littlewood got the actresses to lug around heavy suitcases in order to help them convey the tiredness and irritability called for by the parts.

Another important feature of their work was that the text was never regarded as a sacred, inviolable object, nor was the writer put on a pedestal, even if it was Shakespeare – 'Bill was not a bad old hack'. During rehearsals the company improvised and altered, seeking to increase the directness and immediacy of the production. 'Once a production's fixed it's dead', said Littlewood and on one occasion she went to check up on a production because she had heard it was getting *in* hand.[32]

But such an approach could cause problems. First of all with the Lord Chamberlain: under the system of censorship established by the Acts of 1737 and 1843 plays were supposed to be agreed upon beforehand and then performed unaltered. On one occasion Theatre Workshop was taken to court on the grounds that they had 'Unlawfully for hire presented parts of a new stage play . . . before such parts had been allowed by the Lord Chamberlain contrary to Section 15 of the Theatres Act 1843', which was inevitable in view of the company's techniques of spontaneity and improvisation. Found guilty, the fines imposed were minimal. A second difficulty with the company changing the text was that some writers objected. Most recognised that a better play emerged, but not all.

A further characteristic of Theatre Workshop productions was their synthesis of different elements: dance, music, mime and so on – contrasting with the commercial theatre's unity of style. Sometimes the ingredients of music hall and popular theatre were drawn upon in an attempt to increase the audience's sense of involvement and participation – although this never became, as some people have later interpreted it, a simple 'knees up'. The footlights were removed, performers mingled with the audience at the bar after the show, and special children's events were held together with 'Ballads and Blues' concerts. In order to lessen the often stultifying mystique surrounding the theatre, Littlewood organised special meetings at which members of the audience could question the performers about their interpretation and playing of roles. The sense of intimacy between stage and auditorium was assisted by the smallness of the Theatre Royal which only held 488.

However Theatre Workshop's financial resources were extremely slender – a full house took less than £200 – and by existing on a shoestring, productions occasionally suffered. For instance, in Brecht's *Mother Courage* staged in 1955, the music which was essential to the play's conception had to be omitted. The radical and iconoclastic thrust of Theatre Workshop also ensured that not a penny of subsidy was received until 1957, and even then the Arts Council's support was meagre and grudging: in an appendix to his *The Theatre Workshop Story* Howard Goorney contrasts the varying amounts received by Theatre Workshop and the English Stage Company at the Royal Court.

Disregarded at first by the commercial theatre, Theatre Workshop was much more highly respected on the continent. In 1955, for example, it was invited to an international festival in Paris where it promptly stole the show. But it found itself ignored by the British Embassy, no doubt suspicious of the left-wing politics of some company members, and in order to save money the troupe had to cart its scenery and costumes through the customs by hand.[33]

But by the middle of the 1950s the tone and attitudes of British drama began to change – an important reminder that it is a mistake to regard the West End as simply a monolithic block – and this transformation affected Theatre Workshop. In 1956 the English Stage Company, led by George Devine, staged John Osborne's *Look Back in Anger* at the Royal Court in London, and a much-publicised 'revolution' was proclaimed by the critics: today some writers like Julian Barnes date the modern British theatre from 8 May 1956.[34] That such a furore could be aroused by Osborne's play demonstrated the stranglehold which the 'well-made play' had exercised for so long, excluding settings other than the drawing-room, and the way in which alternative theatre had often anticipated the West End. Everyone talked of the kitchen sink in *Look Back* but Ena

Lamont Stewart's *Men Should Weep* performed in the late 1940s by Glasgow Unity had already used one as a prop.[35] It also suggests how hard it was for alternative companies to impinge upon the country's theatrical consciousness.

Ted Willis has pointed out how often Unity Theatre in London anticipated many of the themes aired at the Royal Court in the late 1950s, and it is interesting that Osborne was one of the sponsors of Unity's 1962 appeal.[36] But the Royal Court also drew upon a new and younger generation of theatre-goers from the *Lucky Jim* era, often benefiting from the post-war expansion of higher and further education, who were repelled by the stuffiness and irrelevance of the traditional West End. Along with them went a new generation of writers, from Osborne and Pinter to Wesker and Arden, and a much greater variety of performer now that classical profiles and elocution were no longer de rigeur: Albert Finney, Tom Courtenay, Glenda Jackson and so on.

Undoubtedly the impact of all this was beneficial to theatre, enlivening the mainstream, but it was clear too that the 'revolution' did not extend to audience relationships or to the structures of theatre management, nor did the plays concentrate on anyone other than the familiar figure of the frustrated individual. In other words the 'revolution' boiled down simply to an extension of what was now permissible (and commercially viable) on mainstream stages – an episode recalling the Barker–Vedrenne seasons at the Court between 1904 and 1907 which resulted in the acceptance of Shaw's works as commercial propositions.

But the new West End continuously required a fresh injection of plays, and where better to look for them than at the Theatre Royal, Stratford? The commercial stage could of course offer substantial financial rewards and by now many members of Theatre Workshop had spent years eking out a meagre living and had families to support. It was disappointingly clear, too, that the Theatre Royal was still not attracting local audiences: with the underground having reached Stratford, many preferred an evening out in the West End. The West End's allure proved almost impossible to resist, and later on for players like Harry Corbett, Brian Murphy and

Yootha Joyce it would be television which beckoned: as Joan Littlewood wrote in her obituary of Corbett: 'He abandoned theatre and went for telly and the bread.'[37]

Between 1959 and 1961 five Theatre Workshop productions successfully transferred to the West End, leading some to refer to the southern end of Charing Cross Road as 'Littlewood's Corner'.[38] The ensemble quality of the company was inevitably destroyed because, with many of the original and longstanding members elsewhere, Littlewood had rapidly to train up fresh casts. At one point she was responsible for over 180 actors and staff, and the discipline which Brian Murphy has stated was Littlewood's main demand was absent. The financial rewards of the West End transfers began to dominate Theatre Workshop's work and priorities, so that on one occasion a show called *Make Me an Offer* (ironic title) was created with the express hope that it would end up elsewhere than at the Theatre Royal – a far cry from the original intention of pioneering a viable, lively non-commercial drama.

By 1961 Joan Littlewood realised that things had gone seriously wrong and she left the Theatre Royal – her 'Goodbye Note' published in *Encore* said that 'the West End has plundered our talent and diluted our ideas'[39] – but in 1963 she returned to produce *Oh, What a Lovely War!* Once more it transferred. By now the nucleus of the company had dissolved and the whole Theatre Workshop ideal was fading away. After some years working on her Fun Palace idea Littlewood left the theatre in 1968 – never, to date, to return. The Theatre Royal itself was actually closed between 1970 and 1972. Today it is under new management, although still permeated by Theatre Workshop associations and practices.

The history and development of Theatre Workshop indicates what an alternative theatre might look like: irreverent, sprawling, collective, improvisatory, spontaneous, topical – all that the West End usually was not. It also shows up all the perils of creating such an alternative drama, especially the constant ability of the West End to take over and utilise fringe talent and innovations. It does seem that Littlewood never fully analysed the drift of Theatre Workshop's last few years; some of her written statements in particular are vague, eschewing any economic explanation as to why British theatre was as it was and seemingly arguing that determination and will power alone were sufficient. As late as 1960 she was writing: 'The building of a popular theatre is a question of opening new doors. With new material and actors of wit and invention working on it, it is only a matter of time now before we have an extensive new dramaturgy. . . . This future great theatre will, and can, arise everywhere, its achievement requires only work and patience.'[40] If only it did.

Apart from the work of Theatre Workshop there was little non-commercial theatre in the 1950s and early 1960s. London Unity's company had dispersed and the theatre often lay empty and unused for long periods before being hired out to touring companies. Its audience had disappeared. In November 1975 the theatre itself burnt down, a sad end to this venture. Merseyside Unity however kept going.

The continuing lack of interest shown by the labour movement in the theatre was emphasised once more by the saga of the Centre 42 project. In 1960 the TUC passed the following resolution: 'It [Congress] notes that the trade union movement has participated to only a small extent in the direct promotion of plays, film, music, literature and other forms of expression. . . .' The idea was taken up in particular by the writer Arnold Wesker who put forward the plan of re-creating arts centres, a programme first floated during the war but then, as we have seen, quietly forgotten by the Arts Council. Wesker decided to build upon the recruiting weeks held by various trades councils: why should they not hold festivals too?: 'From that point we could move on to festivals under the auspices of a borough or county council, a large housing estate, a vast factory. A whole new tradition could begin.'[41]

The first such festival was held in Wellingborough in 1961 and was followed by five more during 1962. They all offered a mix of poetry readings, plays, jazz, folksong and other music concerts. To get over criticisms that Centre 42 was forcing culture down people's throats, the group only went where it had been specifically invited. With hindsight, however, the aims of Centre 42 now appear wildly over-optimistic, for example Wesker's hope that: 'Perhaps in an industrial area where there is no theatre, a few unions could get together and sponsor the building of it. And they would then be responsible for bringing in the audience as well as keeping the theatre going.'[42]

No new plays came out of the enterprise; a reward of £500 was offered for suitable good material, but as the Annual Report for 1961–2 recounts sadly, none of the 80 manuscripts submitted was acceptable, most of them emulating the worst of television drama. Debts of £40 000 were run up by the festivals and despite much huffing and puffing trade union assistance was virtually non-existent, although it must be said that the organisation of the events hardly inspired confidence: 'Administratively, the festivals were often chaotic, and this resulted in late, sparse, and inadequate publicity. Performances often had to take place in premises totally unsuited to their nature, which were frequently accoustically unsound.'[43] Trades councils proved themselves unable to attract large enough audiences, and Wesker admitted later that the general public found the association between trade unions and the arts rather offputting. The Roundhouse in Camden was acquired in the summer of 1964 but the whole initiative simply fizzled out.

With the demise of both Unity Theatre in London and Theatre Workshop by the middle of the 1960s and the failure of Centre 42 to attract any sustained interest or support, it might have appeared that alternative and experimental drama in Britain was on the verge of extinction. In fact it was just about to embark upon the most fruitful period in its history.

The Royal Court saga of the 1950s had hinted at the dissatisfaction which many theatre-goers felt with the commercial stage. By the 1960s this feeling had deepened and spread. The expansion of higher education, the coming of pop music and boutiques, the realisation that the consumer boom had left a substantial new 'youth' market waiting to be tapped – these and other social changes led to a climate in which old shibboleths were challenged. Within the theatre perhaps the first evidence of this mood was the Royal Shakespeare Company's (RSC) 'Theatre of Cruelty' season in 1964 during which the conventions of moderation and naturalism came under violent attack.

The most obvious throwback to the 'old' West End stage was the continuing existence of the Lord Chamberlain's powers of censorship. Since the Second World War clashes with the censor had increasingly held up his activities to ridicule, and forced him to set up more arbitrary dividing lines. Thus for instance in John Osborne's *Inadmissible Evidence* of 1964 the word 'off' had to be deleted from the line 'Do you have it off with that girl of yours', and 'bum' had to replace 'arse'.[44] Theatre Workshop ran into legal difficulties and the coming of the satire boom in the early 1960s with *Beyond the Fringe*, and television's *That Was The Week That Was* pushed back the boundaries of good taste, making the Lord Chamberlain seem more and more of an anachronism. Finally in 1968 his theatrical veto was abolished, over 230 years after Henry Fielding's burlesques of Walpole, which had prompted the introduction of the Stage Licensing Act in 1737. The laws of obscenity and slander remained.

The radical questioning of traditional drama extended to the challenging of the architecture and shape of theatre buildings. Did they have to possess proscenium arches? Some alternative theatre companies in the past – the Workers' Theatre Movement, the touring Unity groups, the ABCA Play Unit, the early Theatre Workshop – had used non-traditional playing spaces and the Edinburgh Fringe Festival begun in 1947 had only ever offered informal venues. In the 1960s such initiatives multiplied. Joan Littlewood, for example, designed what she called a 'Fun Palace', a reminder of the eighteenth and nineteenth-century pleasure gardens which had provided a wide range of entertainment, even though her plan never came to fruition.

In 1962 the new Chichester Festival Theatre was based on an 'open stage' plan with the audience on three sides of the performers. The tiny Traverse in Edinburgh began in 1963 in what had once been a brothel; its manager Jim Haynes opened the Arts Lab in Drury Lane five years later. Charles Marowitz's Open Space was in Tottenham Court Road and pubs like the Soho Poly and the King's Head in Islington started lunchtime theatre performances. Community centres too were another versatile form of location together with student halls at universities and polytechnics, and favoured also was the use of street theatre as a sure way of playing in front of 'non-theatregoers'.

The discovery of Brecht's works, both his plays and his theoretical writings, offered an alternative to naturalism and the well-made play. Other influences came from abroad with the visit of the two American companies, the Living Theater and the Open Theater. The number of alternative and experimental groups spiralled upwards.

Such a flowering of this tradition makes it more convenient to divide up discussion of its development into three chapters, although there is a certain amount of overlap as regards one or two individuals. The first will concentrate on political drama and the attempt to use the theatre as a means of changing or helping to change the world. The second deals with the growth of community, ethnic and women's theatre as well as alternative theatre's relationship with the major subsidised companies like the RSC and the National Theatre (NT). The last chapter briefly covers alternative theatre's responses and reactions to radio and more especially the potent medium of television: should writers and performers compromise in order to reach the vast audiences regularly attracted to television? As we will see, all three chapters continue on from experiments and ideas raised within alternative and experimental theatre before the 1960s and explored in the previous chapters.

Chapter 10

Political Theatre in Britain Since the 1960s

A major thrust behind political theatre in Britain has always been against the 'apolitical' or 'Establishment' tone of the plays presented in the West End. The drawing-room settings automatically excluded portrayals of members of the working class except as domestic servants, and the talk which took place within these rooms steered clear of political controversies – a policy induced by both the Lord Chamberlain and his Examiner of Plays, and by the self-censorship of managers who took care not to offend their clientele.

Thus alternative theatre sought in contrast to put on plays seen as more directly 'relevant' to the bulk of the population, and the riots and disturbances which greeted not just several of the Abbey Theatre productions but other plays mentioned above – results which no doubt confirmed the fears of West End managers – indicated how comparatively successful they were. Plays by Shaw and members of the Manchester School, for example, broached topical issues usually ignored on stage, and it was when there was a political dimension present that groups like the ABCA Play Unit and Theatre Workshop were most compelling.

However the most longstanding of the political groups, Unity Theatre in London, achieved only limited success, largely because Britain conspicuously lacked a labour movement with more than a marginal interest in cultural provision, unlike say the Soviet Union or Germany. Without this tradition, which had made possible the work of a Piscator or a Brecht, British playwrights found it difficult to create suitable material with political themes, leading groups to depend on plays from abroad such as *Waiting for Lefty*. If one glances back through the pages of this book, not many of the plays discussed are still performed, although it should be noted that in recent years a number have been revived to acclaim: Granville Barker's *Waste*, Malleson's *Six Men of Dorset*, Lamont Stewart's *Men Should Weep* and Joe Corrie's *In Time of Strife*.

But in the 1960s the growing size and influence of the British labour movement (the number of trade unionists rose from just over 9½ million at the end of the 1950s to over 11 million by 1970) pointed to fresh possibilities.[1] It was not that such an expansion led of itself to the creation of secure cultural foundations – the Centre 42 experience disproved that – but it did at least indicate the mounting self-confidence apparent within the movement, a mood underlined by the victory of Harold Wilson's Labour Party at the 1964 and 1966 general elections. New strands of Marxist thought seeped over to Britain from the continent, getting tangled up in the student movement of the time and also in the creation of a 'counter culture'. Within alternative theatre, such as it was in the early and mid-1960s, these new trends did not pass by the 'Old Left'.

Unity Theatre's political affiliations had always rested with the British Communist Party, an identification which had sometimes caused problems for members in terms of priorities: which came first, an effective drama or an efficient political organisation? Links with the Communist Party had necessarily caused difficulties during the Cold War of the late 1940s and 1950s. By the 1960s however Unity itself seemed staid and conventional as two workers at the theatre, Claire and Roland Muldoon, discovered: 'We weren't in the CP, but we were coming round to Marxism. We were young and we were part of an enormous resistance to established politics – CND, Ban The Bomb, Anti-Apartheid, that sort of thing. We wanted to bring *this* into Unity. We were expelled for our efforts.'[2]

The Muldoons left to form CAST (Cartoon Archetypal Slogan Theatre) in 1965, perhaps the first of the political groups, but they were some years ahead of their time – three years in fact. 1968 was the year in which the student movement both in Europe and in Britain took off. Protests were fuelled both by the American presence in Vietnam and by Harold

Wilson's support for this venture, arousing the large Vietnam Solidarity Campaign demonstrations which ended up in Grosvenor Square, London outside the US Embassy. These marches were part of a political context which also incorporated a series of landlord and tenant disputes which had broken out all over the country and linked up with a number of 'unofficial' strikes. The Labour government's efforts to deal with the latter, based on Barbara Castle's White Paper *In Place of Strife*, further heightened the political temperature.

In 1968 several alternative theatre groups were set up which rejected conventional theatrical settings in favour of playing on the streets and at the new venues springing up in towns and on university and polytechnic campuses. One such company was Portable, formed by writers David Hare and Howard Brenton amongst others. Another which later became Red Ladder was the Agitprop Street Players – the name itself summing up its approach – which grew out of requests from tenants for 15-minute pieces dramatising rent strikes. For the first two years of its existence the Players worked closely with Greater London Council tenants' groups. Yet another new venture was the Brighton Combination which specialised in playlets dealing with the particular problems and methods of obtaining social security payments.

In such circumstances these groups naturally rejected the whole paraphernalia of naturalist theatre which was for them indissolubly connected with the traditional theatre buildings of the West End theatre. Under the influence of Brecht, the social realism of an earlier generation of radical playwrights like Arnold Wesker was scorned. Groups like Red Ladder concentrated specifically on the labour movement for their audiences and not on traditional theatre-goers; this called for much hard graft and many mistakes:

> Through our work in the Tenants' Movement, we made contact with people in the docks and at Ford's of Dagenham [industrial workers were also active in the rent strike]. In early 1969 we made our first attempt to do a play for industrial workers. On our own initiative we constructed an outdoor play, *Stick Your Penal Up Your Bonus* (the title was its only redeeming feature), and took it down to Ford's to show

to the workers collecting their strike pay. There we tried,
unsuccessfully, to get the attention of the workforce. We had
no organisational relationship with the workers at Ford's or
their trade unions. We might just as well have been selling
cut-price carpets as trying to put over socialist ideas within a
theatrical framework (in fact we might have got more
attention if we had). . . . We realised then that we had to
relate to working people through their own organisations
and not stay on the outside of the labour movement.[3]

These agit-prop groups began to draw upon forms and
techniques last used in the 1920s and early 1930s by the
Workers' Theatre Movement: slogans, simplicity, speed,
topicality – these were adapted to open-air presentation. As
another member of what became Red Ladder has remarked,
'Problems of visibility and audibility on noisy street corners led
us to develop a highly visual outdoor style with text to a
minimum.'[4]

Few of the sketches and playlets of the time were ever
published, but an example of the work being done were the
Agitprop Street Players' *The National Cake* and *The Big Con*, both
of which were performed in the early 1970s. *The National Cake*
tried to show by means of a huge cake the inequalities of British
society, a visual metaphor which ended with the demand 'We
don't want more cake; we want the bloody bakery!!' *The Big Con*
focused on what were seen as the limitations of social
democracy, a system in which there were apparently few
differences between the Conservative and Labour parties and
where the realities shaping people's lives were muffled by
parliamentary debate. The Agitprop Street Players saw
themselves as helping to bring about 'a higher degree of class
consciousness', but they carefully avoided using words like
'capitalism', 'communism' or 'socialism' in favour of more
concrete and direct images.[5] An integral part of the
performance was the discussion afterwards with the audience –
another marked contrast with the tradition of West End theatre
in which the illusionary and self-contained nature of the play
is broken at the end of the play by the final curtain that is the
signal for spectators to leave the building.

It would be easy now to look back on these playlets and

deride them for being crude and simple, as they certainly were: but that is what was called for in the circumstances and what was provided. They did reach 'non-theatrical' audiences, although with what effects is debatable. In a statement which could equally well have been made by a member of the Workers' Theatre Movement, individuals saw the political needs of the current situation as paramount: 'The general feeling of the Red Ladder people at that time was that they did not come out of the theatre tradition; they did not see themselves as doing political propaganda in a particular form. The main impetus was political rather than theatrical.'[6]

Political theatre naturally connected very powerfully with wider events, the latter providing the context in which the former existed. In 1970 the Conservatives under Edward Heath unexpectedly won the general election. Heath came to power with a programme that promised to make inroads into the mixed economy which had prevailed in Britain since the 1940s. A key plank within this was restrictions on trade union rights and privileges, introduced by the government as a series of Industrial Relations Acts. The furore which greeted these Acts – the marches and rallies, the imprisonment of five dockers and their subsequent release – did seem to present the issues in stark black and white terms as a fight to the finish between 'Capital' and 'Labour'.

These struggles were grist to the mill of the political theatre groups, enabling them to plug into concerns and topics animating millions of people. Agit-prop on the street was exactly what was called for. Older groups received new life, new ones were formed such as the General Will in Bradford and the Broadside Company put together by two former members of Red Ladder. Their sketches retained the simplicity and bluntness of agit-prop: General Will's *State of Emergency*, for instance, has been called 'a constantly developing Living Newspaper'.[7] Unlike the Workers' Theatre Movement or Unity, these groups were not identified with any single political organisation.

In a sense these agit-prop troupes could congratulate themselves on having played a small part in the downfall of the Heath government when, after a series of miners' strikes, the Conservatives lost the two elections of 1974. However the new

Wilson administration could hardly be regarded as an especially radical outcome to the militancy of the early 1970s, particularly when its incomes policy or 'Social Contract' presided over a general defusion of the political situation which in turn posed further problems for the political theatre groups. Since the 1960s they had fed off the rising temperature of the situation, but now the tide was flowing in the other direction. The 2-D figures of agit-prop seemed increasingly inappropriate – a process similar to that in the middle of the 1930s when Unity superseded the WTM – and groups found themselves isolated, even allowing for the exhaustion and tiredness resulting from several years' hard work. A member of Red Ladder has written of the problem of finding that 'our "correct analysis" stifled our ability to create living characters . . . desperate attempts to humanise these political Frankensteins with injections of colloquiality and the odd joke failed.'[8]

Some companies began to question whether their isolation from the theatrical mainstream was necessary or effective: Portable, for example, turned their back in the mid-1970s on touring and on trying to reach 'non-theatrical' audiences. For David Hare, Portable had in any event only been playing to sympathetic and already 'converted' middle-class spectators, and the natural corollary of this attitude was to go the whole hog and write instead for large-scale auditoria whether they be provincial repertory companies, subsidised organisations like the National Theatre or, if possible, television. An early indication of this trend – and Portable writers were some years ahead of their counterparts – was the premiere of Hare and Brenton's *Brassneck* at the Nottingham Playhouse in the autumn of 1973, a play which signalled the new willingness to use more accessible forms in its chronicling of the post-war saga of the Bagley family; David Edgar has written that '*Brassneck* is, in fact, that hoary old stand-by, the chronicle of a family through three generations. . . .'[9]

Another response to the changed political climate was simply: so what? Some groups such as Broadside continued to produce plays which covered topics in a direct manner: its *The Lump* was written together with the building workers themselves who formed its subject. And if there was not enough suitable material to hand then 'history' was to be raided for

examples of 'socialist revivalism'. Foco Novo for instance
produced the *Arthur Horner Show* about the Welsh miners'
leader and also *The Nine Days and Saltley Gates* which linked the
General Strike of 1926 with the miners' strike of 1972. Joint Stock
staged a version of Robert Tressell's *The Ragged Trousered
Philanthropists.*

There were also pressures making themselves felt which had
not been experienced by earlier alternative theatre groups,
most notably the effects of public subsidy. At first the Arts
Council had ignored the work of fringe theatre just as in
previous decades they had turned their back on the Unity
Theatre movement and on Theatre Workshop. But in 1971 the
Arts Council's Fringe and Experimental Drama Committee
was introduced and by 1976 a total of nearly £½ million was
being given to 18 alternative theatre groups. It injected an
element of professionalism and inevitably offered the
tantalising prospect of a 'career', particularly in such an
overcrowded occupation as acting. Up to this point companies
had been largely composed of amateurs, members tending to
subsidise their activities by accepting a very low standard of
living – one writer referred to social security as being 'the poor
person's Arts Council'.[10] The influx of money led to a degree
of bureaucratisation – offices, administrative staff, other
overheads – and to a perspective which now stressed financial
considerations at the expense of political ones. Distinctions
between performers and audiences were heightened.

This process of professionalisation led to some companies
having to change their procedures. For instance the collective
nature of companies had prevented the identification of
individuals, this being viewed as a step on the road towards the
despised West End 'star syndrome'. But now some performers
began to demand credits for their work as a useful security for
the future. In the 1979 introduction to its published play *Taking
Our Time*, Red Ladder wrote that within its organisation such a
request for credits had been 'hotly contested' but finally
accepted.[11]

Several of the groups were aware that the receiving of
subsidy threatened to sever their links with the audiences on
which they had concentrated and to pull them into a
London-based role duplicating the metropolitan tendencies of

the West End stage. It was the familiar tension between the merits of touring and of having a permanent base, and if so, where? Red Ladder left London in order to establish a headquarters in Leeds with a view to building up a Northern circuit, and John McGrath's 7:84 (Scotland) focused its efforts on venues and audiences in Scotland.

The problem for a company like Red Ladder was that efforts to develop an alternative circuit based on Northern working men's clubs could lead to substantial compromises in an attempt to appeal to club audiences who were invariably offered a diet of reactionary and sexist material. Sympathisers expressed alarm: at a performance conference of the Association of Community Theatres late in 1978 an observer criticised the show: 'Using all the customary techniques, idioms and cliches of club cabaret, they became at times almost indistinguishable from the type of act that you might see on the Mike Yarwood Show – except for their eccentric socialist lyrics.'[12]

The difficulties facing Red Ladder by the late 1970s – namely how to react and respond to a political situation very different from the days when they worked as the Agitprop Street Players – were endemic throughout political theatre. In particular the Conservative Party's victory under Mrs Thatcher at the 1979 election heralded a downturn in the fortunes of the labour movement and therefore a further questioning of the part that political drama could play. Several factors were at work.

One perennial stumbling block lay in the grudging and meagre support of the official labour movement. Some officials were suspicious of the 'far left' views of the touring companies, and certainly a number of shows castigated the 'reformist' trade unions as being integral to the general political problem. It was also true too that, as Chris Rawlence of Red Ladder once acknowledged, 'many of these companies approach their audiences from the outside. They are not immediately of the class and communities they wish to play for.'[13] Bookings there may have been, but nothing more. Nor had Labour governments when in office embarked upon the sweeping cultural programmes initiated in, say, France by André Malraux whose *Maisons de la Culture* were in fact a reincarnation of British ideas floated in the 1940s regarding arts centres.

Levels of subsidy provided by the Arts Council were much lower than elsewhere in Europe.

However it should also be pointed out that some of the companies seem hardly to have welcomed audiences with open arms; David Hare for example explained of Portable: 'Our aggressiveness is immensely conscious. I suppose it stems from a basic contempt for people who go to the theatre. It gets worse when we get near population centres. I loathe most people as individuals and, en masse, I find people particularly objectionable.'[14]

The critic John Lahr has written of how many political theatre groups treated their audiences with disdain – if, that is, they thought of them at all: Edward Bond does not 'at all' when writing his plays.[15] The crude slogans of early agit-prop put off many potential allies who regarded the shouted simplicities as an insult to the intelligence as well as being deeply patronising. This was especially the case when most people's point of comparison had become the slick and glamorous entertainment seen on television. The personal invective hurled at older theatre workers such as Arnold Wesker and Peter Brook was also indicative of an 'holier than thou' attitude which held back political theatre at this time.

Another difficulty lay in the very nature and consequences of collective organisation. Although Foco Novo for instance came together afresh for each production, most companies were run on a permanent basis in which decisions were discussed at length by everyone, often in a situation in which the financial deprivations of life on the road – low wages, poor working conditions, long periods spent travelling, the lack of security – shortened tempers. John McGrath has written of 7:84 (Scotland) and (England) that, in the years 1977–8: 'While the audiences continued to want the shows, internal wrangling in England, and in Scotland the break-up, mainly through sheer exhaustion, of the nucleus of people who created the company's identity in the early years, led to great difficulties and strains.'[16] And to quote from Red Ladder's experiences again (it remains the best documented of all theatre companies of the period):

Essentially the group was structured so that every decision, however small, needed the unanimous agreement of every individual in it before it could be acted upon. Of course, in theory, this seems the perfect democratic approach. In practice it meant that those with the strongest personalities (the more pushy men) dominated the group. Through the course of an argument those in a minority would eventually put up their hands and make the decision unanimous even when they did not agree with it, just so the work could continue. This method of working itself created personality antagonisms and often reduced arguments to the level of personality differences. When resentments built up to an intolerable level, explosions occurred, and often we would sit down for days in order to work out the problems. Because we believed there could be nothing wrong with the structure, since it was so democratic, this working-out led us into people's individual personalities and psychologies. The effect of this ultra-egalitarianism, this idealistic-democracy, was in fact to individualise everything.[17]

Often, too, groups would engage in a collective creation of productions, hoping thereby to escape from the Romantic and West End conception of the individual 'Artist'. This process also necessitated discussion and examination of personal motives and inclinations. One example of this was Joint Stock's *Cloud Nine* put on at the Royal Court in London in 1979. The writer Michelene Wandor has provided a diary of this gruelling six-month workshop period, the company's egalitarianism making it important that at the end the nominal writer Caryl Churchill produced seven parts of roughly equal weight for members of the company.[18] Likewise has John McGrath described the writing process for 7:84 (Scotland)'s *Boom*: 'Ideas poured out – of all kinds, from all directions. This part of the process of writing was opened wide. Not only were my ideas up for scrutiny, discussion, amendment, but the whole company was throwing in their ideas which were taken up, knocked down, analysed by everyone else and fed into the growing pool of unrealised material that was to be the basis of the show itself.'[19] In such circumstances it is hardly surprising that the turnover in membership of the political theatre groups was so high.

A further obstacle facing companies was the overall lack of organisation between them. Groups were rightly suspicious of centralisation and proud of their hard-won autonomy but this attitude could be detrimental. The magazine *Time Out* proved vital in publicising meetings and events, and yet when Catherine Itzin in her 1975–6 handbook of British alternative theatre tried to compile a list of 'alternative venues' she found that companies either could not or would not volunteer the necessary information.[20] Nor did it prove possible to set up a central booking agency for the touring groups.

Another problem, but this time of a longstanding nature: the lack of new plays and writers. One reason for this was that the collective character of many groups' working discouraged individuals; another lay in the fact that the financial rewards were minimal. It was understandable that writers hoping to make a full-time living out of their talents should turn instead to mainstream theatre where the financial rewards were appreciably higher, or to television. The promising Pluto Playscripts series which began publication in 1978 had to be stopped.

A significant factor in the disappointment of many of the hopes of the 1960s was that they were highly over-optimistic. No one had thought that the production of left-wing plays would directly spark off working-class revolt, but it was thought that they could at least prepare the ground. As Mrs Thatcher's Conservative administration was confirmed in office in the general election of 1983, even this modest aspiration appeared naive. Too often statements echoed this mistaken approach: for example the playwright Steve Gooch complained that everything had gone right – 'All that we needed now was a working-class audience.'[21] Too late people realised that a play could only be, as was written after the production of John McGrath's *Trees in the Wind* in Exeter, 'a mere drop in the ocean'.[22]

In some ways the political theatre companies were caught in a double bind: if agitation was their objective and drama merely a convenient means to that end, then why not simply forget the drama? It is worth recalling Karl Marx's comments to Engels on reading a play written by the socialist Lassalle in 1859: 'Incredible that a man at this time and in these circumstances of world history not only finds time to write such stuff, but demands our time to read it . . .', and Marx was complaining less about the quality of Lassalle's play than its very act of creation.[23]

Some of the plays written by those active within political theatre were thoroughly impractical, most notably John Arden and Margaretta d'Arcy's *The Non-Stop Connolly Show* which, if produced in its entirety, would run some 26 hours. This play is also flawed by the simplicities of early political theatre, for instance the stereotyped figure of Grabitall the 'demon king' who appears throughout the play as various grasping capitalist characters but always wearing the same mask. Few of the plays have risen above this level of crudity. Several which have are those by Trevor Griffiths whose *The Party*, first staged in 1973, analyses the political culture of Britain by means of contrasting personalities arguing in a television producers's flat some time in 1968 after the failure of the Paris 'May events' – a reversion to Shaw's 'discussion play'. Griffiths' *Comedians* drew upon the tradition of the Northern stand-up comic in order to discuss political change, comparing two approaches to humour: that which reinforces the audiences' prejudices, and that of Gethin Price whose bizarre black humour is dismissed as 'cranky' or marginal. Another excellent play of the period is David Edgar's *Destiny*, which offers a thoughtful analysis of the then rise of the National Front.

Both *Comedians* and *Destiny* were adapted for television, thus reaching audiences of millions, as was John McGrath's *The Cheviot, The Stag and the Black, Black Oil*, which depicted past events from Scottish history such as the eighteenth-century land clearances, linking them with contemporary issues. When originally toured by 7:84 (Scotland), the company travelled 17 000 miles and played to over 30 000 spectators – a number dwarfed by the televised version's two transmissions.[24] Clearly viewers in their homes watched and received the play in very different circumstances from those experienced at a public performance, but many of the major figures within political theatre began to transfer their efforts into productions which could be certain of reaching large numbers of people whether in the venues of the major subsidised companies or on television. These moves reflected the depressing overall political situation for socialists, the umbilical cord to which political theatre workers were inextricably attached. Others focused increasingly on 'community theatre', as we will see in the next chapter.

This loss of confidence in political theatre did not detract in any way from the lasting contribution which it had made. One achievement, for example, was the assertion that, contrary to the commercial stage, politics and art could not be separated. It was noticeable that the old 'Loamshire' drawing-room play disappeared almost completely. Working-class characters too now did more than murmur 'Yes, Sir', 'No, Sir' and tug their forelocks. The social dimension of drama – the 'public' which had been ignored by the West End stage and even by writers like Beckett and Pinter with their concentration on the anguished individual – was also an essential part of political theatre. Questions relating to the methods and means of organisation, stressing the value often of collective decision-making, had been asked. Although 'stars' and 'stardom' were still an integral part of the West End, within parts of it and elsewhere in the subsidised theatre the area of consultation and participation had been widened.

Finally, political theatre in Britain did try to take drama back to the people, touring and playing in front of audiences who had never been theatre-goers – unlike earlier writers such as G. B. Shaw who failed to match his words with his deeds. Never again would theatre and drama automatically be equated with traditional theatre buildings.

Chapter 11

Community Theatre Since the 1960s and 'the Majors'

The disillusion felt by many during the course of the 1970s with the strident agit-prop of earlier years prompted a search by groups and individuals for forms of venue and drama which would be firmly rooted in the community. The disadvantages of interminable touring with its succession of one-night stands was that companies were unable to establish relationships with audiences. It was clear too that whole sections of the population were simply being ignored by British theatre, that women and black people for instance found little of relevance in most productions – even if they ventured inside the theatres in the first place. The 1970s saw a determined effort on the part of many companies to address peoples and themes usually excluded from the boundaries of 'legitimate' theatre. One of the most significant was the women's theatre movement.

Although particular women such as Joan Littlewood had played important parts in the development of alternative theatre, not since the collapse of the Actresses' Franchise League during the First World War had general issues relating to a 'woman's theatre' been talked about or acted upon. Within the theatre world as a whole there were and had been very few women directors, women playwrights or women in positions of power or responsibility. But during the 1960s the creation of 'the women's movement' led to an increasing awareness that this situation could and should be challenged, especially by fighting back against the pervasive hold of certain stereotypes.

In 1970 protests at the 'Miss World' beauty contest held in London led to the formation of the Women's Street Theatre

Group which, reflecting alternative theatre's preoccupation at the time with agit-prop on the streets, began to demonstrate and perform in the open air, insisting on talking about what had been essentially 'private' activities: the *Sugar and Spice* show in Trafalgar Square in March 1971 involved the use of giant-size sanitary towels and deodorants as props. Another of its productions, *The Amazing Equal Pay Show* which tried to show up the inequalities between rates of pay for men and women, was toured in 1972.

The Women's Street Theatre Group did in some ways provide a counter to the existing men's agit-prop companies which had possessed, in Michelene Wandor's words: 'an economist tendency, which sees the main protagonists of the class struggle as male and the workplace as the main site of struggle. The home is a place of retreat and emotional support, within which waits the little woman (sometimes the little woman is converted to the class struggle, and then she simply joins the lads).'[1]

Women's agit-prop was not a very promising development, but in 1973–60 years after the Actresses' Franchise League's 'Woman's Theatre' season – a festival was held at the Almost Free venue in London. Although it was revealing that the male director of the Almost Free, Ed Berman, had the final say as regards the choice of plays, the festival represented the growing self-confidence of women workers within the theatre. Out of the festival came the Women's Theatre Group. Realising that the establishment of stereotyping and of reactionary attitudes to women's roles in society need to be combated at the grassroots level, the Women's Theatre Group has since concentrated on taking productions into schools and youth clubs. Their *My Mother Says I Never Should* of 1975 discussed the question of female teenage sexuality and of being clear about various decisions which inevitably have to be made. In 1975 this pioneering group was followed by the formation of Monstrous Regiment and then by other groups such as Cunning Stunts, Beryl and the Perils, and Clapperclaw.

One substantial difficulty was that there was simply no canon of women's plays on which these new companies could draw. Few of the earlier companies working within experimental theatre had even recognised this as a problem.

The only play which was revived and did seem to speak specifically to women in the audience was Ena Lamont Stewart's *Men Should Weep*, toured by 7:84 (Scotland) in 1983. Elizabeth MacLennan has described the experience of performing this work:

> everywhere we go, in every town, you can feel the women in the audience right behind you. You can sense their support, you can hear the special quality of their laughter – because the play's so observant about women's lives and full of women's jokes – and you can see them at the end giving you little nods and smiles and thumbs-up signs. It's been a unique experience for me, and for all the other women in the cast.[2]

But *Men Should Weep* was the exception, and women's groups had to fashion their own plays, concentrating in particular on two forms, the history play and popular entertainment. Examples of the first trend were Caryl Churchill's two plays on seventeenth-century events, *Light Shining in Buckinghamshire* and *Vinegar Tom*. The first was produced with and by Joint Stock, the second by Monstrous Regiment who have put on record the collaborative process involved: 'First we discussed what we wanted to say with the character, and what scenes were needed for it. Then, whilst we rehearsed something else in one part of the rehearsal room, Caryl sat in a corner and wrote the extra scenes. At the end of the day, bingo, two new scenes.'[3] Songs punctuated both plays and were used to comment on the action.

That Monstrous Regiment was prepared to employ a full-time writer like Caryl Churchill indicated the growing realisation that women's theatre groups needed to move away from the amateur 'anything goes' attitude of the first years and instead cultivate certain skills. Its ability to do this was a by-product of the process of subsidy whose effects were explored in the preceding chapter. Groups like Cunning Stunts argued that without entertaining their audiences – in its case by the use of juggling and acrobatics – then any implicit or explicit 'message' would be ignored.

Women's theatre did and still does have to surmount a

number of problems intrinsic to itself. The difficulties of touring, for instance, which is in practical terms open only to 'the relatively young and childless'.[4] The longstanding tradition within British drama which sees women as interpreters or 'extras' rather than creators remains powerful: there are still very few women playwrights – Michelene Wandor has pointed out both that 'between the years 1956–75, only 17 out of 250 produced plays at the Royal Court Theatre (known for its championship of new writing) were written and/or directed by women' and that in the *British Alternative Theatre Directory* of 1980 only 38 of the 327 playwrights are women.[5] A study published in 1984 found that 'the more prestige and money a theatre has, the less women will be employed as directors and administrators, the less likelihood that a play written by a woman will be commissioned or produced (except Agatha Christie) and the less women will be on the board.'[6] Only in the field of radio drama – where both Caryl Churchill and Pam Gems, author of *Piaf*, received their grounding – do women writers maintain some kind of parity, if only because 'the dominantly female radio audience as well as the relative ease of production has proved to be a release rather than a constraint.'[7]

Another hurdle is that, like other alternative theatre groups, rates of subsidy have been cut back in the 1980s, reducing Monstrous Regiment sometimes to casts of just three. As the founder Gillian Hanna has complained, 'No one is paid sufficiently and instead of being able to use our work as a springboard we find ourselves getting physically exhausted.'[8] This had led to a high turnover of members. Performers have also had to face up to the traditional feeling that women should 'look good' on stage. Groups like Cunning Stunts have faced this head-on: 'Women as well as men ask us why we don't like to look pretty on stage. We wanted to shed our anxieties about our looks, so we shoved our bulging bottoms and slack stomachs up front and got over them. It gave us a great deal of confidence.'[9]

But whatever the difficulties, the women's theatre movement has undoubtedly succeeded as it intended in 'raising consciousness' about women and drama whether it be in commercial theatre, subsidised theatre or on the fringe. Other mixed-sex companies like Red Ladder have produced works which raise related issues in their plays *Strike While the Iron is Hot* and *A Woman's Work is Never Done*, and a male playwright, Steve Gooch, has written *Female Transport* about the perils of transportation to Australia and also *The Women Pirates*.

Another area of life in which alternative theatre intervened, in this case for the first time, was in gay drama. Before 1967, of course, homosexual conduct had been illegal and although a few British films such as *The Victim* and plays like John Osborne's *A Patriot for Me* had dealt tentatively with this topic, both the film and theatre censors discouraged such material. However the 'Gay Liberation' movement followed in the wake of the women's, and in 1975 a festival at the Almost Free led to the setting up of the Gay Sweatshop company.

At first the very concept of 'gay theatre' was rejected by some theatre workers who were themselves gay; as Simon Callow has recalled: 'a friend suggested me for the lead in Gay Sweatshop's third production. I was deeply sceptical about the whole enterprise. Ghetto theatre, I said. What next? Plays by chartered accountants, about chartered accountants, for chartered accountants? I regarded gay liberation as shrill, exhibitionist and counter-productive.'[10] In fact, as Callow continues, he did perform in Martin Sherman's *Passing By* at the Almost Free and has written of the 'deeply moved' audience: 'It was as if a secret that had been kept for too long were finally being told to people who knew it individually but had never seen it acknowledged.'[11]

Like women's theatre, several of the plays dealt either with historical subjects – Sherman's *Bent* about gay people under the Nazis or Noel Greig and Drew Griffiths' *Dear Love of Comrades* about the pioneer socialist Edward Carpenter – or sent up and used popular forms: *Jingle Ball* of 1976 was a spoof of Cinderella. Although the existence of a gay theatre has encouraged gay theatre workers to 'come out' and feel more confident – a 'Gay Pride' week was held at the Drill Hall, London in 1980 – the continuing AIDS scare has indicated how entrenched popular feeling remains about homosexuality.

The majority of the country's repertory companies whether by choice or through financial necessity confined themselves to the presentation of London successes. But there were a few which tried to build up local audiences and introduce original material. One such was the Victoria Theatre in Stoke-on-Trent which had been an old cinema but was remodelled in 1962 into a 'theatre in the round'.

One way of developing an indigenous following was by dramatising the history, as was done in the Victoria's *The Jolly Potters, The Staffordshire Rebels* and *The Knotty*, the latter for instance dealing with the construction of the local railway. The plays were created collectively, as the theatre's director Peter Cheeseman has explained: 'The documentaries are not written, but constructed from primary material gathered during a preliminary research period, and then rehearsed collectively by researchers, consisting of the resident dramatist, myself and the company in committee. They are then created on the floor at rehearsal.'[12]

The Liverpool Everyman under the direction of Alan Dossor was another regional theatre which from the middle of the 1970s offered a lively programme, often making use of music to accompany the dramatic action. This theatre proved particularly successful as a launching pad for writers and performers now known nationally, from Willie Russell and Alan Bleasdale to Antony Sher and Jonathan Pryce. But this yet again demonstrated how the fringe and the reps are regarded as suitable training grounds for hopefuls, making it hard for them to sustain their own distinctive forms of theatre.

The People's Theatre in Newcastle has managed to expand its activities and now possesses a 600 seat auditorium as well as an art gallery, a cinema and a restaurant. The Scottish dramatic tradition has been nurtured by the Citizens' Theatre which retains a strong local identification. Under the playhouse's three directors, the Citizens has always tried to attract a wide section of the population by means of its relatively cheap seats and single-price system. Local links are fostered by means of schools and council organisations and its annual pantomime is a major attraction.

The Traverse in Edinburgh, originally housed in a brothel called 'Kelly's Paradise', boasted an auditorium capable of holding only 60 spectators; in the mid-1960s the maximum take possible in a week was only £112.[13] In 1969 Traverse moved to a theatre which could accommodate 120 spectators and under resident directors such as Max Stafford-Clark the company conducted workshops and put on several new productions, specialising in the staging of foreign plays. As for touring, John McGrath's 7:84 (Scotland) was committed to a nomadic existence in a struggle to reach 'non-theatrical' audiences. The group's plays drew upon aspects of Scottish history as in *Little Red Hen*; on older native forms of entertainment like the ceilidh in *The Cheviot, The Stag and the Black, Black Oil*; and more recently they have disinterred plays by Ena Lamont Stewart and Joe Corrie.

Another form of theatre which was revived during the 1960s and 1970s was what was described as 'ethnic drama', of which there had been little since the decline of the Yiddish theatre. A study by Naseem Khan published under the aegis of the Arts Council in 1976 with the title *The Arts Britain Ignores* revealed the substantial quantity of 'non-English' drama. For example, the Polish community could boast of four theatre groups in London alone with additional companies in Nottingham, Slough and Rochdale. The Greek–Cypriot Theatro Technis had existed in London since 1957, and Khan reported on two ad hoc Indian theatre groups and a Bangladeshi theatre group in East London staging 'social dramas'.

The most significant strand has been the Black theatre movement, with groups such as Temba and the Dark and Light Company of Brixton dating from 1970 and Mustapha Matura and Farrukh Dhondy's Black Theatre Co-operative formed in 1979. But if the movement has succeeded, like women's and gay theatre, in increasing theatrical consciousness a degree or two, formidable obstacles remain. It has not proved easy to build up either an audience or the necessary black skills or self-confidence, especially when the poor working conditions and rates of remuneration leave performers susceptible to other offers. As Naseem Khan observed, 'Many a black theatre group has fallen apart because members have had the opportunity to do both lucrative and prestigious television or West End theatre work.'[14]

It is clear that the above organisations have tried to appeal to and rely on particular sections of the population – as has for instance youth theatre which is estimated to involve at least 10 000 young people in Britain – as well as practising a form of 'community theatre' in which they attempt to establish and then sustain contacts with the neighbouring area and its people. One of the first projects which did pioneering work in this field was Ed Berman's Interaction, founded in 1967, which spawned a range of activities from festivals at the Almost Free to lunchtime plays, children's groups and City Farms.

Such an assortment of work led away from the concept of 'theatre' pure and simple – certainly away from the West End play as a self-contained entity – and towards forms of community activity in which drama did not necessarily play a dominant part. Just as Theatre Workshop under Joan Littlewood had decided that touring was not per se a good thing and that the Theatre Royal, Stratford had to become the focus of the whole community, other groups in the 1970s also came off the road and put down roots. In 1973 for example, the Combination, a group formed in 1967, opened the Albany Empire in Deptford, South London, emphasising the multi-media aspects of their work:

> When we realise it is better to produce a poster than a bit of theatre, then we produce a poster. If people come and say to us can you do a show on something, nine times out of ten we say, look go and use the video project – it's much better, faster, cheaper and you don't have to spend eight weeks with eight people shut up in a room rehearsing a play. We can say, you don't need a play but a film, slide show, tape, series of posters, pamphlet. And as an arts project we can help them get all that together. I think we have been lucky because we have been liberated from the need to try to make our art do *everything* political.[15]

Offering rock concerts, jumble sales, a restaurant and a bar, the Albany Empire had to learn not to be blinkered by 'the flat cap image', to understand that its work has had to be smart and professional because audiences compare it with the glossy, slick productions on television.[16] The Albany Empire was rebuilt after it had been burnt down in the summer of 1978 – but a bigger threat looms currently with the demise of the Greater London Council and the shortfall in funds for arts projects.

Another permanent theatre was the Half Moon in the East

End of London. Beginning in a disused synagogue in 1972, the venture then moved into new premises along the Mile End Road. The director at that time, Robert Walker, indicated how several theatre companies emphasised the 'community' aspects and distrusted notions of 'alternative' theatre:

> Our aim is to create a popular theatre combining new works and classics; to offer people a clean, comfortable building to come to; and to make it a social centre where you can eat, drink or simply buy a book or a newspaper. We don't want to be Fringe, we don't want to be an Alternative; we want to be a real people's theatre that proves by its very design that society itself is malleable and changeable.[17]

Walker's regime was responsible for a mix of productions ranging from Toller's Expressionist *The Machine Wreckers* to Brecht's *The Resistible Rise of Arturo Ui* to the local and topical *George Davis is Innocent OK?* (although Walker did not direct all of them himself). In the summer of 1985 the new Half Moon, extensively redesigned and rebuilt, opened at a cost of nearly £1 million – an indication of just how far the initiatives of alternative theatres in the 1960s and early 1970s had moved on – although the designer Florian Beigel has tried to retain the flexibility of experimental theatre by ensuring that there is no fixed seating: 'The idea is that we have made a scenic street – theatre in the street with a roof over it.'[18]

Both the Half Moon and the Albany are agreed that the aim of entertaining their audiences must be in the forefront. Other groups too have also moved away from the attitude which equated socialist purity with amateurishness, realising that they need to develop certain dramatic skills and techniques. As Richard Seyd of Red Ladder has expressed it:

> This belief that skills and the use of entertaining forms is irrelevant is rooted in the argument that as socialist theatre workers we merely happen to use theatre to communicate political objectives. This disrespect and mechanical relegation of the forms used do a disservice to the ideas being communicated. No craftsman would disregard the tools of

his trade to the extent that socialist theatre workers often disregard theirs.[19]

But if such views ruled out agit-prop, which everyone agreed was alienating when performed in front of politically uncommitted audiences, and if the West End well-made play was irrelevant, then what was left? And here we see some theatre workers turning to one of the other traditions sketched out in the first chapter, that of popular theatre. A number of groups had from the earliest days of alternative theatre staged almost fantasy or science-fiction plays. The Welfare State, for instance, founded by John and Sue Fox in 1968, had created what was described as 'performance art' which took place all around the spectator and stressed the visual at the expense of the verbal. As a Welfare State leaflet put it, 'We offer assistance to the national imagination, rather than agit-prop. People have a need for ceremony in their lives. Our vision is to make theatrical celebration a reality and available to all.'

A recent book on this troupe called them 'Engineers of the Imagination' and their productions in the 1970s often traversed the country, the 1972 tour of *Lancelot Quail* ending up in Cornwall. A summary of their March 1970 *Spring Event* at Exeter brings out the anarchic qualities of Welfare State performances:

A composition with a series of all round simultaneous performances in a gymnasium to herald the first day of spring. With the Mike Westbrook Band, racing cyclists, fencers, climbers, weight lifters, army radio operators, model aircraft, scaffold towers, giant projected images and films plus a parade of thirty drum majorettes leading a fancy dress pageant and an enormous 20 foot home-made dragon-fly.[20]

Clearly Welfare State's effect could, on this scale at least, only be diffuse and infrequent, but the People Show, set up in 1967, organised more structured events. All four members are versatile and skilled performers whether as musicians, acrobats or comedians. Running through their shows are references and allusions to popular culture: the 1981 Christmas show was based around an intended performance of Glenn Miller's 'In the Mood' which was repeatedly sabotaged by one of the group. Albert Hunt's group at Bradford College of Art and Technology staged an historical re-enactment in the street of the Russian Revolution and fought out the Cuban Missile Crisis as a Hollywood western. The Bubble Theatre Company put on Shakespearean adaptations in London parks with an irreverence smacking of the penny gaffs. Hull Truck has always emphasised the importance of music and of improvisation in its productions. 7:84 (Scotland)'s *The Game's a Bogey* drew upon pantomime and song, and its *Boom* was modelled on the concert party form. And so on.

In fact it seems at times as if every alternative company has experimented almost as a matter of course with popular entertainment. The attraction is that as a form the popular theatre plays down the notion of illusion: both performer and spectator acknowledge each other's presence unlike the West End's 'Fourth Wall' convention. Claire Luckham has explained of the genesis of her *The Return of Trafford Tanzi*:

> I doubt whether I'd have written it, if I'd been writing for a conventional audience. I don't follow any sport. But I went to see the wrestling. I was amazed by the audience. It was an opportunity for them to work out their frustrations. The audience was so vocal, so clever, the inter-relation between the wrestlers and the audience was exciting and vital.[21]

But there do seem to be problems in using the popular theatre, as most of the groups tried to, as a politically progressive form. David Edgar has recalled of the General Will's three chronicle plays produced in the early 1970s about Heath's Conservative government that 'the images the audiences related to (in the sense of those that they remembered and commented on afterwards) were not those that were drawn from popular-cultural traditions. It was rather those images that we drew from bourgeois popul*ist* culture (films and television) that created the greatest resonances.'[22] Michael Billington, drama critic of the *Guardian*, has also referred to the patronising tendency of some supposedly radical groups to bung in a song or two – that'll keep the workers happy.

The most sustained justification for the use of popular dramatic forms has been advanced by two experienced theatre workers, John McGrath and Dario Fo. McGrath first made his name writing the scripts for the *Z Cars* series on television, but unlike most other writers he left this medium and has since concentrated on live theatre. Setting up his 7:84 Company in 1971, McGrath's plays have always discussed and explored contemporary political issues but with a degree of characterisation and narrative skill that marked his work off from agit-prop. In 1980 McGrath gave a series of lectures at Cambridge which were later published as *A Good Night Out* – the title itself indicates the general shift which had occurred in alternative theatre away from the didactic and towards the entertaining.

In the lectures McGrath took particular issue with the ideas of Brecht which had exercised a formative influence on the British theatre since the 1960s: Peter Brook in *The Empty Stage* for instance had considered that 'Brecht is the key figure of our time, and all theatre work today at some point starts or returns to his statements and achievement.'[23] Brecht rejected the notion of dramatic illusion, insisting that spectators should always be aware that they were in fact watching a play and by means of the alienation or 'A-effect' be presented from identifying with the characters portrayed. They would thus retain their critical and political faculties and perhaps be stimulated to action outside of the playhouse.

Few of Brecht's plays have been notably successful in Britain and supporters of his 'Epic Theatre' have often therefore referred to Joan Littlewood's *Oh, What a Lovely War!* as an example of a successful Brechtian production incorporating music, film, comedy and short sketches in order to underline the carnage of the First World War. The problem with this play was that, as Peter Davison has pointed out, English audiences are unaccustomed to thinking politically in a theatre and tended to interpret *War!* as a great show, although this did not necessarily detract from its effectiveness:

> Its pierrots and gaiety, its newsflashes and bitter ironies, may well have affected attitudes, but not through 'thought', 'detachment', the A-effect. It was not just a romp, it did

touch nerve centres; but its message came across through subconscious feeling, not detached thought. It was, for that reason, far more successful theatrically and 'politically' than plays more overtly attempting Brechtian techniques with the intention of directly effecting changes of response.[24]

McGrath in *A Good Night Out* argues along similar lines by attacking Brecht's prescriptions for Epic Theatre because of their hostility to the audience, pedagogics being the passing down of information and judgements: 'Distance, in place of solidarity, pseudo-scientific 'objectivity' in place of the frank admission of a human, partisan and emotional perspective – coldness, in place of shared experience: politically, Stalinism rather than collectivism.'[25] McGrath then goes on to outline the elements from which he believes a popular and radical drama can be created, amongst them being directness, comedy, music, emotion, variety, localism, and a sense of identity.

The other person who has argued in favour of the use of popular theatre is the Italian actor Dario Fo who, like McGrath, turned away from television to live theatre. At first Fo and his wife Franca Rame performed in traditional and mainstream playhouses. But in 1968 Fo and Rame decided to build up a circuit of 'alternative' venues, feeling that they had been incorporated into the establishment as licensed jesters: 'This bourgeoisie did not mind our criticism, no matter how pitiless it has become through our use of satire and grotesque technique, but so long as the exposure of their "vices" occurred exclusively within the structures they controlled.'[26]

Building upon the network of Italian workers' clubs and their cultural programmes which were singularly lacking in Britain, Fo has toured his own one-man show which dissects and comments upon contemporary topics – but always bearing in mind his own maxim, 'Entertain first, then instruct'. He has also written *Accidental Death of an Anarchist* about the 'suicide' in custody of a young railway worker at Milan police headquarters in 1969 and another political farce *Can't Pay? Won't Pay!*: 'What are the laughs we put in there? We could take them out if we wanted to. But they provided a breathing space to make the audience pay attention. An audience which isn't used to following continuous discussion with no pauses, would grow bored after a while and lose its contact with what's being discussed.'[27]

Both plays have been translated and staged in London, the fringe production of *Accidental Death* transferring to the Wyndham theatre in the West End for a run of nearly two years, and Fo has toured Britain with his *Mistero Buffo*. The show combined slapstick and mime with philosophical disquisition in a largely improvised performance – although none of the adlibs can have been so compelling as those during a show in Vicenza in a storm with Fo talking to the thunder, casting it as the voice of God.[28] Although some of *Buffo's* humour inevitably passed by a predominantly non-Catholic audience, Fo's secret has always been, as Brian Glanville has observed, to include people rather than to alienate them.[29] But there is only one Dario Fo and no English performer has yet come anywhere near the sustained inventiveness of his work.

Other critics and playwrights, notably David Edgar, have not been convinced that importing popular theatrical techniques into the context of alternative theatre can bring forth the anticipated results: 'we don't have a popular tradition that is still feasible, or a revolutionary artistic tradition much beyond Brecht on which to draw. So one of the mistakes that agit-prop and a lot of left-wing groups have made is to say we will relate to ordinary people by taking on their forms, as a kind of passport into their consciousness – "We will write a left-wing *Coronation Street*".'[30]

Edgar has also pointed out that although remnants of the music hall tradition survive in working men's club entertainment, these club acts are by and large reactionary in content and the clubs themselves 'bourgeois in essence' – 'it is no coincidence that the uniform costume of club entertainers is the evening wear of the upper middle-class.'[31] McGrath furiously repudiated Edgar's views in his own *A Good Night Out*, arguing that 7:84's *Cheviot* had taken those 'grossly reactionary club show elements' and transformed them.

But whatever the radical tendencies or otherwise of popular drama – and the concentration on this form has led to the neglect of expressionist or non-realist theatre – the whole debate is undermined by Trevor Griffiths' brutally frank observation that 'the people' are in fact those 97 per cent of the

population who never set foot inside a theatre today.[32] As
Barrie Keefe has said, 'the people I'm writing about, writing
for, wouldn't be seen dead in a theatre.'[33] Alan Ayckbourn is
the only playwright in Britain who might justifiably claim the
label 'popular'. Thus the talk of whether or not popular
techniques are progressive theatrically and politically needs to
be dealt with again in the next chapter on television drama, but
it should be commented upon how yet again the fringe's use of
the popular has often resulted in the transfer of successful productions to the commercial West End stage: *Accidental Death*,
Claire Luckham's *The Return of Trafford Tanzi*, Hull Truck's
Up and Under, and so on. Shades of a process which started
back with J. T. Grein's Independent Theatre of the 1890s.

The recent use of popular dramatic forms has not managed
to cover up the fact that alternative theatre has produced few
good works of its own; and the future looks increasingly bleak,
primarily because the economic squeeze on fringe theatre has
led to fewer companies being able to commission new plays.
Even if they can afford to do so, the works themselves are
normally on a limited scale: the Theatre Royal, Stratford, for
instance is unable to produce plays demanding a cast of more
than seven people.[34] Similarly the Bush theatre is also facing the
prospect of putting on fewer new plays with ever smaller casts.
If one of the achievements of the fringe was to restore the public
dimension to drama – 'theatre as an extension of a public
meeting' in John Arden's words[35] – then this is under
increasing threat because of financial considerations.
Companies are bound to favour the staging of plays not in
copyright, i.e. not new works, and schemes to encourage new
writing have been largely unsuccessful. In any case, the
monetary remuneration accruing to playwrights from live
theatre are meagre when compared with television or even
radio, despite the efforts of the Theatre Writers' Union. But it is
worth bearing in mind that the 'little theatres' of the 1930s
coped without subsidy, although they often had support from
private individuals.

But there are some 'non-West End' theatres which do
possess relatively large resources: the subsidised 'majors' such
as the National Theatre, the Royal Shakespeare Company and
the Royal Court – all three of them based in London. The

paucity of the Arts Council budget of the 1940s had grown in the following decades, funded by accelerating economic expansion. The total figure in 1946 was just £235 000, but in 1967–8 alone the Exchequer allocated over £7 million to the Arts Council and in 1969–70 over £9 million. Even allowing for inflation the rise indicated the extent to which government subsidy of the arts had become accepted across the political spectrum. The drama budget rose from under £200 000 in 1960–1 to nearly £1 million in 1965–6 and over £1½ million in 1966–7.[36] Private patrons like Miss Horniman and Barry Jackson had been superseded.

The mixed effects of this growth on political theatre groups have already been outlined, but of course the major sums were awarded to the NT, RSC and the Royal Court. All three balanced uncertainly between the experimental and West End traditions, but their greater resources enabled them to pick up on fringe developments. One example of this has been the greater flexibility regarding traditional ideas of theatre buildings and architecture, a change to which alternative theatre contributed enormously. In 1969, for instance, the Royal Court opened its small-scale Theatre Upstairs. In 1974 the RSC started its Other Theatre in Stratford and in 1977 the Warehouse in central London, both venues reflecting the antipathy felt towards fixed seating and proscenium arch theatre. There has also been the Cottesloe at the NT, the use of the NT's foyer by various groups and activities, and the Pit at the RSC's new home in the Barbican. As Colin Chambers amongst others has pointed out, these 'Other Spaces' sprang from the pioneering fringe work.[37]

The subsidised theatre companies have also drawn upon the new writers and plays brought forth by alternative theatre – in contrast to the West End which, influenced always by the economics of competition, has never 'brought on' playwrights, a process which demands an investment on a long-term basis. The fringe on the other hand has always specialised in premiers. John Elsom has noted of the 480 new plays staged in Britain in 1971–2: 'Of these new plays, 300 were staged in fringe theatres, and London fringe theatres alone staged 238 premieres. More than half of the total output of new plays was produced in London fringe theatres. . . .'[38] And as Alistair

Moffat has written in his history of the Edinburgh Fringe, 'More new plays and dance pieces are done in those weeks in Edinburgh than are done in the West End in an entire year.'[39]

As early as the autumn of 1969 Bill Gaskill was organising a 20-day 'Come Together' jamboree of alternative and performance theatre at the Royal Court, and ever since many fringe events or writers have made their homes at the 'majors'. The NT's resources, for example, have just permitted them to open a studio theatre under Peter Gill which by means of workshops and select 'try out' performances will nurture individual writers – a policy which Unity Theatre had failed to carry out in the past because of economic reasons. The majors can also afford to mix the presentation of modern plays with fresh interpretations of the classics and works from abroad, a programme which Joan Littlewood had tried to introduce. Peter Daubeny launched his 'World Theatre' seasons in 1964 under the aegis of the RSC.

The 'Big Three' have exploited staging techniques introduced by the fringe, in particular the ability to escape from the restraints of the well-made play which required a certain unity of style and the fostering of the illusion that the performers were not in fact acting in front of spectators. At the NT's Cottesloe for instance, several 'promenade' productions have been put on in which the action takes place in amongst the audience. The RSC director Adrian Noble has staged several Shakespearean plays such as *King Lear* and *A Comedy of Errors* in which popular dramatic elements like farce, slapstick and juggling were highlighted, and the RSC's *Nicholas Nickleby* has been called a 'participatory epic'.[40] Similarly the company's *Macbeth* of 1983 emphasised the use of music with the two players being clearly visible from the auditorium.

The NT and the RSC also offer much greater status for those who work within these institutions, an important attraction when the fringe's financial rewards are so meagre. Productions are extensively reviewed in the national press, widening the possibilities for lucrative parts in television drama. The majors' access to larger audiences was and is bound to be tempting: Howard Brenton, for example, spoke in 1975 of the reasons why he was turning his back on the fringe, attacking it for being 'a licence for saying small things in a small room': 'I want to get into bigger theatres because they are, in a sense, more public. Until that happens you really can't have any worth as a playwright.'[41] David Edgar has talked of the ambition he felt when moving into the large companies.[42]

Clearly, too, the NT and the RSC can build up productions over a period of months – six in the case of *Oresteia* – because of their substantial resources; in the case of *The Mysteries* the plays developed over a number of years before ending up at the Lyceum in the summer of 1985. The majors' casts can also be bigger: when Peter Barnes first sent his *Red Noses* to theatre managements they returned it saying there were too many parts; when the RSC took it they said 'Look, we've got a company here. There aren't enough characters!'[43] The majors can keep a number of plays in production at the same time – six at the NT – which represents a realisation of Miss Horniman's repertory ideals that alternative theatre companies have been unable to implement.

But if the large subsidised theatres have taken hold of and incorporated into their work ideas developed within the framework of alternative theatre, there are several significant aspects which have not been appropriated. The first is that fringe companies have always stressed the virtues of openness and of democratic and collective decision-making, even if this has sometimes been to the detriment of productions. The NT on the other hand is run on strictly hierarchical lines, as Peter Hall's *Diaries* suggest. The actor Simon Callow has written of the NT: 'The involvement of the company in decisions is non-existent. Not a single actor, stage manager, scenic artist, designer or musician sits on any National Theatre committee. It is in these subsidized theatres that the directocracy is at its most unqualified.'[44] Antony Sher in his *The Year of the King* sketches out the fearful atmosphere at the RSC when everyone is waiting for the results of the 'Directors' Meetings', and Colin Chambers has indicated that the elected subcommittees have little power.[45]

Secondly, the alternative theatre's mistrust of London-based drama has not been accepted. Although the NT and the RSC do undertake provincial tours, they are predominantly London-oriented – inevitably because that is where the critics, the tourists and a substantial audience are. As a letter in the

Observer remarked: 'The so-called National remains, unfortunately, an irrelevance to the majority of the British theatre-going community. In no way can it be considered accessible. Even the touring aspect is only an adjunct rather than a forceful form of contemporary theatre.'[46] Although neither the NT nor the RSC is actually situated in the West End of London, both the South Bank and the Barbican possess their own distinctive associations which exclude large sections of the population.

Finally, a third element within recent alternative theatre also not taken up by the major subsidised companies has been the issue of feminism. Michelene Wandor has observed that few of the Royal Court's plays have been by women, and the NT produced not a single play by a woman playwright before 1980 and since then only the one work by the American Lillian Hellman. Although there are plenty of female administrative staff, the positions of power and influence are dominated by men.

It does seem therefore that on balance the subsidised theatres have done very well out of fringe theatre, leading one to ask whether this is not simply a repetition of the old story: alternative drama as a fruitful laboratory for the mainstream. It is worth pointing out here that an American commentator in his study of political theatre in the United States in the 1930s concluded that it was the government-sponsored Federal Theatre which undermined its left-wing competitors.[47] A number of fringe plays and personnel have also made their way into West End theatre.

Of course most alternative theatre companies have been all too aware of this process of incorporation, and some have tried to resist the trend. The most obvious way is by deliberately performing certain material in certain ways that simply can not be transferred. The abolition of the Lord Chamberlain's censorship powers in 1968 made this less straightforward, but Pip Simmons and his troupe, for instance, played up the topic of pornography: 'The English are great at absorbing everything – I mean they've absorbed us for instance. It could indicate that there isn't sufficient tension in England for the underground to be in any way a threat to society. The nearest we've got to becoming dangerous is by being pornographic.'[48] Violent images abound in alternative drama and a feminist group like Beryl and the Perils flaunt their bad taste.

The drawbacks to this approach are that, first of all, it is subject to the law of diminishing returns: the grotesque and hideous becomes so familiar and natural that it ceases to shock, forcing performers to step up the dosage – a policy which has sometimes led to the verbal and physical abuse of spectators. Powerful yes, but not calculated to increase the influence or appeal of alternative theatre. A further difficulty is that the theatre, rather like the music industry and its exploitation of punk rock, is adept at turning controversy into profit – as was the case with shows like *Oh! Calcutta!*

Today, therefore, the boundaries between alternative and subsidised theatres have become increasingly hard to define, especially when the Half Moon, for instance, undergoes rebuilding at a cost of nearly £1 million. Even the West End is not as isolated and self-enclosed as it once was, although the ubiquitous proscenium arch and select audiences restrict the type and range of productions which it can stage. Some individuals retain a fierce hostility towards a mainstream drama – John McGrath has written of the 'nausea' he feels in the presence of 'dominant' theatre events[49] – but most do not.

However even McGrath has spoken of the 'popular apathy' enveloping live theatre, and when the RSC has had to cancel shows in certain boroughs because the company has lacked sufficient 'stars' (i.e. television 'names') then it is right to wonder about the relevance and impact of live drama in Britain today.[50] It is telling that whereas Sir Robert Walpole's reaction to Henry Fielding's skits in the 1730s was to impose a stringent censorship, Mrs Thatcher went off quite happily to see the play *Anyone for Dennis?* Even if the latter was much less blunt and abusive, it does indicate the loss of the theatre's power and influence. The final chapter must deal therefore with the relationship such as it is between alternative theatre and the mass media.

Chapter 12

Alternatives within Radio and Television Drama

The mass media today – radio, cinema and especially television – attracts enormous audiences, many times larger than the followers of experimental theatre. The average viewer in Britain, for example, is supposed to watch something in the region of 22 hours television each week; many children spend more hours in front of the television than they do in school. Virtually everyone has access to one set and many households now have two. Even radio, which is not thought of as a particularly 'mass' form of listening, can notch up audiences of 800 000 for its plays – a total which would require many live theatre performances even to approach. Clearly there are implications here for alternative theatre in Britain. Albert Hunt like many others has found that whereas the theatre is remote from the lives of young people, television is 'taken for granted'.[1]

And yet despite this obvious popularity, or perhaps because of it, those individuals concerned to create a non-commercial drama have never felt comfortable with the manifestation of popular entertainment. For instance Arthur Bourchier, a theatre manager prominent within the Independent Labour Party Arts Guild of the 1920s, wrote in a 1926 pamphlet of 'inane, vulgar, and disappointingly trashy' American films and of the 'crude, savage cacaphonous jazz that we hear on every hand today'.[2] A Marxist literary critic like Christopher Caudwell working in the 1930s was also dismissive of popular culture. Over the last twenty years there has been a vigorous debate over the advisability of radicals trying to use the radio and television for their work.

When radio drama started in the 1920s it consisted largely of broadcasting live West End plays or of reading aloud texts – there was no understanding that radio offered certain opportunities not available to the theatre. Like its putative parent, radio drama faced a stringent censorship; Val Gielgud, the head of radio drama at the BBC for over 30 years until 1963, has written: 'Apart from having to observe the amber warning lights at the cross roads Sex, Religion and Politics, I could drive straight ahead with reasonable confidence of security.'[3]

One of the first writers to grasp the possibilities of the medium was Clifford Odets who began his career writing for an American radio station and used his experiments to fashion the influential *Waiting for Lefty* in the mid-1930s. In England it was the producer Archie Harding who was based in the BBC Manchester and started just before the outbreak of the Second World War to explore the medium by means of 'drama-documentaries'. He worked with both Ewan MacColl and Joan Littlewood on *Coal* in 1938, a collaboration which, despite the clumsy and cumbersome recording apparatus then in use, allowed 'ordinary people's voices' to be heard – nearly 20 years before *Look Back in Anger* began the process by which different dialects and diction became accepted on the mainstream stage. Littlewood continued to work in radio during the war.

However radio drama still clung to theatrical conventions before a two-pronged attack in the 1950s threw off these shackles. The first assault was delivered by radio comedy, heralded by the wartime programmes *ITMA* with Ted Kavanagh, which attracted up to 16 million listeners and has been likened to the *commedia dell' arte* in its exuberant topicality and irreverence.[4] *ITMA* was followed by *The Goons*. The second innovation came once again in the field of drama-documentary and was facilitated by the introduction of portable tape recorders, allowing impromptu and unscripted dialogue. The first programmes which emerged from this source were the 'radio ballads', the first being *The Ballad of John Axton*, which was broadcast in 1959 as a selection from some 70–80 hours of recorded material. MacColl, Peggy Seeger and Charles Parker worked on this first ballad together and Parker has spoken of the freedoms which the tape recorder now permitted other than 'a formal interview of only three minutes': 'Apart from working-class speech we used folk song or songs conceived in the folk tradition. None of the speech, I should add, was scripted or delivered by actors. It was all from the horse's mouth.'[5] Other radio ballads were *The Big Hewer* about coalminers, *The Fight Game* about boxing, *Singing the Fishing* on the North Sea herring industry, and *The Travelling People* about gypsies.

Under this disruption of conventional ideas as to the scope and range of radio, the BBC's drama department began to foster work of a high standard, calling upon the talents of writers like Harold Pinter, Tom Stoppard, Samuel Beckett and John Mortimer. Radio functioned as an important breeding ground for these and other writers in the 1950s, particularly when it is remembered that there was no National Theatre or Royal Shakespeare Company and that the Lord Chamberlain continued to cast his baleful shadow on live theatre.

Today radio drama stands out if only because it broadcasts over 1400 plays each year, one-third of which are premieres. Being a great deal cheaper than television, radio producers have more room for experiment and less anxiety as to what a failure will mean for their careers. As we saw in the last chapter, several women dramatists like Caryl Churchill and Pam Gems received their early grounding in radio. BBC Radio Ulster has also played a significant part in encouraging Irish playwrights and would-be writers. Finally, not the least of radio's attractions is that it can excel in producing forms of theatre such as verse-drama which have almost completely vanished from the West End stage.

But radio drama also suffers from a number of drawbacks. In terms of remuneration it is only half as financially rewarding as television, although comparable to theatre payments. Budgetary constraints limit the possibilities open: even a highly successful serial like *The Archers* with a regular listening public of 5 million has to work within these restraints, as the producer William Smethurst has pointed out: 'We can only afford seven characters a day. . . . Towards the end of a week you may hear strange combinations of people . . . you'll probably hear a lot of one-sided telephone conversations. That's because the

scriptwriters have used up all the other people early in the week
and there are very few left in the allocation!'[6]

Radio can also be used by television as a convenient training
school; as the *Economist* has written, 'The growing strength of
radio drama is reflected in the way television producers are now
turning to the radio for new products, where once they would
be scouring the fringe theatres.'[7] The speed of production and
reception of radio drama can exacerbate its ephemeral nature,
especially as studies have shown that most listeners to the radio
do so when engaged in other tasks.

Finally, radio has always suffered in terms of critical
disregard. Few radio plays from the over 40 000 broadcast
since the 1920s have been published or even thought of in terms
of publication, and fewer still recorded and issued as
cassettes.[8] It is revealing that a writer like Louis Macneice who
was peripherally associated with the Group Theatre in the
1930s but who went into radio drama has never received the
acclaim accorded to his colleagues Auden and Isherwood,
despite the excellence of his radio plays. Somehow the idea of
reaching large numbers of people makes both those within
alternative theatre and academic critics uncomfortable and
disdainful. It is true to say therefore that, unfortunately,
alternative and experimental theatre's relationship with radio
other than through a few isolated examples such as Joan
Littlewood and Caryl Churchill is almost non-existent.

However there is more to say as regards television drama. In
Chapter 3 we saw how the rise of the West End theatre had
elbowed out melodrama, but only so far as the early films and
comic papers. When television drama restarted after 1946 –
there had been a number of productions before the Second
World War – it suffered like radio from an inferiority complex
concerning the live theatre, thus inheriting certain theatrical
conventions, certainly as regards naturalism. Since that was
the West End tradition, then the popular surfaced as 'soap
opera', the distinction between the serious and the popular
reflecting the split or dichotomy which characterises much
thinking about culture: whether it be 'high' or 'low'. In
television terms the difference approximates to that between
the 'one off' and the serial or series.

Until recently radical critics and commentators tended to

dismiss the 'soaps', whether they were of the American or more down-to-earth and 'believable' British variety, but now it is sometimes argued that any form of entertainment reaching so many millions of people directly in their own homes would or should have possibilities for exploitation by radical playwrights. For example, it was noted of the early episodes that 'By and large *Coronation Street* had wisps of socialism blowing through the cracks, but it gradually became a stupendous fairy story.'[9] Likewise John McGrath has written of the genesis of *Z Cars* in terms of the BBC Drama Department's antipathy to series:

> Right then, we thought, let's take the series as a form worth bothering about. Let's go for the pace, the relationship with an audience, of *Highway Patrol*, but let's go for something that will unfold in narrative form all the minor stories that will make the fabric of our own society so alive. Use cops, OK, but as a device for getting into the small but important realities of the lives of the people who are going to be watching. No master-criminals, super-sleuths, gentlemen experts, cunning detectives – the police are *not* our heroes: the people are the heroes.[10]

Recent soaps have also attracted praise: Dorothy Hobson in her study of *Crossroads* has commented that this serial can indeed introduce issues of social concern or importance so long as they are related to particular characters and are not abstract. Similarly Channel 4's *Brookside* has dealt with issues of divorce and unemployment. It is also clear that British soaps in particular have given women the opportunity to play significant roles on screen – although there are few women television writers. In *Coronation Street* invariably it is the women who hold the local community together and middle-aged women are often involved in romantic situations, a topic which the Hollywood cinema for instance generally ignored.[11] As regards *Crossroads* Dorothy Hobson has written of the furious public response to the sacking of Noele Gordon (Meg Richardson) as indicating the strength of this positive female image.[12] The recent serial *Widows* also portrayed the women characters as active rather than passive, and Gillian Skirrow has argued that the programmes succeeded in bringing the feminist debate away from the margins and into the mainstream.[13] Also of importance is the ensemble playing of most British soaps.

Experienced television writers and directors have put forward the opinion that the melodramatic action series can offer distinct possibilities. Trevor Preston for instance, the writer of *Out* and *Fox* as well as episodes for other series, has spoken of mixing together plot and characters into a popular form. As he said of the character Frank Ross in *Out*:

> So you take a popular form like a good kick bollock and scramble about a man who comes out of jail but you weave these other things in, you weave in what happens to a criminal's family. It destroys a family when he goes to prison, it's like a hand grenade, his family blows up. All these sort of things. So you've got to have a text to pull them in – what's going to happen to Frank Ross; and then you've got a sub-text underneath (for those who want to take it) which is saying something.[14]

The critic Albert Hunt has likewise praised the subversive aspects of popular television comedy in which performers undercut notions of seriousness and pomposity.

But clearly there are deep-seated problems as to just how powerful or direct television drama can possibly be: even the 'sub-text' can only exist within the constraints of television production and reception. As David Edgar has put it:

> The inherent problem with television as an agent of radical ideas is that its massive audience is not confronted in masse. It is confronted in the atomised, a-collective arena of the family living room, the place where people are at their least critical, their most conservative and reactionary (the dwelling-addressed postal vote will always get a more reactionary response than any other form of balloted decision).[15]

Workers within American alternative theatre such as Joan Holden of the San Francisco Mime Troupe have also noted that television 'keeps people isolated in their homes, keeps their focus on personal problems and private issues to the exclusion of public or community issues'.[16]

A second difficulty is that television series and serials, like radio programmes, are put together at great speed – three episodes a week in the case of *Crossroads*, two weeks for a *Minder* – which means that producers and directors find themselves falling back into traditional and generally accepted methods of working, back to 'the formula' tried and tested. Case studies of series such as *Hazell* and *Minder* have emphasised the lack of room or time for experimentation or improvisation: in *Hazell* for instance an initial plan was to emphasise the role of one of the female parts, but in the rush of production this failed to occur and the women in the series were more or less stereotyped.[17]

Thirdly, the nature of what has been called 'the flow' of television also mitigates against the impact of any particular programme, the way in which hour after hour the show relentlessly goes on. The BBC's Drama Department, for example, is responsible for 220 hours of television each year. On commercial television, too, and possibly BBC in the near future, advertisements punctuate the action at regular intervals; Theodore Shank has commented: 'In one sense television commercials might be considered the theatre of capitalism. Like political theatre they are intended to influence action.'[18] The need of companies to maintain their respective ratings is also of overriding importance. Finally, television performers are surrounded by the trappings of stardom reminiscent of the West End stage and against which alternative theatre has always struggled, a process which is testified to by the amount of coverage given to certain actors and actresses in the popular press.

Despite these reservations however, a number of individuals have argued that we are stuck with television as it is – Dennis Potter has referred to it as the 'biggest platform in world's history' and our 'true national theatre'[19] – and that alternative and experimental theatre is largely irrelevant. In Trevor Griffiths' blunt words about live theatre, 'I don't really think it's more important than doing a rather high status crossword or playing a rather subtle game of Scrabble'; in another interview he stated: 'I am not interested in talking to 38 university graduates in a cellar in Soho.'[20]

Trevor Griffiths is the most articulate and forceful exponent of the merits of working within television rather than live theatre, especially as he originally wrote for the latter. He acknowledges the drawbacks of television but has always maintained that radicals have no option but to work with generally accepted forms: 'It interfaces with the whole problem of form, which is to do with realistic modes as against non-realistic alienating modes. I choose to work in these modes because I have to work now. I have to work with the popular imagination which has been shaped by naturalism.'[21]

Although it is generally recognised that 'one-off' television dramas offer more scope, Griffiths wrote the serial *Bill Brand* which was shown at peaktime viewing and then repeated at a later date during the afternoon. It portrayed the personal and political career of a young Labour MP and concentrated on what Griffiths saw as the perils of parliamentary Labourism. Much of its impact came from the way in which events and personalities were modelled on their 'real-life' counterparts then being enacted by the Wilson and Callaghan administrations of 1974–9. *Bill Brand* certainly represented arguments, opinions and debates of a character not usually seen and heard on television – unlike the news, television drama is not constrained by any need for 'objectivity'. *Bill Brand* was watched by an audience far exceeding that which visits alternative theatre, but with what effect it is impossible to say.

Griffiths has managed to build up an informal network of people responsible for the production of his work – there have been only three directors so far of his major television work[22] – approximating to the ensemble methods sought by alternative theatre companies. Another loose grouping has been based around the producer Tony Garnett and includes the director Ken Loach and the writer Jim Allen. Garnett has always worked within what he calls 'social realism' in order to reach millions of viewers, and certainly a play like *Cathy Go Home* touched a public nerve. The four-part *Law and Order* (1978) examined corruption in the police force and *The Spongers*, directed by Roland Jaffé, depicted those at the receiving end of the welfare state and was directed at certain newspapers' preoccupation with those 'sponging off' social security. Jaffé has claimed that 'After *The Spongers* the word "spongers" practically disappeared and that whole virulent campaign mounted every week in the *Daily Mail* went too.'[23] *United Kingdom* (1981), directed by Jaffé and written by Allen, portrayed the clash between a militant council and the forces of government.

One of Garnett's most ambitious productions was the four-part *Days of Hope* (1975) which was once again written by Allen and followed the fortunes of a particular family, dealing with such issues as pacifism in the First World War, the behaviour of the Black Tans in Ireland, and the General Strike of 1926. The serial aroused much controversy and several socialist and Marxist commentators attacked *Days of Hope* vociferously, arguing that viewers could not help but identify with the particular individuals shown and thus in a most un-Brechtian manner the programmes exaggerated the personal at the expense of the social and the political. This was a complaint levelled at *Bill Brand* too.

It may well be that television drama as a form contains an inherent tendency in this direction. For instance John McGrath left *Z Cars* because 'after the cops kept appearing week after week, people began to fall in love with them, and they became stars. So the pressure was on to make them the subjects, rather than the device.'[24] However Roland Jaffé has put forward the view that one can only deal with the structures of political and social life by coming to them via individuals' experiences, and this view has been supported by Dorothy Hobson's work on *Crossroads*: 'One of the most important elements in the inclusion of social problems in *Crossroads* is that the audience do find it acceptable and they do not reject the messages. It is perhaps because the social problems are always related to a character within the serial and not introduced in an abstract way they do seem to have an impact with the audience.'[25]

Clearly the whole argument as to whether those in alternative theatre should not instead be trying to work within more mainstream structures is bedevilled by the lack of any real evidence as to what influence, if any, television drama can exercise on viewers. However a specially commissioned report by the BBC following *Days of Hope* tentatively found that two-thirds of those questioned following the serial felt that they themselves 'should be more active in trying to make this country a better place in which to live'.[26] Alan Bleasdale's *Boys from the Blackstuff* clearly struck a huge if unquantifiable public chord. Likewise Trevor Griffiths' *Through the Night* about breast cancer, which was seen by over 11 million people: 'the Corporation's duty officer logged close to a hundred phone calls, the producer's office and the *Radio Times* received many letters, and Griffiths personally some 180. Marjorie Proops in the *Sunday Mirror* opened her columns to readers with experience of mastectomy and received over 1800 letters in ten days.'[27] It is revealing that such a response was aroused by an intensely personal and not a social or political issue.

It would be a mistake to think of viewers as a passive body sitting there through programme after programme. Viewers do talk to each other, flit from channel to channel, move around. No programme is ever unambiguously 'this' or 'that' but is made up of often contradictory elements, allowing viewers a certain freedom to pick and choose. A recent case concerns Trevor Griffiths' play *Oi for England* which was first shown on television. It includes a fierce and gripping racist speech by a character called 'The Man', so powerful that despite Griffiths toning it down South Yorkshire County Council withdrew funds from a touring version on the grounds that it might promote racism. Griffiths himself helped to fund this touring version but as two sympathetic critics of his work have suggested, the experience showed the limited radicalising effects of network television: 'even after lengthy group discussions, the kind of 'recognitions' he [Griffiths] sought from *Oi for England*'s audience remained at best inchoate.' Another commentator noted that 'the play's central issues often seemed to be too complex for audiences.'[28]

One area in which neither Griffiths nor Garnett have experimented is in that of non-naturalism, contending that such an approach would jeopardise the chances of their holding the audience. However both practitioners like Troy Kennedy Martin and John McGrath and academics such as Raymond Williams and Stuart Hall have attacked naturalism for its feeling of 'closure', for depicting things as they are and not as they might be. It is also unclear whether viewers are indeed irrevocably wedded to conventional and naturalistic techniques, particularly if one recalls comedy programmes like *Monty Python* and *The Goodies* or some of the ingredients in *Rock Follies* and *Pennies from Heaven*. As Albert Hunt has said, there is no one 'language of television'.[29]

Ultimately the potential of television drama is heavily influenced by questions of economics and politics. The latter centres around the topic of censorship. Famous instances include Peter Watkins' film *The War Game* and Dennis Potter's *Brimstone and Treacle*. Because the BBC is dependent on ministerial control of the size of the licence fee it is bound to tread warily. Trevor Griffiths has recently asserted that: 'television undeniably is closing down to people like us. It's even harder to get work done now than it was five years ago when there was a genuine pluralism about the commissioning process. Since Thatcher, there has been a sheer panic inside most people who run TV services.'[30] But even bearing in mind the possibilities of self-censorship, it is perhaps more obvious that on the surface at least television drama has remained largely free of overt censorship. The prolific socialist television writer Alan Plater has remarked that 'out of those [Plater's] two hundred and some scripts, only one has run into serious censorship trouble, to the extent that it was filmed but never transmitted.'[31]

More important are the economics of television production and the need to attract international co-production finance. Television drama is expensive: one hour of filmed material costs around £300 000. Such investment is bound to inhibit innovation; as David Cunliffe, Yorkshire Television's head of drama has said: 'You used to be able to have a 50 per cent success rate. Now every show must be a smash. And the bigger the investment, the safer the writer and director and producer and actors you go for.'[32] One-off plays which allow greater scope because they are not inheriting 'set' characters or situations are harder for television companies to schedule or to sell abroad. The pressures are in favour of serials, and, where international deals are concerned, in favour of costume dramas performed by stars. The critic Richard Last has pointed out that not only do 'declared' soaps occupy a weekly total of 7½ hours of screen time, but that co-production is leading to many more which in fact masquerade as television drama:

> Virtually no BBC production of any stature now gets made without outside financial assistance. The end credits mostly proclaim inputs from American and Australian sources, but plenty of other nationalities – German, Canadian, Italian – are in the co-production business. Time was when the BBC could claim that they alone exercised editorial control over co-produced drama. It is still the official Corporation line, but producers, and programmes, tell a different tale, of pressures, choices, compromises.[33]

The upshot of this trend is that the single play is likely to disappear from our screens. Channel 4 seemed to offer possibilities for independent production companies to explore new methods and techniques of programme-making, and in certain cases this has happened. But Channel 4 is funded by advertising revenue and thus is subject also to the pressure induced by the ratings. Companies are also discovering that because Channel 4 is in this area a monopolistic organisation it can strike hard bargains.

In such unpromising circumstances it seems as if the argument which focuses on whether people within alternative theatre should try and work for television is becoming academic. Trevor Griffiths and Tony Garnett have well-established records and will always attract commissions. But for everyone else – assuming one ignores the advice of Stuart Hood that 'those who cannot accept the dominant codes of their society will be well advised to resign themselves to working elsewhere than in the mass media'[34] – opportunities for the production of television drama will be few and far between.

Conclusions

Although these last pages are headed 'Conclusions', it might have been better to have called them something less definite. Any and every history, however copiously backed up with thousands of footnotes and references, is a reflection of the writer who has selected some facts or events and not others in order to bear out his or her argument. What this preamble is leading up to is that when I began researching *Other Theatres* seven or eight years ago I was not only convinced that there had been in Britain a fruitful tradition of alternative and experimental theatre (I still think that), but that it had a future too. Now I am much less sure of the latter proposition.

Alternative and experimental drama has undoubtedly enriched the history and development of British theatre over the last hundred years, challenging amongst other conventions the distinction between performers and audience and between professional and amateur. It has questioned traditional ideas as regards theatre buildings which possess proscenium arches and fixed seating, asking whether drama needs to be equated with the bricks and mortar of permanent 'theatres'. It is notable that many of the venues mentioned in *Other Theatres* boasted a varied existence before being given over to drama: the Abbey in Dublin had been a morgue, the Maddermarket and Unity chapels, the Gate a skittles alley, the Cambridge Festival Theatre a boys' club. Attempts have also been made by the proponents of alternative drama to attract a much wider range of audience than that going to the West End. The well-made play with its limited subject-matter and unity of style has been undermined.

But alternative theatre has also made a positive

contribution, arguing for the need to involve audiences whether during the performance or afterwards. The importance of ensemble acting and collective forms of organisation has been stressed as has the recognition of diverse groups of the population usually ignored by the conventional drama: women, blacks, gays. A mix of elements including music, mime and dance has been advocated and acting styles have been less 'stagey' and more versatile. Venues are informal and accessible.

And yet, despite these achievements and successes, the tradition of alternative and experimental theatre has never been able to overcome certain major drawbacks, most notably the limited role that theatre plays in most people's everyday lives. Not since the early sixteenth century has more than a fraction of the country ever attended live theatre. Writing in *The Peoples' Year Book* of 1936, Ivor Brown considered that 'the British Working Class have no tradition of play-going. Our theatre has been largely a middle-class institution and it takes a great deal to alter a tradition'.[1] Alternative theatre in Britain has barely dented this state of affairs, resulting in, for instance, the perennial complaints about the lack of new plays or writers. The labour movement has been of little or no help, and the attempt to introduce theatre into schools is being undermined by a lack of funds.[2] What is more, with the coming of television and now of video it is difficult to see how this 'middle-class' tradition can be altered.

If this is one reason for my pessimism about the prospects for a distinctive alternative theatre, the second focuses on the ability of the major subsidised companies – and in certain cases the West End too – to make use of fringe innovations and experiments. There will always be a live theatre in Britain – in 1979 alone for example over 14 million tickets were sold to amateur performances, and the West End at the present time is undergoing something of a revival in terms of audience figures with 10 million tickets sold in 1985 and a substantial increase likely with the 1986 figure. But as Robert Hewison, Michael Billington and others have pointed out (The *Sunday Times Weekly Review* 16 September 1984; *Guardian* 29 December 1985) much of this increase can be accounted for by the expansion of tourists taking advantage of a favourable exchange rate, which may be short-lived.[3]

The cost of presenting a play in the West End is rising astronomically: *Cats* alone costs £70 000 each week to produce and a hit musical like *On Your Toes* took more than a year before starting to make a profit. Seat prices are now nudging through the £10 barrier. It is revealing to look across the Atlantic to Broadway for signs perhaps of what is to come. There the average seat costs £24 (excluding, of course, transport, programmes, a meal out), and the massive cost of putting on plays is leading to corporate co-operation between television and theatre. In the words of the *Economist*: 'it will still cost a lot of money to present a straight play or musical – $5 million or more for a musical – and it is becoming extremely difficult to interest individual investors, or "angels", because the chances of profits are so small. Most musicals are backed by television or film companies which can afford high risks'.[4]

Such a trend is already becoming apparent in Britain: just as in television drama the 'one-off' is being edged out by the series or serial, in the West End it is the musical which is taking the place of the straight play. Michael Attenborough of the Hampstead Theatre has said, 'What most concerns me is that if all the theatres are full of musicals, we could get to the point where straight plays are a forgotten species' (*Guardian*, 2 August 1985). The cause of those little theatres like the Hampstead Theatre is not being helped by the cuts in public subsidy.

The future therefore seems to indicate a triad of big West End shows, of radio, television and video, and of a large but unambitious amateur movement, together with two major subsidised companies able to pick up on such fringe activities as will exist. If *Other Theatres* is the first history of alternative and experimental drama in Britain, then sadly it may also be something of an obituary notice too.

Guide to Further Reading

Bibliographies which simply list title after title have never seemed to me particularly useful. This essay tries to survey the material available on the various individuals and theatres covered in the book. The place of publication is London unless stated otherwise.

General

There is no general account of the history of alternative and experimental theatre in Britain. The nearest to it is David Bradby and John McCormick *People's Theatre* (Croom Helm, 1978); this covers Britain, France, the Soviet Union, the United States and Germany in less than 160 pages, so the observations as regards Britain are necessarily brief. *Theatre Quarterly* (vol. 1, no. 4, October–December 1971) is devoted solely to articles on 'People's Theatre'. *History Workshop* (4, Autumn 1977) contains some wideranging articles on the Workers' Theatre Movement. Expanded versions together with new work are in R. Samuel, E. MacColl and S. Cosgrove, *Theatres of the Left 1880–1935* (Routledge and Kegan Paul, 1985). Look too at the essays in D. Bradby, L. James and B. Sharratt (eds), *Performance and Politics in Popular Drama* (Cambridge University Press, 1981). The journal *Theatre Quarterly*, published from 1971, often included interesting historical material.

1 The Great Bard and All That

What is needed is a book which looks at just how Shakespeare's plays have been staged and interpreted since the sixteenth century. Until then we have to rely on Gamini Salgado's *Eyewitnesses of Shakespeare* (Sussex University Press, 1975). Peter Brook in his *The Empty Space* (Penguin, 1972) distinguished certain strands within the theatre, but I don't think his model is as helpful as mine (yes, well, I wouldn't, would I?). John Pick's view of the West End stage is apparent from his title alone: *The West End: Mismanagement and Snobbery* (Eastbourne: John Offord, 1983).

2 Stage Melodrama in the Nineteenth Century

There are several good histories of stage melodrama, among them Frank Rahill, *The World of Melodrama* (Pennsylvania University Press, 1967), M. R. Booth, *English Melodrama* (Herbert Jenkins, 1965) and a number of older books by M. W. Disher including *Blood and Thunder* (Muller, 1949). A. E. Wilson's *East End Entertainment* (Arthur Barker, 1954) is a lively but unreliable account of the minors in the East End. Useful essays with copious footnotes are in the Bradby, James and Sharratt collection (see above). Some Victorian melodramas have been reprinted, for example James L. Smith, *Victorian Melodrama* (Dent, 1976).

3 The Rise of the West End

The standard histories – George Rowell's *The Victorian Theatre* (Cambridge University Press, 1978), J. C. Trewin's *The Edwardian Theatre* (Blackwell, 1976) and Allardyce Nicoll's volumes – are of only moderate use. Much more illuminating are Michael Baker, *The Rise of the Victorian Actor* (Croom Helm, 1978) and Peter Bailey, *Leisure and Class in Victorian England* (Routledge and Kegan Paul, 1978). Anna Miller's *The Independent Theatre in Europe* (reissued New York, Blom, 1966) is indispensable. John Stokes, *Resistible Theatres* (Paul Elek, 1972) should be better known.

As for Morris and Shaw, consult the various biographies. A Marxist view of Shaw's plays is in Alick West, *A Good Man Fallen Among Fabians* (Lawrence and Wishart, 1950). Ian Britain, *Fabianism and Culture* (Cambridge University Press, 1982) is important. Brief but revealing is the chapter in Holbrook Jackson, *The Eighteen Nineties* (Penguin, 1939). The only book devoted to the Court Theatre under Barker and Vedrenne is D. MacCarthy, *The Court Theatre 1904–1907* (Bullen, 1907) – another is needed.

4 Regional, Nationalist and Yiddish Theatre

There are several good accounts of the Abbey Theatre whether by participants such as Lady Gregory (*Our Irish Theatre*, Putnam, 1914) or Lennox Robinson (*Ireland's Abbey Theatre*, Sidgwick and Jackson, 1951; he also edited *The Irish Theatre*, Macmillan, 1939); or in more general histories: Una Ellis-Fermor, *The Irish Dramatic Movement* (Methuen, 1939), Peter Kavanagh, *The Irish Theatre* (Ireland: Kerryman, 1946), Michael O hAodha, *Theatre in Ireland* (Blackwell, 1974).

For the various repertories see the individual histories cited in the footnotes. But see in particular P. P. Howe, *The Repertory Theatre* (Secker and Warburg, 1910), Cecil Chisholm, *Repertory* (Peter Davies, 1934) and Rex Pogson, *Miss Horniman and the Gaiety Theatre, Manchester* (Rockliff, 1952). A good starter for the history of the Scottish theatre is David Hutchison, *The Modern Scottish Theatre* (Glasgow, Molendinar Press, 1977). Norman Veitch in *The People's* provides an excellent account of the life and struggles of a little theatre (Gateshead, Northumberland Press, 1950). There is no general account of the Clarion movement let alone its cultural activities.

Nor is there of the Yiddish theatre. A good chapter in M. J. Landa, *The Jew in Drama* (P. S. King, 1926) is devoted to the topic; otherwise see Lulla Rosenfeld's biography of Jacob Adler, *Bright Star of Exile* (New York, Crowell, 1977) and the useful essay by A. B. Levy in the *East London Papers* of July 1963 together with numerous memoirs and autobiographies. But all in all, another gap waiting to be filled.

5 Women in the Theatre

Excellent on the Actresses' Franchise League is Julie Holledge, *Innocent Flowers* (Virago, 1981). A general history is Rosamond Gilder, *Enter the Actress* (Harrap, 1931) and a more recent account, Michael Sanderson, *From Irving to Olivier* (Athlone, 1984). Lively as always is Richard Findlater, *The Player Queens* (Weidenfeld and Nicolson, 1976). A valuable short essay is Elizabeth Robins, *Ibsen and the Actress* (Hogarth Press, 1928). Autobiographies by Robins, Lena Ashwell, M. W. Nevinson and Cicely Hamilton – see footnotes – tell us much about theatrical attitudes of the time regarding actresses. Otherwise I read my way through the suffragettes' weekly, *Votes for Women*. Some AFL documents and plays are in the British Library but more particularly in the Fawcett Library at the City of London Polytechnic.

6 Between the Wars: the 'Little Theatre Movement'

Norman Marshall, *The Other Theatre* (John Lehmann, 1947) is an excellent survey of the inter-war period. A contemporary account is Huntley Carter, *The New Spirit in the European Theatre 1914–24* (Benn, 1925). Of the various initiatives discussed see Michael Sidnell's thorough *Dances of Death* (Faber, 1984) about the Group Theatre which should be complemented by the more personal and moving Robert Medley, *Drawn from the Life* (Faber, 1983). For Terence Gray see Richard Cave, *Terence Gray and the Cambridge Festival Theatre* (Cambridge, Chadwyck-Healey, 1980) which accompanies a set of 50 slides. There are several articles and essays about the Maddermarket in Norwich, most of which can be consulted at the Norwich Public Library, but no full-length book other than the collected reviews by Charles Rigby, *Maddermarket Mondays* (Norwich, Roberts, 1933). For the repertories, see the footnotes.

7 Between the Wars: the Political Theatre Groups

In recent years there has been an explosion of interest in the
Workers' Theatre Movement – see for example *History Workshop*
(4) and R. Samuel etc. (above). The first book was Ness
Edwards, *The Workers' Theatre* (Cardiff, Cymric, 1930) of which
a copy exists at the British Library. Unity Theatre has not been
so well covered but Colin Chambers is engaged on writing what
should be a definitive account to be published by Lawrence and
Wishart. There are numerous pamphlets issued at the time: the
Unity Theatre Handbook of 1939 and *People's Theatre* of *c*. 1946. For
good studies of local Unity theatres see Angela Tuckett, *The
People's Theatre in Bristol 1930–45* (Our History 72, no date) and
Jerry Dawson, *Left Theatre* (Liverpool, Merseyside Writers,
1985). Also look at Ray Waterman on Proltet in *History
Workshop* (5 Spring 1978), Malcolm Page on the early history of
Unity in *Theatre Quarterly* (Vol. 1, no. 4, October–December
1971), and the two essays by André van Gyseghem and Jon
Clark in J. Clark *et al.* (eds) *Culture and Crisis in Britain in the '30's*
(Lawrence and Wishart, 1979). The three articles by Dr Len
Jones are referred to in the footnotes.

   I also read my way through the newspapers and periodicals
of the 1930s – *Daily Worker, Left Review, Left News, New Leader,
Clarion, New Statesman, Amateur Theatre, Drama* – which does
throw up much information on the period even if it takes quite
some time. Relevant material is held at the Victoria and Albert
Museum and at the Marx Memorial Library in London, e.g. a
copy of the thesis by Ron Travis on Unity between 1936 and
1946.

8 The War Years

Nor very much to report, unfortunately because this is a highly
illuminating saga. Best to start with Ann Davies, *The Theatre*
(Bodley Head, 1948), Mary Glasgow and Ifor Evans, *The Arts
in England* (Faber, 1949) and Robert Speaight's essay in *Since
1939* (Phoenix, 1949). Informative is Peter Noble, *The British
Theatre* (British Yearbooks, 1946). Revealing is Jack Lindsay's
pamphlet, *British Achievement in Art and Music* (Pilot Press, 1945)

and his *After The Thirties* (Lawrence and Wishart, 1956). Broader cultural overviews are in Janet Minihan, *The Nationalization of Culture* (Hamish Hamilton, 1977) and Robert Hewison, *Under Siege* (Quartet, 1979); for the overall picture see Angus Calder, *The People's War* (Panther, 1971) and my more slender *Where Did the Forties Go?* (Pluto, 1984).

9 After 1945

For London Unity see the sources mentioned above in Chapter 7. For Glasgow Unity John Hill's article in *Theatre Quarterly* of Autumn 1977 and some of the articles in *New Edinburgh Review* (no. 40, February 1978). The Theatre Conference episode is chronicled in *New Theatre* and in J. B. Priestley's books and essays of the time. As regards Theatre Workshop, Howard Goorney's *The Theatre Workshop Story* (Eyre Methuen, 1981) is indispensable, giving a feel of the whole venture which is sadly missing from most theatre histories. Also read Ewan MacColl's article on the early days of Theatre Workshop in *Theatre Quarterly* of January 1973 and Oscar Tapper's *The Other Stratford* of 1962, held at West Ham Public Library. A short history of the theatre itself is in Michael Coren, *The Theatre Royal: 100 Years of Stratford East* (Quartet, 1984). A general survey of the post-war years is John Elsom, *Postwar British Theatre* (Routledge and Kegan Paul, 1976). For further references look at E. H. Mikhail, *Contemporary British Drama 1950–1976: A Bibliography* (Macmillan, 1976). Only Frank Coppieters in an article in *Theatre Quarterly* of March–May 1975 has provided an account of Centre 42.

10 and 11 Political, Community and Subsidised Theatre Since the 1960s

Start with Catherine Itzin, *Stages in the Revolution* (Eyre Methuen, 1980) which is a history as well as including much valuable interview material. Sandy Craig (ed.), *Dreams and Deconstructions* (Amber Lane Press, 1980) is a collection of essays of variable quality. As regards various aspects, look at

Naseem Khan, *The Arts Britain Ignores* (Arts Council, 1976) for
'ethnic drama'; Colin Chambers, *Other Spaces* (Eyre Methuen,
1980) for the RSC; Helen Keyssar on *Feminist Theatre*
(Macmillan, 1984) together with Michelene Wandor's
invaluable *Understudies* (Eyre Methuen, 1981). Red Ladder is
probably the best documented of the groups (see footnotes for
references) and there is also a full-scale account of the Welfare
State in Tony Coult and Baz Kershaw, *Engineers of the
Imagination* (Methuen, 1984).

The journal *Theatre Quarterly* is indispensable; less so is *Plays
and Players* although a former editor, Peter Ansorge, wrote the
helpful *Disrupting the Spectacle* (Pitman, 1975). Best for the feel of
contemporary subsidised work in the 'majors' read Simon
Callow, *Being an Actor* (Penguin, 1985), Antony Sher, *Year of the
King* (Chatto and Windus, 1985) and Jim Hiley, *Theatre at work*
(Routledge and Kegan Paul, 1981).

12   Alternatives within Radio and Television Drama

For radio drama see Ian Rodger, *Radio Drama* (Macmillan,
1982), Peter Lewis (ed.), *Radio Drama* (Longman, 1981) and
John Drakakis (ed.), *British Radio Drama* (Cambridge
University Press, 1981).

There are individual essays on some of the major television
dramatists in George Brandt (ed.), *British Television Drama*
(Cambridge University Press, 1981). A useful collection of
articles and essays is *The Screen on the Tube* (Norwich, Cinema
City, 1983). Peter Buckman deals with 'the soaps' in *All for Love*
(Secker and Warburg, 1984). More specifically, refer to
Alvarado and Buscombe on *Hazell*, Hobson on *Crossroads*,
Richard Dyer et al. (eds) on *Coronation Street* and Alvarado and
Stewart (eds) on Euston Films in *Made for Television* – for full
references see footnotes. There are interviews and essays in
Frank Pike (ed.), *Ah! Mischief: The Writer and Television* (Faber,
1982). On Trevor Griffiths see Mike Poole and John Wyver,
Powerplays (British Film Institute, 1984). *Screen* and *Screen
Education* contain some provoking articles and essays, if, that is,
you can decode the language into something resembling
English – the former being infinitely the worse offender.

International Theatre

For references see Bradby and McCormick (above); but also John Willett, *The Theatre of Bertolt Brecht* (Eyre Methuen, 1967), Cecil Davies, *Theatre for the People* about the Volksbuehne (Manchester University Press, 1977) and C.D. Innes, *Erwin Piscator's Political Theatre* (Cambridge University Press, 1972). For the United States look at Gerald Rabkin, *Drama and Commitment* (Indiana University Press, 1964), Morgan Himelstein, *Drama was a Weapon* (Rutgers University Press, 1963) and more recently Theodore Shank, *American Alternative Theatre* (Macmillan, 1982). For the Soviet Union an interesting start is André van Gyseghem, *Theatre in Soviet Russia* (Faber, 1943). James Roose-Evans, *Experimental Theatre from Stanislavsky to Peter Brook* (Routledge and Kegan Paul, 1984) is a comprehensive survey of European developments this century; it also includes a section on 'Recommended Further Reading'.

References

Preface

Raphael Samuel's remarks are in R. Samuel, Ewan MacColl and Stuart Cosgrove, *Theatres of the Left 1880–1935* (London: Routledge and Kegan Paul, 1985) xi. The Joan Littlewood quote is from Howard Goorney, *The Theatre Workshop Story* (London: Eyre Methuen, 1981) p. 130. Eric Bentley's gibe is in the book he edited called *The Theory of the Modern Stage* (London: Penguin, 1976) p. 401. R. H. Tawney's statement is from his lecture 'Social History and Literature' reprinted in *The Radical Tradition* (London: Allen and Unwin, 1964) pp. 187–8.

Introduction

1. J. D. A. Ogilvy, 'Mimi, Scurrae, Histriones: Entertainers Of The Early Middle Ages', in *Speculum*, 38 (1963) pp. 603–19.
2. Anne Righter, *Shakespeare and the Idea of the Play* (London: Chatto and Windus, 1962), see opening chapter on 'The Audience as Actor'.
3. Allardyce Nicoll, *Masks, Mimes and Miracles* (London: Harrap, 1932) pp. 179–80.
4. Glynne Wickham, *The Medieval Theatre* (London: Weidenfeld and Nicolson, 1977) p. 4.
5. Christopher Hill, *Reformation to Industrial Revolution* (London: Penguin, 1969) p. 89.
6. Alwin Thaler, 'The Elizabethan Dramatic Companies', in *Publications of the Modern Language Association*, 35 (1920) pp. 123–59.
7. Alfred Harbage, *Shakespeare and the Rival Traditions* (Indiana University Press, 1970) pp. 24–5.
8. M. C. Bradbrook, *Shakespeare the Craftsman* (Cambridge University Press, 1979) and the chapter on 'The New Clown: Twelfth Night'.

9. See Stephen Orgel, *The Illusion of Power* (California University Press, 1975).
10. Margot Heinemann, 'Popular Drama and Leveller Style', in M. Cornforth (ed.), *Rebels and their Causes* (London: Lawrence and Wishart, 1978) p. 88.
11. Cecil Price, *Theatre in the Age of Garrick* (Oxford: Basil Blackwell, 1973) p. 23.
12. Allardyce Nicoll, *British Drama* (London: Harrap, 1932), p. 271.

1 The Great Bard and All That

1. Frank Aydelotte, *Elizabethan Rogues and Vagabonds* (1913, republished London: Frank Cass, 1967) pp. 110–11.
2. Quoted in J. Dover Wilson, *Life in Shakespearean England* (London: Penguin, 1944) p. 231.
3. L. L. and F. O. Marker, 'Sources in Audience Research,' from *Das Theater und sein Publikum* (Wien, 1977) p. 26.
4. Gilbert B. Cross, *Next Week – East Lynne* (London: Associated University Presses, 1977) p. 229.
5. Sir Barry Jackson, 'Barnstorming Days', in *Studies in English Theatre History* (London: Society for Theatre Research, 1952) p. 116.
6. A. E. Green, 'Popular Drama and the Mummers' Play' in D. Bradby, L. James and B. Sharratt (eds), *Performance and Politics in Popular Drama* (Cambridge University Press, 1980) p. 157.
7. *The Times*, 5 February 1985.
8. Both Morley's and Archer's remarks come from Michael R. Booth, 'East End and West End: Class and Audience in Victorian London', in *Theatre Research International*, vol. II, no. 2 (February 1977) pp. 99–100.
9. John Pick, *The West End: Mismanagement and Snobbery* (Eastbourne: John Offord, 1983) p. 17.
10. Richard Findlater, *Joe Grimaldi* (Cambridge University Press, 1978) pp. 11–12.
11. Peter Lewis, 'Introduction', in P. Lewis (ed.), *Radio Drama* (London: Longman, 1981) p. 1.
12. George Brandt, 'Introduction', in G Brandt (ed.), *British Television Drama* (Cambridge University Press, 1981), p. 2.
13. See his essay 'The Politics of Popular Culture' in C. W. E. Bigsby, *Approaches to Popular Culture* (London: Edward Arnold, 1976) pp. 3–26.
14. Colin Chambers, 'Socialist Theatre and the Ghetto Mentality', in *Marxism Today* (August 1978), p. 249.
15. D. P. Miller, *The Life of a Showman* (London, 1849) p. 111.
16. R. D. Altick, *The English Common Reader* (London: University of Chicago Press, 1957) p. 243.
17. Rev. J. Panton Ham, *The Pulpit and the Stage* (London, 1878) p. 73.
18. Derek Longhurst, 'Reproducing a National Culture: Shakespeare in Education', in *Red Letters*, no. 11 (n.d.); also Derek Longhurst, 'Not For

All Time, But For An Age' in Peter Widdowson (ed.), *Re-reading English* (London: Methuen, 1982) pp. 150–63.

2 Castles, Ghosts and Chartists

1. The phrase 'non-books' comes from Leslie Shepard, *The History of Street Literature* (Devon: David and Charles, 1973), see p. 14.
2. See W. D. Howarth's essay, 'Word and Image in Pixerecourt's Melodramas', in D. Bradby, L. James and B. Sharrat (eds), *Performance and Politics in Popular Drama* (Cambridge University Press, 1980) p. 17.
3. Asa Briggs, 'The Language of "Class" in Early Nineteenth-Century England', in A. Briggs and J. Saville (eds), *Essays in Labour History* (London: Macmillan, 1967) pp. 53–73.
4. Derek Forbes, 'Water Drama', in Bradby et al, op. cit., p. 92.
5. Robert Blatchford, *My Early Life* (London: Cassell, 1931) p. 19.
6. Joseph Donohue, *Theatre in the Age of Kean* (Oxford: Blackwell, 1975) p. 155.
7. Emrys Bryson, *'Owd Yer Tight* (Nottingham: Roy Palmer, 1967) p. 32.
8. Errol Sherson, *London's Lost Theatres of the Nineteenth Century* (London: Bodley Head, 1925) p. 12.
9. John Hollingshead, *Ragged London in 1861* (London: Smith Elder, 1861) p. 180.
10. Leon Faucher, *Manchester in 1844* (London: 1844) p. 21 and n. 7 on p. 23.
11. F. G. Tomlins, *Remarks on the Present State of the English Drama* (London: 1851) p. 14.
12. The play is reprinted in James L. Smith, *Victorian Melodramas* (London: Dent, 1976).
13. Frank Rahill, *The World of Melodrama* (Pennsylvania University Press, 1967) p. 151.
14. Richard Findlater, *Banned!* (London: MacGibbon and Kee, 1967) p. 55.
15. See David Mayer, *Harlequin in His Element* (Harvard University Press, 1969) pp. 165–237 but NB p. 23.
16. Sally Vernon, 'Trouble up at T'Mill', in *Victorian Studies* vol. xx (Winter 1977) p. 133.
17. Shepard, op. cit., p. 126.
18. Victor Neuberg, *Popular Literature* (London: Penguin, 1977) p. 137.
19. *Anglo–Soviet Journal* (Autumn 1958) p. 15.
20. George Rowell, *The Victorian Theatre* (Cambridge University Press, 1978) p. 3.
21. R. K. Webb *The British Working-Class Reader 1790–1840* (London: Allen and Unwin, 1955) p. 128; George Spater, *William Cobbett* (Cambridge University Press, 1982) vol. ii, p. 602, n. 4.
22. Spater, ibid.
23. Eileen Yeo, 'Robert Owen and Radical Culture', in S. Pollard and J. Salt (eds), *Robert Owen* (London: Macmillan, 1971) p. 84.
24. J. F. C. Harrison, *Robert Owen and the Owenites in Britain and America* (London: Routledge and Kegan Paul, 1969) p. 255.

25. Quoted in Y. V. Kovalev, *An Anthology of Chartist Literature* (Moscow, 1956) p. 311.
26. A. Temple Patterson *Radical Leicester* (Leicester: University College, 1954) p. 331.
27. In Kovalev, op. cit., p. 376 – translation from the Russian.
28. John Booth, *The Old Vic 1816–1916* (London: Stead, 1917) p. 36.
29. Raphael Samuel, Editorial Introduction to Documents on the Worker's Theatre Movement in *History Workshop* (4, Autumn 1977) p. 103.

3 The Rise of the West End

1. Ernest B. Watson, *Sheridan to Robertson* (Harvard University Press, 1926) p. 5.
2. Asa Briggs, *Victorian Cities* (London: Penguin, 1968) p. 314.
3. See Francesca Wilson, *Strange Island* (London: Longmans, 1955) p. 174.
4. Quoted in Julie Holledge, *Innocent Flowers* (London: Virago, 1981) p. 9.
5. Quoted in 'Jenny Marx as Critic' in the *Quarterly Bulletin of the Marx Memorial Library*, no. 75 (July/September 1975) p. 8.
6. Donald Roy, 'Theatre Royal, Hull' in K. Richards and P. Thomson, *Nineteenth-Century British Theatre* (London: Methuen, 1971) p. 35.
7. See for example Peter Bailey's chapter on the music hall in his *Leisure and Class in Victorian England* (London: Routledge and Kegan Paul, 1978).
8. Cicely Hamilton and Lilian Baylis, *The Old Vic* (London: Cape, 1926) p. 185.
9. Colin Watson, *Snobbery with Violence* (London: Eyre Methuen, 1979) p. 109.
10. Cecil Davies, *Theatre for the People* (Manchester University Press, 1977) p. 5.
11. G. B. Shaw, *Our Theatres in the Nineties* (London: Constable, 1932) vol. 2, p. 211; and May Morris, *William Morris. Artist Writer Socialist* (Oxford: Blackwell, 1936) p. 390.
12. Shaw, *Our Theatres*, p. 213.
13. Jack Lindsay, *William Morris* (London: Constable, 1975) p. 324.
14. Quoted in Yvonne Kapp, *Eleanor Marx. The Crowded Years* (London: Lawrence and Wishart, 1976) p. 100.
15. Elizabeth Robins, *Ibsen and the Actress* (London: Hogarth Press, 1928) p. 10–11.
16. Quoted in Chushichi Tsuzuki, *The Life of Eleanor Marx* (Oxford University Press, 1967) p. 181.
17. From the paper given by Lawrence Marlow, 'Clubs and Leisure in the Early 1890's' at the Society for the Study of Labour History Conference, 1975.
18. Tim Ashplant's paper, 'The Provision of Entertainment in London Working Men's Clubs, 1890–1914' at conference mentioned in n. 17. Also see Barry Burke and Ken Warpole *Hackney Propaganda* (London: Centerprise, 1980).

19. See Ian Britain, *Fabianism and Culture* (Cambridge: University Press, 1982), pp. 180, 186.
20. Holbrook Jackson, *The Eighteen Nineties* (London: Penguin, 1939) p. 211.
21. Quoted in Anna Miller, *The Independent Theatre in Europe* (New York, 1931) p. 164.
22. Miller, op. cit., p. 185.
23. Shaw, *The Quintessence of Ibsenism* (London: Walter Scott, 1891).
24. Shaw, *Our Theatres*, vol. II, p. 70.
25. B. Shaw, *The Quintessence* p. 202.
26. Shaw, *Our Theatres*, p. 79.
27. Emma Goldman, *The Social Significance of the Modern Drama* (Boston, Mass., 1914) p. 195.
28. H. Jackson, op. cit., p. 213.
29. Quoted in Grace Wyndham Goldie, *The Liverpool Repertory Theatre 1911–1934* (London: Hodder and Stoughton, 1935) p. 10.
30. Hesketh Pearson, *Bernard Shaw* (London: Reprint Society, 1948) p. 254.
31. Desmond MacCarthy, *The Court Theatre 1904–1907* (London: Bullen, 1907) p. 17.
32. Harley Granville Barker, *The Exemplary Theatre* (London: Chatto and Windus, 1922).
33. Annette T. Rubinstein, *The Great Tradition in English Literature* (New York: Modern Reader Paperbacks, 1969) p. 926.

4   Regional, Nationalist and Yiddish Theatre

1. See Asa Briggs, *Victorian Cities*, op. cit.
2. Malcolm Bradbury, 'London 1890–1920' in M. Bradbury and J. MacFarlane (eds), *Modernism* (London: Penguin, 1976) p. 179.
3. Richard Fawkes, *Dion Boucicault* (London: Quartet, 1979) p. 117.
4. Raymond Williams, *Drama from Ibsen to Brecht* (London: Penguin, 1973) p. 124.
5. Peter Kavanagh, *The Story of the Abbey Theatre* (New York, 1950) p. 11.
6. Lady Gregory, *Our Irish Theatre* (London: Putnam, 1914) p. 24.
7. Rex Pogson, *Miss Horniman and the Gaiety Theatre, Manchester* (London: Rockliff, 1952) p. 11.
8. Lady Gregory, op. cit., pp. 113, 115.
9. Lady Gregory, op. cit., p. 47.
10. Lennox Robinson, *Ireland's Abbey Theatre* (London: Sidgwick and Jackson, 1951) pp. 58–9.
11. Emmet Larkin, *James Larkin* (London: New English Library, 1968) p. 99.
12. Sean O'Faolain, *The Irish* (London: Penguin, 1980) pp. 128–9.
13. Allardyce Nicoll, *British Drama* (London: Harrap, 1932) p. 391.
14. Rex Pogson, op. cit., p. 26.
15. Rex Pogson, op. cit., p. 189.
16. Rex Pogson, op. cit., pp. 129 ff.
17. *Votes for Women*, 2 August 1912.

18. C. Hamilton and L. Baylis, op. cit. p. 236.
19. P. P. Howe, *The Repertory Theatre* (London: Secker and Warburg, 1910) p. 66.
20. David Hutchison, *The Modern Scottish Theatre* (Glasgow: Molendinar Press, 1977) p. 18.
21. Goldie, op. cit., p. 123.
22. Bache Matthews, *A History of the Birmingham Repertory Theatre* (London: Chatto and Windus, 1924) xiv and xv.
23. T. C. Kemp, *Birmingham Repertory Theatre* (Birmingham: Cornish Brothers, 1948) p. 2.
24. Howe, op. cit., p. 153.
25. Cecil Chisholm, *Repertory* (London: Peter Davies, 1934) p. 15.
26. Goldie, op. cit., p. 74.
27. Goldie, op. cit., p. 120.
28. Harley Granville Barker, *The Exemplary Theatre* (London: Chatto and Windus, 1922) p. 261.
29. St John Ervine, *The Organised Theatre* (London: Allen and Unwin, 1924) p. 149.
30. Judith A. Fincher, *The Clarion Movement* (Manchester University MA Thesis, 1971) p. 19, n. 12.
31. Norman Veitch, *The People's* (Gateshead: Northumberland Press, 1950) p. 4.
32. James Sexton, *Sir James Sexton Agitator* (London: Faber, 1936) p. 217.
33. Paul Magriel (ed.), *The Memoirs of the Life of Daniel Mendoza* (London: Batsford, 1951) p. 17.
34. M. J. Landa, *The Jew in Drama* (London: P. S. King, 1926) pp. 286–7.
35. Lulla Rosenfeld, *Bright Star of Exile* (New York, 1977) pp. 199–200.
36. Israel Zangwill, *Children of the Ghetto* (London: White Lion Editions, 1972) pp. 197–202.
37. Harry Blacker, *Just Like It Was* (London: Valentine Mitchell, 1974) p. 173.
38. Landa, op. cit., p. 288.
39. Lloyd P. Gartner, *The Jewish Immigrant in England 1870–1914* (London: Allen and Unwin, 1960) p. 261.
40. A. B. Levy, 'The Jewish Theatre' in *East London Papers*, vol. 6, no. 1 (July 1963) p. 28.

5 Women in the Theatre

1. Quoted in Christina Hole, *English Sports and Pastimes* (London: Batsford, 1949) p. 140.
2. Rosamond Gilder, *Enter the Actress* (London: Harrap, 1931) pp. 142–3.
3. Robert Latham (ed.), *The Illustrated Pepys* (London: Bell and Hyman, 1976) p. 158.
4. Cecil Price, *Theatre in the Age of Garrick* (Oxford: Blackwell, 1973) p. 37.
5. Quoted in F. Wilson, op. cit., p. 175.

6. Quoted in Richard Findlater, *The Player Queens* (London: Weidenfeld and Nicolson, 1976) p. 127.
7. Pearson op. cit., p. 249.
8. Michael Baker, *The Rise of the Victorian Actor* (London: Croom Helm, 1978) p. 106.
9. Cicely Hamilton, *Life Errant* (London: Dent, 1935) p. 60.
10. Lena Ashwell, *Myself a Player* (London: Michael Joseph, 1936) p. 164.
11. In Shaw, *Ibsenism*, p. 92.
12. Helen Crawfurd, manuscript autobiography held at the Marx Memorial Library, London, p. 62.
13. Edith Craig in *Votes for Women*, 15 April 1910.
14. M. W. Nevinson, *In the Workhouse* (London: International Suffrage Shop, 1911) p. 21.
15. M. W. Nevinson, *Life's Fitful Fever* (London: A. and C. Black, 1926) pp. 225–6.
16. Holledge, op. cit., p. 72.
17. V. Buchanan-Gould, *Not Without Honour* (London: Hutchinson, n.d.) pp. 67–8.
18. *AFL Report*, June 1912–June 1913, p. 8.
19. *Votes for Women*, 3 February 1911.
20. *Votes for Women*, 29 August 1913.
21. Holledge, op. cit., p. 99.
22. Goldie, op. cit., pp. 92–3; also see Sexton, op. cit., pp. 215–16.
23. Holledge, op. cit., p. 3.

6 Between the Wars: the 'Little Theatre Movement'

1. Asa Briggs, *Mass Entertainment: The Origins of a Modern Industry* (Adelaide, Australia, 1960) p. 16.
2. Richard Findlater, *Banned!* (London: MacGibbon and Kee, 1967) p. 141.
3. Allardyce Nicoll, *The English Theatre* (London: Nelson, 1936) p. 188.
4. *25 Years of the British Drama League* (London: BDL, 1945) no pagination.
5. O. Brockett and R. Findlay *A Century of Innovation* (New York: Prentice-Hall, 1973) p. 470.
6. David Hutchison *The Modern Scottish Theatre* (Glasgow: Molendinar Press, 1967) p. 32.
7. L. du Garde Peach, 'Your World Has No Right to be Rosy' in *Amateur Theatre*, 25 September 1936.
8. Norman Marshall, *The Other Theatre* (London: John Lehmann, 1947) p. 88.
9. Michael O hAodha *Theatre in Ireland* (Oxford: Blackwell, 1974) p. 110.
10. Matthews, *Birmingham Repertory Theatre*, p. 71.
11. Goldie, op. cit., p. 214.
12. Sybil and Russell Thorndike, *Lilian Baylis* (London: Chapman and Hall, 1938) p. 56.
13. See Robert Speaight in Harcourt Williams (ed.), *Vic-Wells: The Work of Lilian Baylis* (London: Cobden-Sanderson, 1938) p. 20.

14. Veitch, op. cit., p. 54.
15. Philip Lorraine, 'Yiddish Theatres in London' in *Drama* (June 1939).
16. N. Monck, 'The Maddermarket Theatre and the Playing of Shakespeare's in *Shakespeare Survey* (Cambridge University Press, 1959) p. 72.
17. Charles Rigby, *Maddermarket Mondays* (Norwich, Roberts, 1933) p. 4.
18. See *The Maddermarket Theatre, Norwich* (issued by the theatre; no date or pagination).
19. Terence Gray, *Dance-Drama* (Cambridge: Heffer, 1926) p. 27.
20. Marshall, op. cit., p. 63.
21. Rigby, op. cit., p. 105.
22. Richard Cave, *Terence Gray and the Cambridge Festival Theatre* (Cambridge: Chadwyck-Healey, 1980) p. 36.
23. Quoted in B. J. Utting, *The Festival Theatre* (unpublished volume of 1973 held at Cambridge Public Library) p. 10.
24. Utting, op. cit., p. 38.
25. Marshall, op. cit. p. 44.
26. *Of Course We Remember the Gate*, programme broadcast on BBC Radio 4, 12 August 1984.
27. Nigel Playfair, *The Story of the Lyric Theatre, Hammersmith* (London: Chatto and Windus, 1925) p. 9.
28. Hamilton and Baylis, op. cit., p. 16.
29. Giles Playfair, *My Father's Son* (London: Geoffrey Bles, 1937) p. 29.
30. Stuart Samuels, 'English Intellectuals and Politics in the 1930s', in Philip Reiff (ed.), *On Intellectuals* (New York, 1969) p. 227.
31. Letter of 1965 from Auden quoted in N. Jacobs and P. Ohlsen (eds), *Bertholt Brecht in Britain* (London TQ Publications, 1977) p. 67
32. Group Theatres programmes held at the British Library: *The Agamemnon of Aeschylus*, November 1936.
33. Robert Medley, *Drawn from the Life* (London: Faber, 1983) p. 139.
34. Michael Sidnell, *Dances of Death* (London: Faber, 1984) p. 76.
35. St John Ervine, op. cit., p. 156.
36. Noreen Branson and Margot Heinemann, *Britain in the Nineteen Thirties* (St Albans: Granada, 1971) pp. 274–5.
37. O. Brockett and R. Findlay, *A Century of Innovation*, op. cit., p. 509.

7   Between the Wars: the Political Theatre Groups

1. Charles Madge, 'Pens Dipped in Poison', in *Left Review*, vol. 1, no. 1 (October 1934) p. 17.
2. Foreword to Miles Malleson and H. Brooks, *Six Men of Dorset* (London: Gollancz, 1934).
3. Letter from Alex McCrindle in the *Guardian*, 16 March 1984.
4. *Trades Union Congress Report 1937*, p. 109.
5. 'Co-operative Drama', in *The Co-operative Review* (August 1937) p. 239; (December 1937) pp. 374–5.

6. André van Gyseghem, 'British Theatre in the Thirties' in J. Clark et al. (eds) *Culture and Crisis in Britain in the '30s* (London: Lawrence and Wishart, 1978) pp. 217–18.

7. See Miles Malleson, *The ILP and its Dramatic Societies* (London: ILP, n.d., but *c*.1925).

8. R. E. Dowse, *Left in the Centre* (London: Longman, 1966) pp. 83–4, 129.

9. L. A. Jones, 'The Workers' Theatre Movement in the Twenties' in *Zeitschrift für Anglistik und Amerikanistik* (January 1966) p. 273.

10. *New Leader*, 15 November 1929.

11. Harold Scott in the *Socialist Review* (January 1930).

12. Ness Edwards, *The Workers' Theatre* (Cardiff, Cymric, 1930) p. 37.

13. R. P. Dutt, 'The Workers' Theatre', in *Labour Monthly* (August 1926).

14. Philip Poole in *Red Letters*, no. 10 (n.d.) pp. 4–5.

15. Malleson, op. cit.

16. Tom Thomas, 'A Propertyless Theatre for the Propertyless Class' in *History Workshop*, 4 (Autumn 1977) p. 118.

17. Letter in *Our Time* (June 1948) p. 242.

18. Quoted in Leonard Jones, 'The General Strike and the Worker's Theatre', in *Essays in Honour of William Gallacher* (Berlin, 1966) p. 155.

19. L. A. Jones 'The Workers' Theatre Movement in the Twenties', op. cit., pp. 227–9.

20. *Daily Worker*, 10 February 1930.

21. *Daily Worker*, 11 June 1930.

22. See Thomas Dickinson, (ed.), *The Theatre in a Changing Europe* (London: Putnam, 1938) p. 16.

23. Ewan MacColl, 'Grassroots of Theatre Workshop', in *Theatre Quarterly* (January 1973) p. 59.

24. Ray Waterman, 'Proltet', in *History Workshop*, 5 (Spring 1978) p. 176.

25. Quoted in C. D. Innes, *Erwin Piscator's Political Theatre* (Cambridge University Press, 1972) p. 21.

26. See e.g. *The Plebs* (October 1925) pp. 401–4.

27. Poole, op. cit., p. 9.

28. See the journal *International Theatre*, published in the first half of the 1930s.

29. *Daily Worker*, 3 October 1934; *International Theatre* 3–4 October 1934.

30. Marie Seton, *Paul Robeson* (London: Dobson, 1958) pp. 99–102.

31. van Gyseghem, op. cit., p. 211.

32. Norman Marshall, *The Other Theatre* (London: John Lehmann, 1947) pp. 221–2.

33. Letter from Malleson, Nixon and van Gyseghem in *New Statesman*, 23 March 1935, p. 417.

34. Montagu Slater, *New Way Wins* (London: Lawrence and Wishart, 1937).

35. Ivor Brown, 'Left Theatres' in *New Statesman*, 6 April 1935, p. 487.

36. *New Leader*, 5 March 1937.

37. *Daily Worker*, 19 September 1935, also 15 November 1935.

38. Malcolm Page, 'The Early Years at Unity', in *Theatre Quarterly*, vol. 1, no. 4 (October–December 1971) p. 60.

39. Vincent Flynn, 'Looking Back', in *New Edinburgh Review*, no. 40 (February 1978) p. 19; Norman Veitch, op. cit., pp. 180–1.

40. Vernon Beste, 'Unity Theatre's Repertory', in *Million* (Glasgow: n.d.) p. 28.
41. *Amateur Theatre*, 25 September 1936, p. 35.
42. Honor Arundel, *The Freedom of Art* (London: Lawrence and Wishart, 1965) p. 43.
43. Herbert Hodge, *Draughty in Front* (London: Michael Joseph, 1938) p. 254.
44. Roger Gullan and Buckley Roberts *Where's that Bomb?* (London: Lawrence and Wishart, 1937); Arthur Calder Marshall, *The Changing Scene* (London: Chapman and Hall, 1937) p. 67.
45. *New Theatre*, January 1938, no. 3; *Drama*, April 1937.
46. Hugh D. Ford, *A Poet's War* (University of Pennsylvania Press, 1965) p. 142.
47. Mark Clifford, 'Workers' Circle Theatre', in *The Circle* (November 1937) p. 9.
48. *Daily Worker*, 25 November 1937.
49. *Amateur Theatre*, 20 May 1938, p. 28.
50. Tom Foster, 'No Slump in this Theatre', in *Daily Worker*, 28 September 1937.
51. John Lehmann, *The Whispering Gallery* (London: Longman, 1955) p. 303.
52. Bootman in Page, op. cit., p. 64.
53. Quoted in Ron Travis, *The Unity Theatre of Great Britain 1936–1946* (thesis for the University of Southern Illinois 1968, copy held at Marx Library, London) p. 87.
54. *Theatre for the People*, no. 4–5 (June–July 1939) p. 28.
55. *Left News*, no. 19 (November 1937) p. 588.
56. John Allen, 'Where are those New Dramatists?', in *Daily Worker*, 21 June 1937.
57. Ray Waterman, 'Proltet', in *History Workshop*, (Spring 1978) p. 177.
58. Angela Tuckett, *The People's Theatre in Bristol 1930–45* (London: Our History 72, n.d.) p. 10.
59. Figures from the *Unity Theatre Handbook*, 1939.
60. *Daily Worker*, 5 June 1939.
61. Bootman in Page, op. cit., p. 63.
62. Samuel, op. cit., p. 232.

8 The War Years

1. Robert Hewison, *Under Siege* (London: Quartet, 1979) p. 29.
2. W. A. Darlington, *The Actor and His Audience* (London: Phoenix House, 1949) p. 170.
3. 'A Violinist', 'A Tour with CEMA' in *Our Time*, no. 7 (September 1941) p. 18.
4. See 'The Arts in War and Peace' in Janet Minihan, *The Nationalization of Culture* (London: Hamish Hamilton, 1977).
5. John Casson, *Lewis and Sybil* (London: Collins, 1972) p. 218.

6. Edward J. Dent, *A Theatre for Everybody* (London: Boardman, 1945) p. 125.
7. Unity Theatre leaflet held at Marx Memorial Library, London.
8. Travis, op. cit., pp. 107–8.
9. Travis, op. cit., p. 130.
10. John Hill, 'Towards a Scottish People's Theatre: the Rise and Fall of Glasgow Unity' in *Theatre Quarterly* (Autumn 1977) p. 62.
11. Minihan, op. cit., p. 226.
12. Bernard Miles, *The British Theatre* (London: Collins, 1948) p. 10.
13. Donald Wolfit, *First Interval* (London: Odhams, 1954) p. 215.
14. A. C. T. White, *The Story of Army Education 1643–1963* (London: Harrap, 1963) p. 112.
15. N. Scarlyn Wilson, *Education in the Forces* (London: Year Book of Education, 1948) p. 70; Army Education Scheme, *Arts, Crafts, Music and Drama* (London: War Office, 1945) p. 75.
16. William Harrington and Peter Young, *The 1945 Revolution* (London: Davis-Poynter, 1978) p. 51.
17. T. H. Hawkins and L. J. F. Brimble, *Adult Education: The Record of the British Army* (London: Macmillan, 1947) p. 172.
18. Jack Lindsay, *After the Thirties* (London: Lawrence and Wishart: 1956) p. 61.
19. Churchill's intervention – interview with Jack Lindsay, July 1979; Ernest Sigler quoted in Robert Hewison, op. cit. p. 163.
20. Tuckett, op. cit., p. 1.
21. Kemp, op. cit., p. 112.
22. Jack Lindsay, *British Achievement in Art and Music* (London: Pilot Press, 1945) p. 21.
23. Eric Capon, 'A Citizen's Theatre is Founded' in *Million* (Glasgow: n.d.) p. 37.
24. Many are detailed in Ann Lindsay, *The Theatre* (London: Bodley Head, 1948).
25. e.g. by Lindsay, op. cit., p. 45.

9 After 1945

1. Anthony Howard, 'We are the Masters Now' in M. Sissons and P. French (eds), *Age of Austerity 1945–1951* (London: Hodder and Stoughton, 1963) p. 31.
2. John Elsom, *Post-war British Theatre* (London: Routledge and Kegan Paul, 1976) p. 12.
3. Kenneth Tynan, *A View of the English Stage* (St. Albans: Paladin, 1976) p. 148.
4. Ted Willis, 'The Labour Movement's Challenge' in *New Theatre* (July 1946) p. 18.
5. See 1946 folder of Unity material held at the Victoria and Albert Museum, London.
6. Travis, op. cit., p. 143.

7. Travis, op. cit., pp. 146–7.
8. Malcolm Page, *London's Theatre of the Left: Unity 1936–1975* (unpublished manuscript).
9. Richard Findlater, *The Unholy Trade* (London: Gollancz, 1952) p. 151.
10. John Hill, 'Towards a Scottish People's Theatre: the Rise and Fall of Glasgow Unity', in *Theatre Quarterly* (Autumn 1977) p. 63.
11. Hill, op. cit., p. 64.
12. Montagu Slater, 'Glasgow Unity Theatre', in *Our Time* (July 1948) p. 256.
13. Hill, op. cit., p. 66.
14. Edward Boyd, 'A Word on a Blackboard' in *New Edinburgh Review*, no. 40 (February 1978) p. 34.
15. Jerry Dawson, *Left Theatre* (Liverpool: Merseyside Writers, 1985) p. 26.
16. Jankel Sonntag, 'The Yiddish Theatre', in *Our Time* (December 1946) p. 105.
17. Robert Sinclair, *East London* (London: Robert Hale, 1950) p. 284.
18. Judah Waten, 'Yiddish Culture in East and West', in *Labour Monthly* (August 1968) pp. 377–8.
19. *New Theatre* (March 1948) p. 8, and John Pick, *The West End: Mismanagement and Snobbery* (Eastbourne: John Offord, 1983) p. 159.
20. John S. Harris, *Government Patronage of the Arts in Great Britain* (London: University of Chicago, 1970) p. 196.
21. J. B. Priestley, *Theatre Outlook* (London: Nicholson and Watson, 1947) p. 31.
22. J. B. Priestley, *The Arts Under Socialism* (London: Turnstile Press, 1947) pp. 29–30.
23. Ann Lindsay, *The Theatre* (London: Bodley Head, 1948) p. 63.
24. *New Theatre* (March 1948) p. 7.
25. Norman Marshall, 'Origins and History', in *New Theatre* (August 1948) p. 4.
26. Wilfred Bannister, *James Bridie and his Theatre* (London: Rockliff, 1955) p. 217.
27. Quoted in Richard Stourac, *Revolutionary Workers' Theatre in the Soviet Union, Germany and Britain (1918–1936)* (unpublished dissertation for the University of Bristol, 1978) p. 408.
28. Howard Goorney, *The Theatre Workshop Story* (London: Eyre Methuen, 1981) p. 50.
29. Goorney, op. cit., p. 88.
30. Oscar Tapper, 'Theatre Workshop', in *East London Papers* (July 1963) p. 6.
31. Clive Goodwin and Tom Milne, 'Working with Joan', in *Encore*, 26 (July–August 1960) p. 13.
32. Daniel Farson, 'Where is Joan Littlewood?' in *Sunday Telegraph Magazine* (24 May 1981) p. 49.
33. Goorney, op. cit., p. 150.
34. Julian Barnes *The Sunday Times Magazine* (26 November 1978) p. 24.
35. Hill, op. cit., p. 70.

36. Ted Willis, *Whatever Happened to Tom Mix?* (London: Cassell, 1970) p. 153.
37. Joan Littlewood, 'Lament for a Clown' in the *Guardian*, 27 March 1982.
38. Oscar Tapper, *The Other Stratford* (London: West Ham Public Libraries, 1962) p. 47.
39. Joan Littlewood, 'Goodbye Note from Joan', in *Encore* (September–October 1961) p. 16.
40. Joan Littlewood, 'Plays for the People', in *World Theatre*, vol. VIII, no. 4 (1959–60) p. 290.
41. Arnold Wesker's 1962 *Encounter* essay is reprinted in his *Fears of Fragmentation* (London: Cape, 1970) p. 47.
42. Richard Clements, 'The Wesker Campaign Moves into the Trade Unions' in *Tribune*, 15 July 1960.
43. Frank Coppieters, 'Arnold Wesker's Centre Forty-two', in *Theatre Quarterly*, vol. V, no. 17 (March–May 1975) p. 46.
44. Alan Sinfield, 'The Theatre and Its Audiences', in Alan Sinfield (ed.), *Society and Literature 1945–1970* (London: Methuen, 1983) p. 180.

10   Political Theatre in Britain Since the 1960s

1. Henry Pelling, *A History of British Trade Unionism* (London: Penguin, 1976) p. 296.
2. Catherine Itzin, *Stages in the Revolution* (London: Eyre Methuen, 1980) p. 12.
3. Richard Seyd, 'The Theatre of Red Ladder', in *New Edinburgh Review*, no. 30 (August 1975) p. 36.
4. Chris Rawlence, 'Political Theatre and the Working Class', in C. Gardner (ed.), *Media, Politics and Culture* (London: Macmillan, 1979) p. 65.
5. 'Red Ladder Now' in *New Theatre Magazine*, vol. XII, no. 3, pp. 23–9.
6. Itzin, op. cit., p. 43.
7. Interview with David Edgar in *Theatre Quarterly*, vol. IX, no. 33 (Spring 1979), p. 7.
8. Rawlence, op. cit., p. 66.
9. David Edgar, 'Political Theatre', in *Socialist Review*, no. 2 (May 1978) p. 37.
10. Anon, 'Grant Aid and Political Theatre 1968–77, Part 1', in *Wedge*, no. 1 (Summer 1977) p. 6.
11. Red Ladder, *Taking Our Time* (London: Pluto, 1979) xiii.
12. T. Ilott, 'Tact Together', in *The Leveller* no. 22 January 1979, p. 26.
13. Rawlence, op. cit., p. 70.
14. Quoted in Peter Ansorge, 'The Portable Playwrights', in *Plays and Players* (February 1972) p. 20.
15. John Lahr, 'Living Theatre in Shadow Life' in *New Society* (16 August 1979) pp. 356–7; interview with Edward Bond in *Theatre Quarterly*, vol. II, no. 5 (January–March 1972) p. 12.

16. John McGrath, *A Good Night Out* (London: Eyre Methuen, 1981) p. 125.
17. Seyd, op. cit., p. 42.
18. Michelene Wandor, 'Free Collective Bargaining', in *Time Out* 30 March–4 April 1979) pp. 14–16.
19. John McGrath, 'Boom. An Introduction' in *New Edinburgh Review*, no. 30 (August 1975) p. 10.
20. Catherine Itzin (ed.), *Alternative Theatre Handbook 1975–1976* (London: Theatre Quarterly Publications, 1976) pp. 2–3.
21. Steve Gooch, 'The Commitment to Socialist Theatre' in *Workers and Writers* (publication of papers from conference held at Birmingham University, October 1975) p. 78.
22. Production Casebook of 'Trees in the Wind' at Northcott Theatre, Exeter, in *Theatre Quarterly* vol. v, no. 19 (September–November) p. 100.
23. Quoted in Cecil Davies, *Theatre for the People: the Story of the Volksbughne* (Manchester University Press, 1977) p. 5.
24. John McGrath, 'The Year of the Cheviot', in *Plays and Players* (February 1974), p. 24.

11 Community Theatre

1. Interview with Michelene Wandor in *Theatre Quarterly*, vol. IX, no. 36 (Winter 1980) p. 29.
2. Joyce McMillan, 'A Miracle from the Gorbals' in the *Guardian*, 2 June 1983.
3. M. Wandor (ed.), *Plays by Women, Volume One* (London: Methuen, 1982) p. 41.
4. Wandor in *Theatre Quarterly*, op. cit., p. 30.
5. Wandor, *Plays by Women*, op. cit., p. 11 and *Understudies* (London: Eyre Methuen, 1981) p. 61.
6. See *The Status of Women in British Theatres* (London: Conference of Women Theatre Directors and Administrators, 1984).
7. Helen Keyssar, *Feminist Theatre* (London: Macmillan, 1984) p. 79.
8. Clare Colvin, 'Women in need of fringe benefits' *The Times*, 27 February 1984.
9. Helen Franks, 'Nice Girls Don't, Do They?' in *The Sunday Times Magazine*, 27 July 1980, p. 51.
10. Simon Callow *Being an Actor* (London: Penguin, 1985) p. 62.
11. Callow, op. cit., pp. 63–4.
12. Peter Cheeseman, 'A Community Theatre-in-the-Round' in *Theatre Quarterly*, vol. I, no. 1 (January–March 1971) p. 79.
13. Alistair Moffat, *The Edinburgh Fringe* (London: Johnston and Bacon, 1978) pp. 54, 59.
14. Naseem Khan, *The Arts Britain Ignores* (London: Arts Council, 1976) p. 93.
15. Catherine Itzin, *Stages in the Revolution* (London: Eyre Methuen, 1980) p. 328.

16. See Naseem Khan, 'The Public-going Theatre' in Sandy Craig (ed.), *Dreams and Deconstructions* (London: Amber Lane Press, 1980) p. 66.
17. Michael Billington 'Fuller Moon' in the *Guardian* , 27 June 1979.
18. Tom Sutcliffe, 'Old Miracles of the Space-age Auditorium' in the *Guardian*, 3 May 1985.
19. Richard Seyd, 'The Theatre of Red Ladder', in *New Edinburgh Review*, no. 30 (August 1975), p. 39.
20. Quoted in *Theatre Quarterly*, vol. II, no. 8 (October–December 1972), p. 8.
21. John Lahr, 'Athletes of the Heart', in *New Society* (29 July 1982), p. 189.
22. Edgar, 'Political Theatre' op. cit., p. 35.
23. Peter Brook, *The Empty Stage* (London: Penguin, 1972) p. 80.
24. Peter Davison, *Contemporary Drama and the Popular Dramatic Tradition in England* (London: Macmillan, 1982) pp. 86–7.
25. McGrath, *op. cit.*, pp. 40–1.
26. Franca Rame, 'Introduction', to Dario Fo *We Can't Pay? We Won't Pay!* (London: Pluto, 1978) vi.
27. Quoted in Russell Southwood, 'Fo: Laugh a Minute', in *The Leveller*, no. 26 (May 1979), p. 16.
28. See Tony Mitchell, 'Dario Fo's Mistero Buffo', in *Theatre Quarterly*, vol. IX, no. 35 (Autumn 1979) p. 11.
29. Brian Glanville, 'Master-class from a Master Clown' in *The Sunday Times*, 1 May 1983.
30. Interview with David Edgar in *Theatre Quarterly*, vol. IX, no. 33 (Spring 1979) p. 14.
31. Edgar, 'Political Theatre', op. cit., p. 35.
32. Griffiths' remark is in D. Bradby, L. James and B. Sharratt (eds), *Performance and Politics in Popular Drama* (Cambridge University Press, 1980) p. 310.
33. Itzin, *Stages in the Revolution*, p. 248.
34. Robert Hewison, 'Case of the Disappearing Playwrights' in *The Sunday Times Weekly Review*, 26 May 1985.
35. Quoted in Ronald Hayman's *The Conversion of John Arden* on BBC Radio 3, 26 August 1980.
36. Figures from John S. Harris, *Government Patronage of the Arts in Great Britain* (London: University of Chicago Press, 1970) pp. 197, 318.
37. Colin Chambers, *Other Spaces* (London: Eyre Methuen, 1980) p. 9.
38. John Elsom, *Post-war British Theatre* (London: Routledge and Kegan Paul, 1976) p. 147.
39. Moffat, op. cit., p. 98.
40. Michael Billington 'A Sandwich Course by the Signpost Man', in the *Guardian*, 22 January 1982.
41. In Michael Coveney, 'Beyond the Fringe', in *The Sunday Times Magazine*, 26 November 1978, p. 73.
42. Interview with Edgar, op. cit., p. 15.
43. Angela Wilkes, 'Desperate Acts on a Large Scale' in *The Sunday Times Weekly Review*, 30 June 1985.
44. Callow, op. cit., p. 131.
45. Sher, op. cit., p. 17 and Chambers, op. cit., p. 18.

46. Letter from David Burrows in the *Observer Review*, 30 December 1984.
47. Morgan Himelstein, *Drama Was a Weapon* (Rutgers University Press, 1963) p. 73.
48. 'Made in USA' in *Plays and Players* (March 1972) p. 24.
49. John McGrath, op. cit., p. 62.
50. John McGrath, 'The Theory and Practice of Political Theatre', in *Theatre Quarterly*, vol. IX, no. 34 (August 1979) p. 54; Chambers, op. cit., p. 82.

12 Alternatives within Radio and Television Drama

1. Albert Hunt *The Language of Television* (London: Eyre Methuen, 1981) p. 94.
2. See his pamphlet, *Art and Culture in Relation to Socialism* (London: ILP Publications, 1926).
3. Val Gielgud, *British Radio Drama 1922–1956* (London: Harrap. 1957) p. 36.
4. Angus Calder, *The People's War* (London: Panther, 1971) p. 416; Francis Worsley, 'Anatomy of ITMA', in *Pilot Papers*, vol. 1, no. 1 (January 1946) p. 42.
5. Charles Parker, 'The Dramatic Actuality of Working-class Speech' in Wilfried van der Will (ed.), *Workers and Writers* (Birmingham: conference papers, 1975) p. 100.
6. Jackie Highe, 'The Archers', in *Living*, 10 July 1985, p. 37.
7. 'The Largest Theatre in the World', in the *Economist*, 4 August 1984.
8. Ian Rodger, *Radio Drama* (London: Macmillan, 1982) p. 156.
9. Malcolm Lynch, 'Pageants for the People' in the *New Statesman* (26 August 1983) p. 9.
10. John McGrath, 'TV Drama: The Case Against Naturalism' in *Sight and Sound*, vol. 46, no. 2 (Spring 1977) p. 103.
11. See Terry Lovell's remarks in her essay 'Ideology and Coronation Street,' in Richard Dyer (ed.), *Coronation Street* (London: British Film Institute, 1981).
12. Dorothy Hobson, *Crossroads* (London: Methuen, 1982) p. 142.
13. Gillian Skirrow 'Widows' in Manuel Alvarado and John Stewart, *Made for Television* (London: British Film Institute, 1985) p. 184.
14. Quoted in Alvarado and Stewart, op. cit., p. 82.
15. Edgar, 'Political Theatre', op. cit., p. 35.
16. Theodore Shank, *American Alternative Theatre* (London: Macmillan, 1982) p. 73.
17. See Manuel Alvarado and Edward Buscombe, *Hazell* (London: British Film Institute, 1978).
18. Theodore Shank, 'Contemporary Political Theatres and their Audiences', in *Das Theater und sein Publikum* (Vienna, 1977) p. 296, n. 15.
19. Philip Purser on Dennis Potter in George Brandt (ed.), *British Television Drama* (Cambridge University Press, 1981) p. 168.
20. Interview with Griffiths in *Theatre Quarterly*, vol. VI, no. 22 (Summer 1976) p. 36; and the *Leveller*, no. 1 (November 1976) p. 12.

21. Interview in *The Leveller*, op. cit., p. 12.
22. Mike Poole and John Wyver, *Powerplays* (London: British Film Institute, 1984) p. 5.
23. John Wyver, 'Real Life Stories' in *Time Out* (23–9 March 1979) p. 18.
24. Interview with John McGrath in *Theatre Quarterly*, vol. v, no. 19 (September–November 1975) p. 43.
25. Dorothy Hobson, op. cit., p. 123.
26. Graham Murdock, 'Radical Drama, Radical Theatre', in *Media, Culture and Society*, vol. 2, no. 2 (April 1980) p. 160.
27. Edward Braun on Trevor Griffiths in George Brandt (ed.), op. cit., p. 71.
28. Poole and Wyver op. cit., p. 179; Stuart Cosgrove, 'Refusing Consent: the Oi for England Project', in *Screen*, vol. 24, no. 1 (January–February 1983) p. 95.
29. See Albert Hunt, op. cit.
30. Interview with Trevor Griffiths in *Marxism Today* (May 1985) p. 40.
31. Alan Plater, 'The Wages of Commitment', in Bob Baker and Neil Harvey, *Publishing for People* (London: Labour Library, 1985) p. 10.
32. Quoted in Philip Purser 'Is the writing on the wall for the TV play?', in *Sunday Telegraph*, 24 March 1985.
33. Richard Last, 'Drama bosses opt for Soap', in *Daily Telegraph*, 2 December 1985.
34. Stuart Hood, 'Dilemma of the Communicators', in C. W. E. Bigsby (ed.), *Approaches to Popular Culture* (London: Edward Arnold, 1976) p. 212.

Conclusions

1. The People's Year Book (London: English and Scottish Wholesale Societies, 1936) p. 133.
2. Tony Coult, 'Agents of the Future' in S. Craig (ed.), *Dreams and Deconstructions* (London: Amber Lane Press, 1980), p. 85.
3. *Guardian*, 29 December 1985; also *The Sunday Times Weekly Review*, 16 September 1984.
4. *The Economist*, 29 June 1985.

Index of People

Index of Theatres, Companies, Cultural Organisations and Statutes

241

Index of Plays (Stage, Radio and Television)